EYEWITNESS TRAVEL

LAS
VEGAS

Main Contributor **David Stratton**

P9-DMW-703

DK

DK

LONDON, NEW YORK,
MELBOURNE, MUNICH AND DELHI
www.dk.com

Managing Editor Aruna Ghose

Art Editor Benu Joshi

Project Editor Shahnaaz Bakshi

Project Designer Kavita Saha

Picture Research Taiyaba Khatoon

Senior Cartographer Uma Bhattacharya

Cartographer Alok Pathak

DTP Coordinator Shailesh Sharma

DTP Designer Vinod Harish

Main contributor David Stratton

Photographer Nigel Hicks

Illustrators Pramod Negi, Arun Pottirayil,
Madhav Raman, Ashok Sukumaran

Printed and bound in China

First American Edition 2005

17 18 19 20 10 9 8 7 6 5 4 3 2 1

Published in the United States by
DK Publishing, 345 Hudson Street,
New York, New York 10014

Reprinted with revisions 2007, 2008, 2009, 2010, 2012, 2015, 2017

Copyright 2005, 2017 © Dorling Kindersley Limited, London

A Penguin Random House Company

Published in Great Britain by Dorling Kindersley Limited.

A catalog record for this book is available from the Library of Congress.

ISSN: 1542-1554

ISBN: 978-1-46546-034-9

MIX
Paper from
responsible sources
FSC™ C018179

Front cover main image: Fountains of Bellagio and the Las Vegas Strip

◀ The bright lights of the Strip

Lucky the Clown outside Circus Circus
(see pp66–7)

Contents

Slot machines at one of Las Vegas's
hotel casinos (see pp150–57)

The spectacular Grand Canal at The Venetian *(see pp60–61)*

A mule trip convoy explores the Grand Canyon's narrow trails *(see p98)*

Bellagio *(see pp50–51)*

HOW TO USE THIS GUIDE

This Eyewitness Travel Guide helps you to get the most from your visit to Las Vegas by providing detailed practical information and expert recommendations. *Introducing Las Vegas* maps the city and region, setting it in its historical and cultural context, and describes events through the entire year. *Las Vegas at a Glance* is an overview of the city's main attractions. *Las Vegas Area by Area* starts on page 36. This is the main sightseeing section, which covers all the important sights, with maps, photographs, and illustrations. *Farther Afield* looks at sights just outside the city, while *Beyond Las Vegas* explores other inviting locations within easy reach of the city. Information about hotels, restaurants, shops, entertainment, and sports is found in *Travelers' Needs*. The *Survival Guide* has advice on everything from using the postal service and the telephone system to Las Vegas's medical services and public transport system.

Finding Your Way Around the Sightseeing Section

Each of the three sightseeing areas in Las Vegas is color-coded for easy reference. Every chapter opens with an introduction to the area of the city it covers, describing its history and character, and has a *Street by Street* map illustrating typical parts of that area. Finding your way around the chapter is made simple by the numbering system used throughout. The most important sights are covered in detail in two or more full pages.

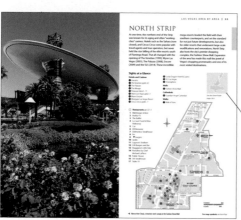

1 Introduction to the area
For easy reference, the sights in each area are numbered and plotted on an area map. This map also shows monorail stations. The area's key sights are listed by category, such as Museums and Galleries, and are also shown on the *Street Finder* on pages 182–7.

A locator map shows where you are in relation to other areas in the city center.

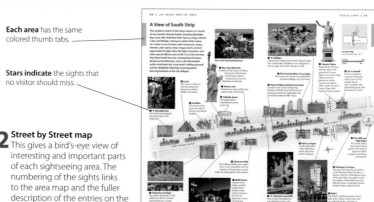

Each area has the same colored thumb tabs.

Stars indicate the sights that no visitor should miss.

2 Street by Street map
This gives a bird's-eye view of interesting and important parts of each sightseeing area. The numbering of the sights links to the area map and the fuller description of the entries on the pages that follow.

Las Vegas Area Map

The colored areas shown on this map *(see inside front cover)* are the three main sightseeing areas used in this guide. Each is covered in a full chapter in *Las Vegas Area by Area (see pp36–93)*. They are highlighted on other maps throughout the book. In *Las Vegas at a Glance*, for example, they help you locate the top sights. They are also used to help you find the position of two walks and a drive *(see pp86–93)*.

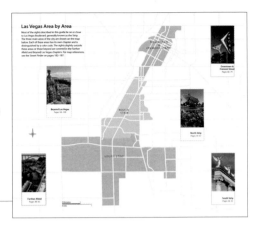

Las Vegas Area by Area

Numbers refer to each sight's position on the area map and its place in the chapter.

Story boxes provide information about historical or cultural topics relating to the sights.

3 Detailed information
All the important sights in Las Vegas are described individually. They are listed in order following the numbering on the area map at the start of the section. Practical information includes a map reference, opening hours, and telephone numbers. The key to the symbols is on the back flap.

The visitors' checklist gives all the practical information needed to plan your visit.

Practical information provides everything you need to know to visit each sight. Map references pinpoint the sight's location on the *Street Finder* map *(see pp182–7)*.

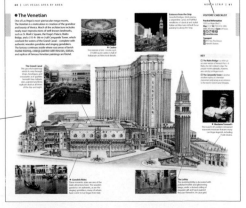

4 Las Vegas's major sights
Important buildings are dissected to reveal their interiors. Some iconic sights have color-coded floorplans to help you get the best from your visit.

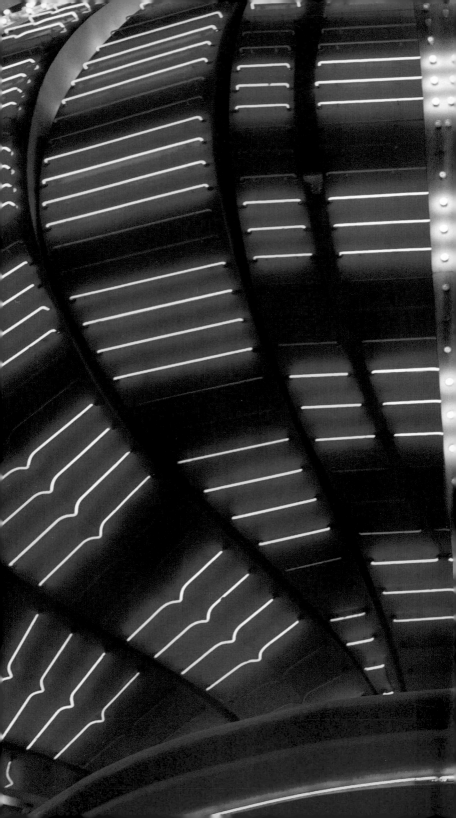

INTRODUCING
LAS VEGAS

GREAT DAYS IN LAS VEGAS

As one of the world's busiest tourist destinations, the city of Las Vegas offers just about everything – grand hotels, spectacular shows, excellent shops and restaurants, theme park attractions, and the natural beauty of the surrounding lakes, parks, and canyons. Most visitors, however, are here for a short period and need to plan their visit efficiently so as to sample the best of all that is available. The following itineraries present suggestions for four distinct days of sightseeing, exploring, and amusement, and offer ideas on where to eat, what to see, and what to do for entertainment.

However, these suggestions are just ideas and can be modified to suit your tastes and requirements. The price guides are indicative of the cost of transport and admission (if any) for two adults or for a family of two adults and two children.

Spectacular setting of Grand Canal Shoppes at The Venetian

Shopping and Sightseeing

Two adults allow at least $300

- Shop at Via Bellagio
- Lunch at the famous Grand Canal Shoppes
- Enjoy light-and-sound shows at Fremont Street Experience
- See "O" at the Bellagio

Morning
Start at **Via Bellagio** (see p129), an upscale shopping promenade that consists of some of the world's most exclusive shops, such as Giorgio Armani, Gucci, Prada, Tiffany & Co., Hermès, and Louis Vuitton. Farther north on the Strip is **Forum Shops at Caesars Palace** (see p128), an eclectic mix of designer shops. Walk across the street, and head for **The Venetian** (see pp60–61). Take some time to admire the magnificent architecture, which re-creates many of the famous sights of Venice. After a brief photography session, head for **Grand Canal Shoppes** (see p129), a chic shopping arcade set along the canal. The complex also boasts a range of eateries suitable for a quick lunch.

Afternoon
A short distance from here is **Fashion Show Mall** (see p128), the city's largest mall, which is anchored by high-end department stores.

For shoppers who prefer to rummage, head downtown to **Retro Vegas** (see p133), a store specializing in retro items from Vegas homes of the past. Also see the light-and-sound shows at the **Fremont Street Experience**, which begin after dusk (see pp74–5).

In the evening, put your feet up and take in the Cirque du Soleil production of **"O"** (see p136) at the Bellagio. Reservations are required for this spectacular, fantastical, water-themed show.

Wild, Weird, and Wonderful

Two adults allow at least $175

- Visit CSI: The Experience
- Try the thrilling rides at Stratosphere Tower
- Ride the VooDoo Zip Line at the Rio

Morning
Begin at **MGM Grand** (see p46), and play the role of a crime-scene investigator at the blockbuster **CSI: The Experience** (see p46). Then head north on the Strip to the **LINQ Promenade** (see p53), a dining, shopping and entertainment district that is also home to the world's largest observation wheel. Just across the street is **The Mirage** (see p58). End the morning with a visit to see the white tigers and the playful dolphins at **Siegfried & Roy's Secret Garden and Dolphin Habitat** (see p58).

Atlantic bottlenose dolphins at play, Dolphin Habitat, The Mirage

Afternoon

Head to **Wynn Encore** (see p64) for lunch at one of its many exceptional restaurants. Walk to **Stratosphere Tower** (see p65) and try the thrill rides, situated nearly 1,000 ft (305 m) above the ground. Nearby is the **Viva Las Vegas Wedding Chapel** (see p160), which performs themed weddings, and the **Little White Chapel** (see p160) with its Drive-Up Wedding Window for quick marriages. In the evening, catch the **VooDoo Zip Line** at **Rio** (see p52), an exhilarating ride from atop the 51st floor of the Masquerade tower. The many restaurants nearby – such as **Café 6** (see p123) at Palms Place – are also superb.

Sheer red sandstone cliffs at Red Rock Canyon

Great Outdoors

Two adults allow at least $50

- Enjoy a hike at Red Rock Canyon
- Picnic at Willow Springs
- Drive up Mount Charleston

Morning

Head out on a 20-minute drive from the Strip to **Red Rock Canyon** (see p82). Take the 13-mile (21-km) scenic loop and view the majestic red sandstone rock formations. Allow time for a hike into one of the many canyons here – a minimum 60-minute walk. **Willow Springs** (see p82) is a good picnicking spot, or visit a coffee shop in **Bonnie Springs** (see p83) for lunch.

Afternoon

After lunch, make your way northwest along Highway 95 to **Toiyabe National Forest** (see p83). Drive up **Mount Charleston** (see p83), which is located within the forest and is a popular year-round destination for hiking, backpacking, picnicking, and overnight camping. Part of the Spring Mountain Range, it is also a popular destination for skiers and snowboarders during winter. Stop at the **Mount Charleston Ranger Station** (see p146) for maps and any information on the area's ecology and history. Dine at a resort restaurant on the mountain for satisfying dishes in comfortable rustic surrounds. Or make your way back to the city lights to indulge in an all-you-can-eat smorgasbord at **Bacchanal Buffet** (see p120).

A Family Day

Two adults and two children allow at least $430

- Rides at Adventuredome
- Eat candy at M&M's World
- Visit BODIES: The Exhibition at Luxor
- Watch the *Tournament of Kings* show

Morning

It is a good idea to get an early start at **Circus Circus: Adventuredome** (see pp66–7), the most popular children's attraction in Las Vegas.

Riders being spun around on Chaos at Adventuredome

This indoor amusement park features many rides, fast-paced as well as toddler-friendly, and a variety of arcade games. Also stop at the big top, **Carnival Midway** (see p66), to enjoy free circus acts such as clowns and trapeze artists. Afterward, take a bus south. Head to the Showcase Mall and savor the chocolates at **M&M's World** (see p46).

Afternoon

Stop at **New York-New York** (see p45) for a Manhattan-style lunch at any one of the myriad cafés, bars, and restaurants set among Greenwich Village brownstones. Take a free tram ride from **Excalibur** (see p44) down to **Mandalay Bay's Shark Reef** (see pp42–3), a huge aquarium with sharks, reptiles, and other marine life. Get back on the tram for a short ride to **Luxor** (see p44) and learn all about the human anatomy at **BODIES: The Exhibition** (see p44). In the evening, walk back to **Excalibur** to feast on a hearty three-course meal while watching jousting knights and sword fights at the **Tournament of Kings** (see p164) show.

Imposing structure of the Great Sphinx and glass pyramid at Luxor

Two Days in Las Vegas

- Marvel at panoramic views of the city from the world's tallest observation wheel
- Enjoy a dazzling display from the dancing Fountains of the Bellagio
- Learn about the role mobsters played in the early history of Las Vegas

The tall High Roller, a landmark of Las Vegas

Day 1

Morning Start your day at **Mandalay Bay** *(see pp42–3)*, a resort on the South Strip with a striking tropical theme. Stroll along the sands of the hotel's artificial beach before visiting the **Shark Reef Aquarium** *(see p43)*. Visitors can see over 2,000 animals and 100 different species of marine life, including sharks, green sea turtles, and crocodiles.

Afternoon Walk or take the tram to **Luxor** *(see p44)*, an Ancient-Egyptian-themed hotel encased in a giant glass pyramid. Visit **BODIES: The Exhibition** *(see p44)*, which displays real human bodies and specimens that have been dissected and preserved. Afterward, head north on the Strip to **The LINQ Hotel & Casino** *(see p53)*, a shopping, entertainment, and dining resort. Enjoy staggering views of the city from the **High Roller** *(see p53)*, the world's tallest observation wheel, before having dinner in the outdoor plaza. Finish your day at the **Fountains of Bellagio** *(see p51)*, a stunning show featuring jets of water set to lights and music.

Day 2

Morning Explore the history of downtown Las Vegas, starting with a guided tour of the **Neon Museum** *(see p79)*, which features signs dating back to the 1950s. Just a few blocks away is the **Mob Museum** *(see p79)*, detailing the history of the law enforcement's battle with organized crime in the early days of Las Vegas.

Afternoon Head to the nearby **18b Arts District** *(see p78)* for lunch, then explore the art galleries, street art murals, and antique and vintage stores in this lively area.

Once it gets dark, take in one of the dazzling light shows on the overhead canopy at the **Fremont Street Experience** *(see pp74–5)*. Afterward, catch a show at the nearby **Smith Center for the Performing Arts** *(see p140)*. If there's time, head to the **Fremont East District** *(see p75)*, an eclectic mixture of bars, clubs and cafés with iconic vintage neon signs.

Three Days in Las Vegas

- View relics recovered from the Atlantic at Titanic: The Artifact Exhibition
- Admire the truly breath-taking scenery at the Grand Canyon
- Watch astonishing acrobatics at a Cirque du Soleil show

Day 1

Morning Start the day at the impressive Shark Reef Aquarium in Mandalay Bay, then journey to **Luxor** for **Titanic: The Artifact Exhibition** *(see p44)*. This features over 250 haunting relics from the doomed ocean-liner. Visitors can also see re-created parts of the ship, such as the Grand Staircase and Promenade Deck.

Afternoon Have lunch in the plaza at The LINQ before taking in dizzying views from the High Roller. In the evening, follow the overhead pedestrian walkway to the Bellagio. See the dazzling Fountains show before heading to the resort's **Conservatory & Botanical Gardens** *(see p50)*, a mesmerizing floral extravaganza.

Day 2

Morning One of the world's greatest natural wonders, the **Grand Canyon** *(see pp98–103)*, is relatively close to Las Vegas. The very best way to experience the grandeur of the Canyon is by helicopter. For those on a tighter budget, the South Rim of the Canyon is a five-hour drive from Las Vegas and there are a variety of bus tours available.

Afternoon If you find yourself back in Vegas with time to spare, head to **The Mirage** *(see p58)*. Among the many attractions at this Polynesian-island-themed resort is **Siegfried & Roy's Secret Garden and Dolphin Habitat** *(see p58)*, home to endangered white tigers, lions and bottlenose dolphins. Have dinner on the resort and look out for the huge artificial volcano that erupts every hour from 8pm to 10pm.

The Fountains of Bellagio, a mesmerizing choreographed water show

Day 3
Morning Hop aboard the **Big Bus Tour** *(see p178)*, an open-top bus that cruises the Vegas Strip and points to many of its most famous landmarks. Exit at the **MGM Grand** *(see p46)* and test your inner crime-solver at **CSI: The Experience** *(see p46)*.

Afternoon Visit the **Downtown Container Park** *(see p78)* on Fremont Street, a unique assortment of boutiques, bars and eateries set in shipping containers. Continue down the road to the vibrant Fremont Street Experience before ending the day with one of the extraordinary Cirque du Soleil shows, *"O"* at Bellagio *(see p136)*.

Five Days in Las Vegas

- Take in magnificent views from a half-scale replica of the Eiffel Tower
- Witness a 19th-century shootout in a replica Western mining town
- See the Hoover Dam, a staggering triumph of engineering.

Day 1
Morning Begin the day at **Circus Circus: Adventuredome** *(see pp66–7)*. With 25 exhilarating rides and attractions, it is America's largest indoor theme park. Afterward, take a ride above the Strip on the High Roller observation wheel at The LINQ.

Afternoon Take a bus to **Paris Las Vegas** *(see p48)* and ride the glass elevator to the top of the half-scale replica of the **Eiffel Tower** *(see p48)*. Enjoy great views of the entire Las Vegas Valley before heading to the Bellagio.

Day 2
Morning Travel west of Las Vegas to the **Red Rock Canyon** *(see p82)*. Follow the Scenic Loop Drive, a 13-mile tour around stunning sandstone formations. Afterward, head south to **Spring Mountain Ranch State Park** *(see p83)*, home to some of the oldest buildings in Southern Nevada.

Afternoon Journey another mile south to **Bonnie Springs Ranch** *(see p83)*, a full-scale replica of an old Western mining town, complete with live 1800s-era melodrama performances and shootouts. Travel back to Las Vegas in time for dinner. If you have time, visit the **Stratosphere** *(see p65)*. Enjoy stunning views from the observation deck and, if you're feeling brave, try one of the four hair-raising rides on offer.

Day 3
Morning Find impressive savings at more than 150 designer and name brand shops at the downtown mall **Las Vegas Premium Outlets** *(see p130)*.

Afternoon Marvel at marine life in the Shark Reef Aquarium at Mandalay Bay and then head to BODIES: The Exhibition at Luxor. In the evening, see a show at the **Smith Center for the Performing Arts** *(see p140)*.

Day 4
Morning Drive or take a helicopter tour of the Grand Canyon. Take time to appreciate the scenery from the **Grand Canyon Skywalk** *(see p99)*, a giant horseshoe-shaped glass bridge that hangs over the Colorado River.

Afternoon If you have time on your return, see one of the spectacular light shows at the Fremont Street Experience.

Day 5
Morning Take a scenic cruise on **Lake Mead** *(see p84)*, the country's largest man-made

New York-New York, a resort dedicated to re-creating the best of the Big Apple

reservoir, followed by a tour inside the power plant of the **Hoover Dam** *(see p85)*, named as one of the world's Top 10 Construction Achievements of the 20th Century. Afterward, walk across the **Mike O'Callaghan-Pat Tillman Memorial Bridge** *(see p84)*, the longest single-arch bridge in North America.

Afternoon Visit Siegfried & Roy's Secret Garden and Dolphin Habitat at The Mirage, and then head to **New York-New York** *(see p45)*, where you'll find, among other attractions, a replica of the Manhattan skyline and Hershey's Chocolate World flagship store. Thrill-seekers should take a ride on the **Big Apple** roller coaster *(see p45)*, which makes high-speed dives overlooking the Vegas Strip. Finish your trip with a relaxing dinner in one of the many Manhattan-themed restaurants.

Insanity, a heart-stopping ride overhanging the Stratosphere Tower

Putting Las Vegas on the Map

Renowned as the "Entertainment Capital of the World", Las Vegas covers 113 sq miles (292 sq km) of the Nevada desert in Southwest USA. Located 270 miles (434 km) northeast of Los Angeles, the population of this city is constantly growing. More than 40 million visitors come to Las Vegas each year, lured by its casinos and other attractions. An international airport and interstate highways connect the city to the rest of the country and the world. Within easy driving distance from the city are lakes, canyons, and vast desert plateaus.

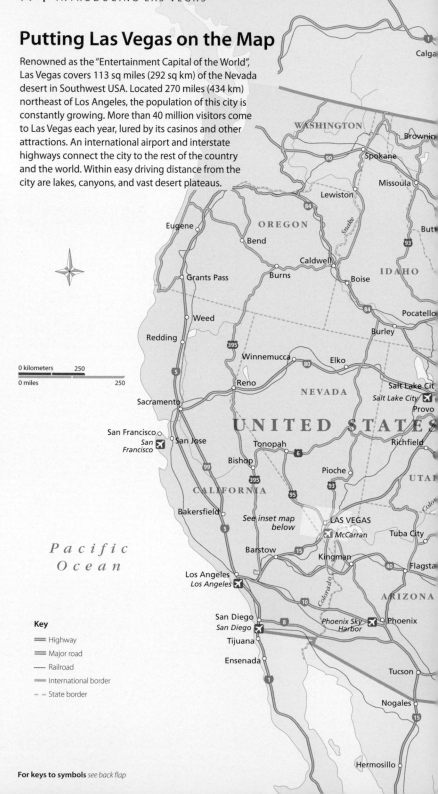

Key

━━ Highway
━━ Major road
── Railroad
━━ International border
-- State border

Central Las Vegas

The Las Vegas valley is split into east and west sections with the Las Vegas Boulevard or the Strip serving as the central divider. The Strip also often acts as a starting point for visitors who want to explore the city's attractions, many of which are located along the boulevard or within a few blocks of it. These include luxurious and grand mega resorts, museums, fantastic shows, massive shopping malls, theme parks, and much more. Towards the north end of the Strip is the downtown area, home to the entertaining Fremont Street Experience and Neonopolis center.

Neon Signs, Downtown Las Vegas
The downtown area and Fremont Street (see pp68–79) feature an interesting collection of restored neon signs, including the old Hacienda's horse and rider.

Fashion Show Mall
The jewel of the city's shopping malls, Fashion Show is home to upscale department stores such as Nordstrom, Saks Fifth Avenue, and Neiman Marcus, as well as more than 225 shops, boutiques, and restaurants (see p59).

Flamingo Las Vegas
The glittering pink-and-orange feather sign outside this hotel is one of Las Vegas's most recognized icons (see p53). Nothing remains of Bugsy Siegel's original resort except a stone pillar and a small plaque in the casino's garden.

Key

◼ Major sights

— Monorail/tram route

House of Blues
This distinguished nightclub in Mandalay Bay is known for its superb jazz, blues, and rock performances by famous stars (see p143).

Fremont Street Experience
Night turns into day as hundreds of visitors stroll under this brightly lit canopy to watch the amazing light-and-sound shows (see pp74–5).

Madame Tussauds
The Vegas branch of this famous wax exhibition in London is located at The Venetian (see pp60–61). More than 100 celebrities, including Hollywood personalities, rock stars, and sports figures are displayed here. Special exhibits feature legends such as Elvis Presley, Frank Sinatra, and Liberace.

***Mystère* at Treasure Island**
The longest running Cirque du Soleil show in Las Vegas, this spectacular production showcases fantastic circus acts, and is a surrealistic celebration of music, dance, acrobatics, mime, and comedy (see p136).

The Orleans
This hotel and casino boasts an impressive array of facilities. These include an 18-screen cinema complex, bowling alley, spa, and a large arena used for concerts and special events (see p45).

THE HISTORY OF LAS VEGAS

One of America's most modern cities, Las Vegas did not exist before the 20th century. Initially an oasis for desert travelers, many people say that it was only after Bugsy Siegel built the Flamingo hotel in 1946 that the town shed its frontier image in favor of ultra-modern neon. Since then, Las Vegas's growth has centered around its reputation as the world's entertainment capital.

Most of the Southwest and the area today known as Las Vegas was once submerged by a huge lake fed by waters from the retreating glaciers of the last Ice Age, 25,000 years ago. The earliest signs of human activity in this region date back 11,000 years to the Paleo-Indian period. Skilled hunters of mammoths and other large animals, the Paleo-Indians roamed the area in small groups between 10,000 and 8,000 BC.

Gradually, the climate began to change and became increasingly warm. As a result, the lake slowly dried up, and the area around today's Las Vegas turned to desert. In order to survive in this new environment, the Paleo-Indians underwent long periods of adaptation. As the large mammals died out, they began hunting small game and harvesting roots and berries. These hunter-gatherers came to be known as Archaic Indians. Though the area they occupied was arid, spring waters were plentiful in places. Anthropologists believe that as the population grew, settled farming societies began to appear. By about AD 800, Anasazi Indians, or Ancient Ones, had settled along the washes, dry beds of intermittent streams, and in the valleys to the north and east of what is now Las Vegas. A highly advanced Native civilization, they grew corn, beans, and squash; hunted with bows and arrows; made baskets; and lived in pit houses. By 1050, however, the area was inexplicably abandoned, possibly due to drought.

Early Explorers

As time passed, the peaceful and semi-nomadic Southern Paiute tribe came to the region, and occupied it for the next seven centuries. They grew corn and squash, and hunted wild animals. Petroglyphs indicate the Paiute had settlements at Red Rock Canyon (see p82), and Valley of Fire (see p83). One of the first Europeans they met was Francisco Garces, a Franciscan friar, who, in 1776, traveled along the Old Spanish Trail, which connected the Catholic-Spanish missions between New Mexico and California.

Garces was followed 50 years later by fur trader and explorer Jedediah Smith, who passed through present-day Southern Nevada and blazed a route that would traverse the Sierra Nevada Mountains.

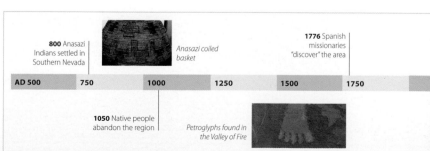

800 Anasazi Indians settled in Southern Nevada

Anasazi coiled basket

1776 Spanish missionaries "discover" the area

AD 500	750	1000	1250	1500	1750

1050 Native people abandon the region

Petroglyphs found in the Valley of Fire

◀ Elvis Presley in *Love in Las Vegas*

Mormon pioneers on the great trek westward

In 1829, Spanish trader Antonio Armijo and his scout Rafael Rivera traveled along the Spanish Trail and found a path that led them through an area with oasis-like springs. They named it Las Vegas, or "The Meadows."

By the mid-1800s, the area had become a popular camping spot because of its source of water. In 1845, John C. Fremont, a cartographer with the US Topographical Corps, led an expedition through the region, and drew accurate maps of the Nevada landscape.

Exploration eventually ended in exploitation with the Paiutes losing control of their land as the Las Vegas Valley's popularity finally resulted in its colonization. In 1855, the Mormon president, Brigham Young *(see p107)*, sent a group led by William Bringhurst to set up a mission in Las Vegas, where they built a fort and developed farmlands. The discovery of lead at nearby Mount Potosi attracted miners from Salt Lake City and led the Mormons to launch a mining operation. Their lack of experience and growing dissension between the groups of missionaries and the miners, coupled with crop failures and harsh summers, forced the Mormons to abandon their mission in 1858. Mining continued, however, and in 1861, the discovery of silver at Potosi led to a fresh influx of prospectors. Among them was Octavius Gass, a failed gold prospector.

The City's Beginnings

Helen Stewart, local ranch owner

A permanent settlement developed in 1865, when Gass seized the opportunity to take ownership of the Old Mormon Fort and set up a ranch – the Las Vegas Ranch – and supply station. Gass succeeded in growing crops by digging irrigation channels on the land. By 1872, he owned most of the land in Las Vegas. However, he eventually slid into debt and was forced to sell his land to Archibald Stewart, a wealthy rancher. Following Stewart's death in 1884, his wife Helen took charge

1826 Explorer Jedediah Smith passes through Southern Nevada

Mormon pioneers

1864 Nevada admitted to the Union as the 36th state

1825	1840	1855	1870	1885

1845 John C. Fremont leads an expedition to Las Vegas

1855–58 Mormons establish a settlement in Las Vegas Valley

1884 Helen Stewart becomes owner of the Las Vegas Ranch

of the land. Over the next 20 years, she acquired more land and ran the ranch as a profitable resort. In 1903, she sold the Las Vegas Ranch to William A. Clark, proprietor of the San Pedro, Los Angeles, and Salt Lake Railroad, who planned to take advantage of its strategic location as an ideal stopping point for trains.

By 1905, the railroad was completed and a train service had begun. In January of the same year, gold was found just south of Las Vegas, attracting yet more speculators to the area. The publicity generated by the railroad created a huge demand for land, and on May 15, 1905, the railroad company auctioned 1,200 lots of land. Almost overnight, the city was transformed as buildings sprang up and businesses were established.

Roulette session in progress at a casino in Las Vegas

Development

The city of Las Vegas, with a population of about 1,500, was officially incorporated as a municipality in 1911. The same year, the railroad built a locomotive repair yard here. The resulting jobs doubled the population. But it was not a model town. There was no sewage system, prostitution was rife in the city's red-light district, Block 16, and gambling, though illegal, was widespread. Some modernization, however, did take place. By 1915, residents had 24-hour electricity, and the Las Vegas Land and Water Company began graveling streets and laying water pipes. In 1931, Nevada legislators legalized quick

divorces and gambling, the latter in an attempt to gain tax revenues.

The Great Depression did not affect Las Vegas much. Building work on the Hoover Dam project (see p85), originally known as Boulder Dam, began in 1931 and employed about 5,100 workers, funnelling millions of dollars into the economy. It even led to the creation of Boulder City (see p84) to house the dam's workers. Completed in 1937, the dam provided the first reliable source of water, along with cheap electricity, to meet the city's demands. It also formed Lake Mead (see p84).

During this period, new casinos were emerging in downtown and spreading south on Las Vegas Boulevard. El Rancho opened in 1941 followed by Last Frontier in 1942. Around this time, the US military set up base in Las Vegas. In a strange turn of events, this led to the closure of Block 16 as the War Department threatened to bar service personnel from the town until "Sin City" cleaned up its act.

The Hoover Dam under construction

1920 Anderson Field, Las Vegas's first airport, opens

1905 Las Vegas township established

1931 Gambling and quick divorces legalized in Nevada

1941 El Rancho Vegas opens as first resort on the "Strip"

El Rancho Vegas

1948 McCarran Field, later McCarran Airport, opens

1900	1915	1930	1945

1911 The city of Las Vegas is officially incorporated

1920 Prohibition era begins

1915 Las Vegas residents have 24-hour electricity

Hoover Dam postcard

1931 Hoover Dam project begins

1946 Bugsy Siegel opens the Flamingo

1941 Army establishes gunnery school near Las Vegas

The Rise and Fall of the Mob

Although gambling was legalized in Las Vegas in 1931, it was not until almost a decade later that it attracted the attention of criminal elements who recognized the full potential of the city's growing gambling industry. The appearance of Bugsy Siegel, a New York mobster, on the city's horizon marked the emergence of the Mafia in Las Vegas, and for several years from the 1940s onward, organized crime and Las Vegas walked hand in hand. The tide began to turn in the 1960s as Nevada state authorities passed new laws in attempts to weaken the mob's hold on the city. However, it was the arrival of billionaire Howard Hughes, and the subsequent advent of legitimate corporations, that finally signaled the end of the mob.

Arrival of the Mob
Bugsy Siegel (left) opened the Flamingo hotel *(see p53)* in 1946 using funds provided by a syndicate of New York mobsters.

Flamingo's Second Opening
After Bugsy's death, successful Phoenix mobster Gus Greenbaum took over the Flamingo, and the second opening of the $5 million casino and resort was a big success. Many other casino-resorts, bankrolled by organized crime, sprang up during the 1950s.

Casino Operator Moe Dalitz
Through the 1950s and 60s, mobster Moe Dalitz opened several casinos along the Strip with the help of Jimmy Hoffa, head of the Teamsters labor union. The union's $269 million fund was used to purchase Circus Circus, Dunes, and Stardust among others.

Gambling Halls and Clubs Along Fremont Street
Bright lights and neon signs of several casinos and clubs illuminate the sidewalks of Fremont Street (1948). Located in the heart of downtown, this street was the city's most-visited and popular area until the rise of the Strip.

Casinos Funded by "the Boys"
By 1959, Americans were starting to understand just how involved the mob was in running Las Vegas. A *Reader's Digest* article told of how casinos such as Desert Inn, Flamingo, Frontier, Sands, Riviera, Sahara, and many others had been funded by "the boys", ie the mobsters, in Detroit, Minneapolis, Cleveland, Miami, New York, and New Jersey.

The Rat Pack
Frank Sinatra, Dean Martin, Sammy Davis Jr, and other members of the "Rat Pack" were regular performers at the Sands and Desert Inn, and sealed Las Vegas's reputation as an entertainment mecca. Sinatra's links to Mafia chieftain Sam Giancana soon brought him to the notice of federal agencies aiming to rid the city of its mob affiliations in the 1960s.

The Apache hotel was bought by Texas bootlegger and gambler Benny Binion, who changed its name to Binion's Horseshoe.

Howard Hughes (1905–76)

Billionaire Howard Hughes arrived in Las Vegas in November 1966, moving into a luxurious suite on the ninth floor of the Desert Inn hotel. When the hotel's management tried to move him out a few months later, Hughes bought the place for $13.25 million. Although he never left his room in four years, he spent some $300 million buying Vegas properties. These included the Silver Slipper hotel and casino across the Strip, whose blinking neon slipper disturbed him – as the owner he had it switched off.

Hughes is credited with bringing legitimate business and a sanitized image to Vegas, sounding the death knell of mob investment in the city. However, as recently as the 1970s and 80s mobsters were caught skimming profits from some Vegas hotels.

Billionaire entrepreneur Howard Hughes

Anthony Spilotro and Wife
Mob figure Anthony "the Ant" Spilotro and his wife, Nancy, leave the federal building in Las Vegas after a session in court on racketeering charges (1986). Charges of corruption and tax evasion were filed against many Vegas mobsters in the 1970s and 80s.

Public Corporations
In 1967, a new law in Nevada allowed public corporations to obtain gambling licenses. This paved the way for companies such as Hilton, MGM, and Holiday Inn to begin legitimate building programs in Las Vegas. Eventually, the influence of corporate America loosened the mob's grip on casinos.

Las Vegas's Changing Face

In 1950, the newly created Nevada Proving Ground, later named the Nevada Test Site, brought the atomic age to Vegas. The periodic nuclear test explosions added to the city's entertainment value. Las Vegans celebrated the tests by holding the Miss Atomic Bomb beauty pageant, as well as picnics at points that afforded a bird's-eye view of the explosions.

At the same time, a construction frenzy, which lasted for more than a decade, seemed to grip the city. Soon, downtown and Las Vegas Boulevard, which later came to be known as the Strip, were packed with casino-resorts that had been built at an incredible pace. Each tried to outdo the other in terms of scale and extravagance. Entertainers such as Frank Sinatra (see p29) and the Rat Pack held sold-out shows at the Sands hotel, which opened in 1952.

Montgomery Clift, Rosemary Clooney and other celebrities in Las Vegas

The nine-story Riviera hotel, which opened in 1955, was the city's first high-rise resort. This was followed by the 15-story Fremont Hotel (see p74) in downtown Las Vegas.

By 1960, the city's population had grown to 65,000. With the advent of air conditioning, interstate highways, and transcontinental travel, Las Vegas was fast becoming a leading tourist destination and a favorite haunt of movie stars, millionaires, and other celebrities.

Las Vegas's gambling industry was also going through an overhaul. In the 1980s, corporate entities implemented tighter cash accounting rules in their casinos. This gave state regulators the impetus to insist on the same statewide. The remaining traces of the mob's influence were gradually being erased. Slowly, but surely, the city's image was changing. Amid the bright lights and the hordes of tourists, Las Vegas was becoming a family destination.

Nevada Test Site

Originally a gunnery range for the US Army Air Corps during World War II, the site became a testing range for nuclear weapons at the end of the war. Located 90 miles (145 km) north of Vegas, the site conducted its first test in January 1951 on a stretch of desert called Frenchman Flat. Over the next 11 years, 126 atomic bombs were detonated above ground. Open-air testing was banned under the First Nuclear Test Ban Treaty, but underground testing went on for the next 30 years. In 1996, President Bill Clinton signed the Comprehensive Test Ban Treaty, which ended all nuclear testing.

Radioactive cloud at the Nevada Test Site

Boomtown

Las Vegas experienced a period of mixed fortunes in the 1970s. MGM Grand – today Bally's (see p53) – opened in 1973 and heralded the age of the mega-resort.

1951 First atomic bomb detonated at Nevada Test Site

1955 Gaming Control Board created to regulate gaming industry

Howard Hughes

1966 Howard Hughes arrives in Las Vegas

1968 Vegas's first family-friendly hotel, Circus Circus, launched

1985 first Natio Finals Roo are h

1950 **1955** **1960** **1965** **1970** **1975** **1980**

1955 Riviera opens as the city's first "high-rise"

1960 The Rat Pack take the stage at the Sands Hotel

1966 Caesars Palace opens as first major, themed resort

Marble Statue, Caesars Palace

1975 Nevada's gaming earnings cross $1 billion mark

With 2,100 rooms the hotel earned the title of "world's largest resort." However, in 1975, flash floods wreaked havoc on the Strip, and in 1978, gambling was legalized in Atlantic City. Both these events had an adverse effect on the city's tourism industry. But it was not long before Las Vegas recovered and entered a phase of large-scale expansion. In 1989, entrepreneur and hotelier Steve Wynn *(see p28)* opened The Mirage *(see p58)* at a cost of $620 million, the grandest resort the city had ever seen. Its success spurred the construction of many theme-based mega resorts, such as Excalibur *(see p44)*, Luxor *(see p44)*, Treasure Island – TI *(see pp58–9)*, and a new MGM Grand *(see p46)*, which had over 5,000 rooms. Wynn struck gold again in 1998 when he launched the $1.6 billion Bellagio *(see pp50–51)* which, along with The Venetian *(see pp60–61)*, is considered to be one of the most opulent resorts in the world.

Unencumbered by the slow-growth ordinances enacted by its neighbor Reno, the Las Vegas boom continued unabated until 2010. While burnishing its reputation as an entertainment capital, it has become home to a growing legion of full-time residents. In 2007 the New Frontier, the second hotel and casino to open on the Strip, was demolished with accompanying fireworks to make way for a new resort, although the project has since been put on hold.

Today, Las Vegas is one of the fastest growing cities in the country. Sunny skies, casinos, world-class restaurants, thrill rides, and a range of entertainment options attract millions of visitors each year. In 2008 The Palazzo *(see p58)* opened at a cost of $2.7 billion, in 2009 the 2,304-suite Encore connected to the already incredible Wynn Las Vegas *(see pp62–3)*, and in 2016 the T-Mobile Arena *(see p52)* and The Park joined the famous skyline.

Amid this amazing ever-changing scene, just two things remain constant: the way the city looks and the type of people who live here.

A lion statue at MGM Grand

The glittering and shimmering vista of Las Vegas in 2005 – its centennial year

1993 MGM Grand, the world's largest hotel, is built

Campanile Tower, The Venetian

1999 The lavish Venetian is built

2004 Las Vegas Monorail opens to the public

2005 Wynn Las Vegas opens

2010 The Cosmopolitan resort opens

2014 Opening of The LINQ, The Cromwell and SLS Las Vegas

1990	1995	2000	2005	2010	2015	2020

1989 Steve Wynn opens The Mirage

1996 Stratosphere Tower, the country's tallest observation tower, is built

1998 Bellagio is built for $1.6 billion, the costliest at the time

2009 CityCenter and ARIA open

2008 The Palazzo opens

2005 Las Vegas celebrates its centennial year

2016 T-Mobile Arena and The Park open

LAS VEGAS AT A GLANCE

A city like no other in the world, spectacular Las Vegas shimmers amid the Nevada desert. Only Vegas can take the best and the most recognized landmarks of other cities, and re-create them in grander and flashier reincarnations than the original. Fueled by tourism, the city is best known for its hotels: huge flamboyant resorts with their own museums, shows, rides, and casinos. The range of attractions extends beyond Las Vegas as well and includes the natural splendor of the Grand Canyon *(see pp98–103)*, and the engineering feat of the Hoover Dam *(see p85)*.

To make your visit as rewarding as possible, the following pages are a quick guide to the best Las Vegas has to offer, down to the city's best wedding chapels and its most celebrated residents and visitors. Below is a selection of the top ten tourist attractions that no visitor should miss.

Las Vegas's Top Ten Tourist Attractions

Cirque du Soleil Shows
See p136 & p139

Fountains of Bellagio
See p51

Gondola Rides at The Venetian
See pp60–61

Shark Reef
See p43

Death Valley
See pp108–9

Red Rock Canyon
See p82

Adventuredome
See pp66–7

Fremont Street Experience
See pp74–5

Hoover Dam
See p85

Grand Canyon
See pp98–103

◄ Fountains of Bellagio

Famous Visitors and Residents

As one of the world's most popular entertainment destinations, Las Vegas is associated with many glamorous personalities. These include movie stars such as Mickey Rooney, Lana Turner, and Leonardo DiCaprio; famous singers such as Frank Sinatra and Elvis Presley; eccentric billionaires such as Howard Hughes; and mobsters such as Benjamin "Bugsy" Siegel. Some have been drawn to Las Vegas from other parts of the country, while others call it home. All have left their mark on the city and future visitors and residents will no doubt continue to do the same.

Welcome sign for Howard Hughes, near Landmark hotel, Las Vegas

Entrepreneurs and Billionaires

The famous Las Vegas Strip came into being when Los Angeles hotelier Thomas Hull (1893–1964) decided to build the El Rancho on the dusty highway, a few miles south of Fremont Street. The idea came to him as he counted the number of cars that passed by on the highway as he waited for his flat tire to be fixed. The hotel was an instant hit, especially with the Los Angeles celebrity crowd. Eccentric billionaire Howard Hughes (1905–76) arrived in Las Vegas in 1966, and moved into a lavish suite at Desert Inn. When the hotel management asked him to move out a few months later, Hughes bought the hotel for $13.25 million. This led to a buying spree of several hotel properties, and an era of corporate ownership of casinos that marked the end of mob investment in the city. The father of the Las Vegas mega-resorts, Kirk Kerkorian, built the world's largest resort hotel three times. The first was in 1969, when he built the 1,500-room International, which is now the Westgate Las Vegas (see p64). However, his crowning achievement was the 5,000-room MGM Grand (see p46), which he built in 1993.

In true pioneering spirit, Kerkorian planned the construction of a huge, multi-billion dollar "urban metropolis" between the Monte Carlo and Bellagio hotels. Opened in 2010, CityCenter (see p49) includes a 4,004-room resort and casino, three 400-room hotels, 1,650 luxury condominiums, and an extensive retail, entertainment, and dining space.

Steve Wynn, Chairman and CEO of Wynn Resorts

Billionaire businessman and hotelier Steve Wynn is credited with building some of the most expensive and most opulent hotels in Las Vegas, such as the amazing Bellagio (see pp50–51) and the Wynn Las Vegas (see pp62–3).

Gangsters and Criminals

Infamous New York Mobster Benjamin "Bugsy" Siegel (1905–47) brought Hollywood celebrity status to Las Vegas, even though the spotlight mostly shone after his violent death in 1947. On one of his many cross-country trips he stopped in Las Vegas and came up with the idea of building a "Miami-modern-type" of casino-resort in the middle of the desert, on what is now the Strip. Built at a huge cost of $6 million, the Flamingo opened in 1946 with posh amenities never before seen in the city. Today, Flamingo Las Vegas (see p53) is among the city's most archetypal resorts.

Underworld crime boss Morris "Moe" Dalitz (1899–1989) came to Las Vegas in the 1940s and soon became a major player in the city's casino business. In 1950, he opened the lavish Desert Inn, which raised the standard of Vegas casinos by offering the best and the most extravagant of all amenities and services. In the following years, Dalitz purchased a string of casinos along the Strip, including Stardust, Dunes, and Sahara, and turned them into highly successful business ventures.

Benjamin "Bugsy" Siegel, gangster turned Vegas hotelier

Andre Agassi, the world-class tennis player, was born in Las Vegas

Texan gambler and bootlegger Benny Binion (1904–89) opened Binion's Horseshoe casino in 1951 and transformed the sawdust-floored casinos into carpeted gambling halls where players were encouraged to place huge bets. By the 1970s, he had raised the betting limit to $10,000. For gamblers with bigger bankrolls, he would gladly remove the limits. At its peak in the late 1980s, Horseshoe was the most profitable casino in town. Binion also established the World Series of Poker (see p33) in 1970, which is one of Vegas's most famed annual events.

Sports Personalities

World-class tennis player Andre Agassi is a native of Las Vegas and was born here in 1970. He was recognized as a tennis prodigy at the age of three and he turned pro at the age of 16. Agassi has won virtually every major tennis tournament, and was ranked number one in the mid-1990s. In 2001, he married acclaimed tennis player Steffi Graf, who has won 22 major championships. The couple, who are now both retired from professional tennis, currently reside in Las Vegas with their two children.

French figure skater Surya Bonaly has won nine French national championships and silver medals at three world championships. She became a US citizen in 2004, and is now a resident of Las Vegas.

Former baseball star pitcher Greg Maddux, who won an unprecedented four straight Cy Young Awards in the mid-1990s and a record 18 Gold Gloves, is also a resident of Las Vegas.

Golfing legend Tiger Woods was once a frequent visitor and high-stakes games player at MGM Grand. The same was true of former basketball player, Charles Barkley, forced to quit the habit due to large debts.

Entertainers

Glitz became a part of Las Vegas's persona when Wladziu Liberace (1919–87) made his debut here in 1944. An accomplished pianist, he was one of Las Vegas's most flamboyant performers, who wowed crowds with his showmanship and portrayal of outlandish "characters." Liberace soon became famous for his multicolored and sequined apparel, as well as for his endearing wit.

He later became a Las Vegas resident and once had his own museum. But, it was popular music legend Frank Sinatra (1915–98) who gave Las Vegas its ultra-hip, cool image. In 1953,

he performed at the now-demolished Sands hotel and was an instant success. Sinatra, Dean Martin, Sammy Davis Jr, and Joey Bishop made up the Rat Pack, and sealed Las Vegas's reputation as an adult playground.

More than a decade later, the undisputed King of Rock 'n' Roll, Elvis Presley (1935–77), arrived in Las Vegas. His debut performance in 1969 at the International Hotel, now the Westgate Las Vegas, was a run-away success. Elvis appeared for a record 837 sold-out shows there.

Other entertainers associated with Las Vegas include renowned comedian Jerry Lewis, singers Celine Dion, Wayne Newton, and Barbra Streisand, and the Illusionists Siegfried and Roy. Other performers, such as Elton John and Rod Stewart, sign up for a certain number of shows over a specified period of time.

Celebrities

Las Vegas's close proximity to Southern California has made it a popular getaway and entertainment mecca for the Hollywood crowd since the early 1940s. Even when it was just a Western-style resort town, many of the movie world's elite enjoyed taking refuge in the solitude of the Southern Nevada desert. Some of the regular visitors were Mickey Rooney, Humphrey Bogart, Rosemary Clooney, Maurice Chevalier, Gary Cooper, and Lana Turner, just to name a few.

Today, a new generation of Hollywood celebrities has made Vegas a kind of extension of Los Angeles – a place to jet to for a weekend rock concert, golf tournament, or championship prize fight. Tara Reid, Leonardo DiCaprio, and Eminem make frequent visits to the city's many nightclubs. And some, such as singer Gladys Knight, have established residence here.

Frank Sinatra receives the "Pied Piper Award" at Caesars Palace

Las Vegas's Best: Wedding Chapels

Weddings are big business in Las Vegas *(see pp158–61)* with more than 120,000 marriage licenses issued annually. Celebrities such as Elvis Presley, Richard Gere, Paul Newman, Bruce Willis, Michael Jordan, Clint Eastwood, and Britney Spears have all got married in Vegas. With an extensive selection of wedding chapels to choose from, ceremonies can range from drive-through affairs to lavish extravaganzas with helicopter rides over the city's skyline, and from simple civil proceedings to themed events amid singing Elvis impersonators. Most of the resorts also have at least one wedding chapel, and many offer elaborate wedding packages as well.

Guardian Angel Cathedral
This Catholic church holds services and the collection plate often receives casino vouchers as offerings *(see p59).*

Paradise Falls
This tropical garden chapel is located at Flamingo Las Vegas *(see p53)*. Beautiful waterfalls, palm trees, and lush surroundings create a romantic setting for weddings.

Bellagio's Wedding Chapel
Stained-glass windows, and fresh flowers form part of the decor at this elegant chapel. Couples can spend up to $25,000 for a lavish ceremony that includes a wide variety of services *(see pp158–9).*

Little Church of the West
The Little Church opened in 1942, making it the city's oldest wedding chapel. This famous redwood-sided chapel has a colorful flower garden, and more than 100 couples get married here each week.

SOUTH INDUSTRIAL RD

NORTH STRIP

WEST FLAMINGO ROAD

LAS VEGAS FREEWAY

SOUTH LAS VEGAS BLVD

SOUTH STRIP

WEST TROPICANA AVE

Graceland Wedding Chapel
This tiny Cape Cod-style chapel stages a ceremony with an Elvis impersonator handling the service, ending with a 15-minute musical tribute to the King of Rock 'n' Roll.

DOWNTOWN & FREMONT STREET

Hartland Mansion
Once visited by Elvis Presley, this expansive mansion is located in a quiet residential neighborhood. The banquet hall can accommodate weddings and receptions of up to 700 people *(see p92)*.

Chapel of the Flowers
This picturesque chapel has a charming outdoor setting with waterfalls, lush greenery, fragrant flowers, a quaint wooden bridge, and garden gazebo. People from all over the world come here to tie the knot.

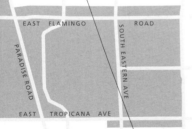

Chapel of the Bells
In service since the 1960s, this intimate chapel has performed marriage ceremonies for many celebrities, including South American soccer champion Pelé, Mickey Rooney, Ernest Borgnine, Kelly Ripa, and Beverly DeAngelo.

0 kilometers 2
0 miles 1

LAS VEGAS THROUGH THE YEAR

Las Vegas enjoys an average of more than 312 days of sunshine each year, allowing for the enjoyment of various outdoor activities almost every day of the year. Spring and fall are the most comfortable seasons as visitors and residents alike revel in the pleasantly warm days, filled with several sporting events, including golf and boxing championships, baseball tournaments, and NASCAR races. June ushers in four, hot months of summer, with daytime temperatures averaging 39°C

(103°F) and numerous festivals. The end of September marks the onset of a very brief fall with an astounding array of colors in the area's forests and national parks. Winter here is a distinctly different season, often close to freezing at times. However, in December the National Finals Rodeo, and New Year's celebrations draw huge crowds and make this one of the busiest times of the year. The city is also a premier destination for conventions all year round.

Spring

The spring months are usually very mild. The days are virtually cloud-free, and outdoor enthusiasts can enjoy the parades, carnivals, and numerous sporting activities that take place during these months.

Racing cars at the UAW-Daimler Chrysler 400 Series, Nextel Cup, Las Vegas

March

NASCAR Weekend (early Mar), Las Vegas Motor Speedway. The Busch Series and the Nextel Cup races are held over three days. This is the largest sporting event of the year, and attracts more than 150,000 racing fans.

March Madness (mid-Mar–early April). College basketball season takes off as teams compete in a lead up to the NCAA (National Collegiate Athletic Association) Championship finals.

St. Patrick's Day Parade (Mar 17). More than 100 entrants and colorful floats

Gwyneth Paltrow at CinemaCon (previously ShoWest) Convention

set off on the city's biggest parade. Resorts use the occasion to run specials on corned beef and cabbage and green beer.

Big League Weekend (late Mar or early April), Cashman Field. Baseball season swings into action with gusto as six major league teams compete against each other.

CinemaCon Convention (late Mar). This huge, motion picture industry event lures celebrities to town.

April

Mardi Gras (early Apr). The Fremont Street Experience and several hotels gear up for special Mardi Gras festivities with live Dixieland jazz, street carnivals, and Cajun cuisine.

May

Cinco de Mayo (Sun closest to May 5). Annual Mexican

celebration with fun-filled activities at parks throughout the city. Casinos and hotels offer food and drink specials, as well as free giveaways.

Snow Mountain Pow Wow (May). Presents dance, drama, and musical performances. An outdoor craft market features over 40 vendors with Native American arts, crafts, and food.

Helldorado Days (early May). This event has developed into a charity fundraiser, featuring a golf tournament, poker championship, trap-shooting contest, and two rodeos. There is also a parade with floats and a fireworks show.

Memorial Day Weekend (last weekend). The city comes alive during three days of parties, outdoor concerts by international performers, sizzling shows, sports events, and appetizing cuisines.

Average Daily Hours of Sunshine

Hours

	Jan	Feb	Mar	Apr	May	Jun	Jul	Aug	Sep	Oct	Nov	Dec

Sunshine Chart
A sunny climate is one of Las Vegas's main attractions. There are very few days with no sunshine at all, even in the winter. The summer sun can be very fierce, and adequate precautions against sunburn and sunstroke should be taken. Sunscreen, a hat, and sunglasses are highly recommended, as is drinking plenty of water.

Summer

Summer begins in earnest in mid to late June as temperatures climb steadily beyond the 32°C (90°F) mark. This is also festival time for Las Vegas with two food and one film festival to look forward to. For racing enthusiasts, the NASCAR Camping World Truck Series is a treat, while gaming lovers enjoy the annual World Series of Poker tournament.

June
World Series of Poker
(Jun 2–Jul 15), Rio. More than 20,000 players match wits in this annual tournament. Buy-ins range from $1,000 for the ladies' game to $10,000 for the No-limit Texas Hold 'em World Championship.
The Electric Daisy Carnival
(mid-Jun). This three-day festival is a celebration of electronic dance music, with art, carnival rides, and all of the top dance music DJs. Held at the Las Vegas Motor Speedway, it attracts more than 400,000 people.

July
Fourth of July *(Jul 4)*.
Fireworks, drinking, gambling, barbecues, and outdoor concerts, as well as high temperatures mark the celebration. Local parks sponsor sports contests, pancake breakfasts, and other events.

August
Men's Apparel Guild in California (MAGIC) *(third week)*. The latest in men's and women's fashion apparel is showcased twice a year – in February and August. Some celebrities also display their own latest lines of clothing.

September
San Gennaro Feast and Street Fair *(mid-Sep)*. The centerpiece of this famous festival is the Italian cuisine feast with over 60 ethnic food vendors. The four-day event also features a carnival midway, Miss San Gennaro beauty pageant, rides, games, live bands, and several stalls of arts and craft.

Greek Food Festival *(mid-Sep)*, St. John's Orthodox Church. Luscious pastries and lip-smacking Greek foods and specialties are available at this festival, which is held in celebration of the Greek Independence Day. Events include authentic Greek music, folk dancing, a huge shopping bazaar, and many other forms of entertainment that take place on the lush grounds of this massive church, which is located near Hacienda Road and Jones Boulevard.

Bread from the Greek Food Festival

NASCAR Camping World Truck Series *(late Sep/early Oct)*, Las Vegas Motor Speedway. This special NASCAR event is held for trucks. More than 70 Chevy, Ford, and Dodge pickups race at speeds of up to 160 mph (257 km/h) in this exciting competition.

Guests enjoy a MAGIC opening night party at the Hard Rock Hotel and Casino

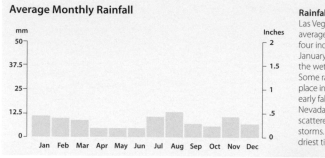

Average Monthly Rainfall

Rainfall Chart
Las Vegas receives an average rainfall of about four inches each year. January and August are the wettest months. Some rainfall also takes place in late summer and early fall, when Southern Nevada experiences scattered electrical storms. Spring is the driest time to visit.

Fall

Although this is probably the shortest season in Las Vegas, it is also one of the most pleasant. The period from mid-October to mid-November is filled with warm days and cool nights, and the ground is covered with leaves in striking colors. The atmosphere is festive with Halloween and Thanksgiving just around the corner. The temperate weather makes it an ideal time for golfing and other outdoor activities.

Brightly colored fall leaves

October
Life is Beautiful *(late Sep)*, Downtown. Renowned music, food and art festival, which also hosts inspiring speakers.
Art in the Park *(early Oct)*, Bicentennial Park, downtown

Watching the action at the Shriners Hospitals for Children Open

Boulder City. This is one of the biggest festivals of the year, as hundreds of craftsmen and artists display their works.
Las Vegas Age of Chivalry Renaissance Festival *(early Oct)*, Sunset Park. Three days of costumed performers and medieval pageantry.
Pro Bull Riders Final *(late Oct)*, T-Mobile Arena *(see p52)*. This thrilling four-day event features the top bull riders of the country.
Halloween *(Oct 31)*. Thousands of revelers fill the streets of Las Vegas in scary costumes. Casinos, hotels, and clubs host night-long parties with music, food, drinks, and dancing.
Shriners Hospitals for Children Open *(late Oct-early Nov)*, Summerlin. Pro golfers from around the world team up with amateur players for this week-long championship.

November
Rock 'n' Roll Las Vegas Marathon *(mid-Nov)*. More than 10,000 athletes from around the globe participate in this annual race.
Thanksgiving *(Nov 24)*. Visitors and local residents get into the holiday spirit with a long weekend of entertainment, delicious food, beverages, and general merriment.

Winter

Like many desert resorts, Las Vegas has winters that are usually mild with bright, sunny days, while the nights are literally freezing. The city is covered in sparkling and glittery

Dangerous antics at the National Finals Rodeo

decorations as everybody prepares for the Christmas and New Year celebrations, and football fans get ready for the Super Bowl weekend.

December
National Finals Rodeo *(early Dec)*, Thomas & Mack Center. This 10-day event is the nation's richest rodeo, and features the top 15 competitors in seven different events – bareback riding, steer wrestling, team roping, saddle bronc riding, calf roping, bull riding, and barrel racing.
Parade of Lights *(mid-Dec)*, Lake Mead Marina *(see p84)*. Fifty boats show off their special lights at this luminous lake event. Trophies are awarded, including a Best of Show award for the most brilliant display. Past parades have drawn up to 20,000 shoreline spectators.
Las Vegas Bowl *(Sat before Christmas)*, Sam Boyd Stadium. College football season kicks off as top teams from Pac-12 Conference and Mountain West Conference compete.

Average Monthly Temperature

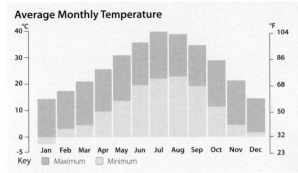

Key: ■ Maximum ■ Minimum

Temperature Chart

As befitting a land of extremes, temperatures in Vegas can range from below freezing on many nights from December through February to an uncomfortable high of 40°C (105°F) during July and August. On rare occasions, Vegas also experiences snowfall. Spring and fall offer the most comfortable weather.

Christmas *(Dec 25)*. Like Thanksgiving, this is another holiday when a large number of families visit Las Vegas, and the city is bursting at the seams. Malls and shopping centers overflow, restaurants host elaborate Christmas dinners, and hotels throw lavish, night-long parties.

New Year's Eve *(Dec 31)*. There is hardly any standing room during the busiest holiday of the year. Casinos stage huge and extravagant New Year's Eve bashes, though many of them are by invitation only for their best customers. One of the biggest parties is on Fremont Street as the block comes alive with fireworks, laser displays, and live bands bringing in the New Year.

Chinese New Year, Bellagio

all over the world convene at this gathering and display the latest high-tech electronic gadgets, including digital cameras, audio and video systems, home theaters, satellite systems, wireless communications, and more. The show is expected to attract approximately 150,000 visitors each year.

Chinese New Year *(late Jan or first half of Feb)*. Celebrate the New Year, oriental style. The occasion is marked by festivities that include entertainers from Asia, with authentic dance performances, including the Lion Dance, which is believed to chase out evil spirits. It also features cultural exhibits, Asian cuisines, and mahjong tournaments. Dates vary from year to year.

January

Consumer Electronic Show (CES) *(early Jan)*. More than 3,200 vendors and manufacturers from

February

Super Bowl Weekend *(last weekend in Jan or first weekend in Feb)*. Football frenzy hits the

A heart-shaped decoration for Valentine's Day, Chapel of Love

city during the Super Bowl weekend, which determines the National Football League champion. Several casinos and resorts celebrate with special football parties.

Valentine's Day *(14 Feb)*. Couples flock to any of the hundreds of wedding chapels *(see pp30–31)* in Las Vegas on this day to tie the nuptial knot or renew their vows. Those planning to wed on this day should make chapel and other reservations in advance.

Public Holidays

New Year's Day *(Jan 1)*

Martin Luther King Jr Day *(3rd Mon in Jan)*

President's Day *(3rd Mon in Feb)*

Memorial Day *(last Mon in May)*

Independence Day *(Jul 4)*

Labor Day *(1st Mon in Sep)*

Nevada Day *(last Fri in Oct)*

Veteran's Day *(Nov 11)*

Thanksgiving Day *(4th Thu in Nov)*

Christmas Day *(Dec 25)*

New Year celebrations light up the sky in Las Vegas

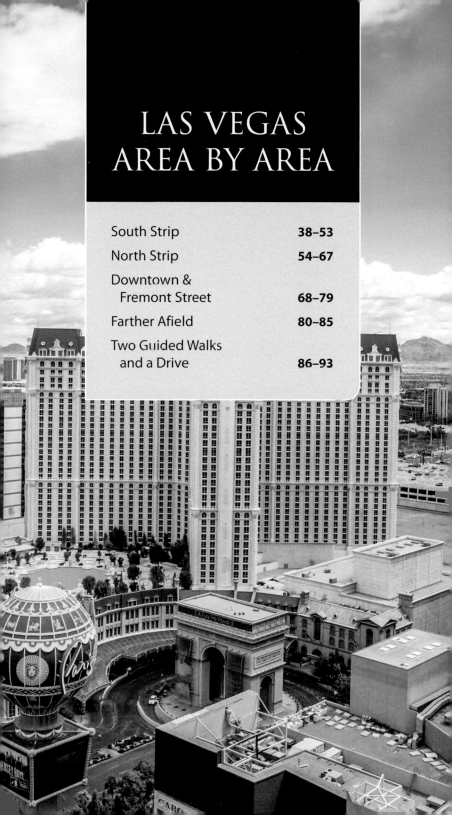

LAS VEGAS AREA BY AREA

Row of trumpeting angels along the entrance gate to Caesars Palace

SOUTH STRIP

The southern section of the famous Las Vegas Strip is a Mecca of sights and sounds that vary from the sublime to the exotic, from the outrageous to the bewildering. The area that stretches from Flamingo Road down to Mandalay Bay contains some of the newest and most lavish of Las Vegas's famed casino resorts. Among the landmarks are Bellagio, one of the city's most expensive and opulent casino hotels, and MGM Grand. Several of the resorts trace their roots to Las Vegas's

earliest days. These include Flamingo Las Vegas, built by the infamous mobster Bugsy Siegel in 1946, and Caesars Palace, which opened in 1966. Many others have managed to re-create not just the appearance, but also the ambience of great cities, such as Paris, New York, Rome, and Monte Carlo, through remarkably meticulous reproductions. Located just a short distance from the Strip is the University of Nevada, Las Vegas (UNLV) – the city's educational center.

Sights at a Glance

Hotels and Entertainment
2 Mandalay Bay pp42–3
3 Luxor
4 Excalibur
5 The Orleans
6 New York-New York
7 Monte Carlo
9 MGM Grand
10 Tropicana Las Vegas
12 Hard Rock Hotel & Casino

13 Planet Hollywood Resort & Casino
14 Paris Las Vegas
15 Bellagio pp50–51
16 The Cosmopolitan of Las Vegas
17 CityCenter and ARIA p49
18 T-Mobile Arena
19 Palms Casino Resort
20 Rio
21 Caesars Palace
22 The Cromwell
23 Flamingo Las Vegas
24 The LINQ Hotel and Casino
25 Bally's

Landmarks
1 Welcome to Fabulous Las Vegas sign

Museums and Galleries
11 UNLV Barrick Museum

Malls
8 Showcase Mall

Restaurants pp120–22
1 Andre's Monte Carlo
2 Aureole
3 Bacchanal Buffet
4 Bobby's Burger Palace
5 The Buffet@ARIA
6 Burger Bar
7 Carmine's
8 D.O.C.G.
9 Emeril's New Orleans Fish House
10 Estiatorio Milos
11 Giada
12 Gordon Ramsay BurGR
13 Gordon Ramsay Pub
14 Guy Fieri's Kitchen & Bar
15 Hakkasan
16 Holstein's
17 Jean-Georges Steakhouse
18 Joël Robuchon
19 Julian Serrano Restaurant
20 Mastro's Ocean Club
21 Michael Mina Bellagio
22 Nobu Caesars Palace
23 Old Homestead
24 Prime
25 Restaurant Guy Savoy
26 Rí Rá
27 RM Seafood
28 Scarpetta
29 Sterling Brunch
30 STK
31 Twist by Pierre Gagnaire
32 The Wicked Spoon
33 Yellowtail Restaurant & Lounge

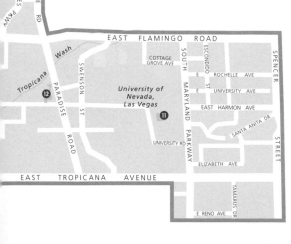

See also Street Finder maps 3 & 4

A View of South Strip

This southern stretch of the Strip is home to a cluster of vast, lavishly-themed hotels, including Mandalay Bay, Luxor, New York-New York, Paris Las Vegas, Monte Carlo, and Bellagio. Aiming to satisfy all the needs of a visitor in one location, with restaurants, shops, theaters, and casinos, these mega-resorts are best appreciated at night when the lights, fountains, and other special effects come to life. It is in the evening that these hotels become a fantasyland of riotous design and architecture, such as the illuminated sphinx that fronts the Luxor hotel's striking pyramid and the delightful, flawlessly choreographed dancing fountains at the chic Bellagio.

View of South Strip from Mandalay Bay

❻ New York-New York
A replica of the Statue of Liberty forms part of the facade of this hotel, which is composed of a host of Manhattan landmarks.

❸ Luxor
The casino is home to two fascinating and interactive exhibits: BODIES and Titanic.

❼ Monte Carlo
Renaissance-style architecture comes to life at this hotel.

❽ T-Mobile Arena
The largest indoor entertainment arena in the city.

❹ Excalibur
The towers at this resort are a kitsch fantasy of those in medieval England.

❷ ★ Mandalay Bay
One of the most popular attractions here is the Shark Reef.

TROPICANA AVE

LAS VEGAS BLVD

❽ Showcase Mall
This striking building has a giant neon Coca-Cola bottle near the entrance. A huge games arcade makes the mall popular with families.

❾ MGM Grand
Symbol of the Hollywood film studio, MGM, the lion statue at this hotel rises 45 ft (15 m) above the corner of Tropicana Avenue.

❿ Tropicana Las Vegas
This casino was given a $180 million face lift in 2010 and transformed into a South Beach theme.

Locator Map
See Street Finder maps 3 & 4

| 0 meters | 300 |
| 0 yards | 300 |

⑮ ★ Bellagio
Lighting the ceiling of the hotel's elegant lobby, this colorful glass installation was designed by famous glass artist Dale Chihuly in 1998.

⑯ The Cosmopolitan of Las Vegas
This hotel's two towers are sandwiched between Bellagio and CityCenter.

⑱ Planet Hollywood Resort & Casino
Located at the center of the Strip, featuring 100,000 sq ft (9,300 sq m) of gaming, restaurants, nightclubs, and encircled by Miracle Mile Shops.

㉑ Caesars Palace
Reproduction Roman statuary adorns the grounds of Caesars Palace. One of the Strip's oldest and most glamorous hotels, Caesars was built in 1966. Inside, the lavish Forum Shops mall features moving statues.

㉒ The Cromwell
Home to Giada De Laurentiis' restaurant, GIADA, and to Drai's rooftop "beach club", complete with shimmering pool; glam beachwear is a must.

⑭ Paris Las Vegas
A half-scale replica of the Eiffel Tower stands tall at this resort's entrance.

㉔ The LINQ and High Roller
The world's tallest observation wheel stands 550 ft (168 m) tall and is found at the LINQ's shopping and dining promenade.

㉓ Flamingo Las Vegas
The pink-and-orange neon plumes of the Flamingo hotel's facade is a famous Strip icon. Redesigned in the 1970s and 1980s, and again in 2012, the original 1946 building was the beloved project of gangster turned hotelier, Bugsy Seigel *(see p28)*.

㉕ Bally's
This hotel's colorful entryway is lined with neon columns, palm trees, and cascading fountains, and gives a futuristic look to this mega-resort.

⑰ ★ CityCenter and ARIA
This massive development was designed to be a city within a city.

❷ Mandalay Bay

Las Vegas may be located in the middle of a desert, but visitors can still get a taste of the tropics at this island-themed mega-resort. The hotel is built around an expansive lagoon, surrounded by lush ferns and other tropical plants, and features a sand-and-surf beach with a wave-generating machine. During the summer months, the beach is the venue for outdoor concerts by well-known bands, including the Beach Boys and the B-52's. Mandalay Bay is also home to one of the city's most popular attractions – Shark Reef, an aquarium specializing in sharks and other aquatic predators.

Aureole
This famous restaurant serves Continental specialties, and hosts a four-story-tall wine tower *(see p121).*

★ **Mandalay Bay Beach**
Beachgoers enjoy the sun, sand, and surf, courtesy of a wave-making machine. In addition to the deck chairs, guests can use the luxurious private bungalows and cabanas, or lounge on a day bed.

Lazy River
This winding river offers swimmers a chance to float through the lagoon while sipping a tropical drink.

KEY

① **Cascading waterfalls** set among palm trees and mystical architecture create a soothing and tranquil ambience.

② **Shark Reef**

③ **Convention Center**

④ **Four Seasons Hotel** occupies the top four floors in Mandalay Bay. Its restaurants and health club are located here.

★ **Pedestrians' Entrance**
The hotel's exterior showcases Asian architectural elements such as pagodas. Stone sculptures of winged dragons stand guard at the sidewalk leading from the Strip to the resort's main entrance.

VISITORS' CHECKLIST

Practical Information
3950 Las Vegas Blvd S. **Map** 3 C5.
Tel (702) 632-7777.
Open Hotel: 24 hrs; Shark Reef: 10am–8pm daily (to 10pm Fri & Sat). 🎫 for Shark Reef. ♿ 🎁 📷 🚿 🅿 w mandalaybay.com

Transport
🚌 RTC bus The Deuce.
🚉 MGM Grand Station; free tram from Excalibur.

House of Blues
This concert venue presents an intimate setting and is an excellent place to enjoy live music by top music artists (see p143).

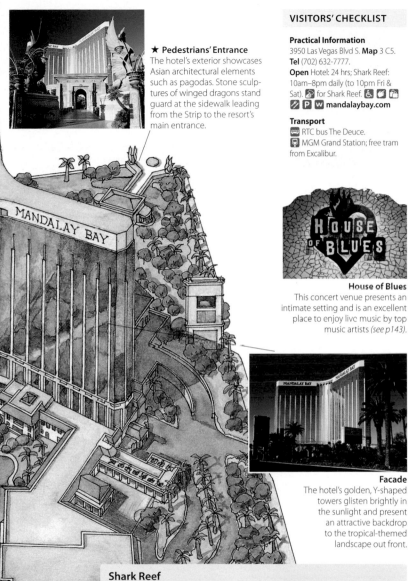

Facade
The hotel's golden, Y-shaped towers glisten brightly in the sunlight and present an attractive backdrop to the tropical-themed landscape out front.

Shark Reef

This massive aquarium and sea life exhibit contains over 1,200 species of aquatic life, including sharks, exotic fish, sea turtles, crocodiles, and more. The attraction begins with an outdoor exhibit of deadly Amazon predators, including the red tail catfish, monkey fish, and black piranha, along with the Komodo dragon. Visitors descend through tunnels into the aquarium section where they can observe a variety of sharks, eels, and other tropical fish. A favorite for kids is the petting pond, the Touch Pool, where they can touch rays and Port Jackson sharks.

Visitors at the Touch Pool, Shark Reef

❶ Welcome to Fabulous Las Vegas Sign

5100 Las Vegas Blvd S.

Erected in 1959, and located on the median just south of Mandalay Bay on the Strip, this 25-ft- (7.5-m-) tall sign receives so many visitors that a small 12-car parking lot was built in 2008 to accommodate the constant queue of those stopping for a photo opportunity. The iconic sign reads "Welcome to Fabulous Las Vegas, Nevada" on the front and "Drive Carefully" and "Come Back Soon" on the back. To access the sign's parking lot you must be driving south on Las Vegas Boulevard heading away from Mandalay Bay.

❷ Mandalay Bay

See pp42–3

❸ Luxor

3900 Las Vegas Blvd S. **Map** 3 B5. **Tel** (702) 262-4444; (877) 386-4658. **Open** 24 hours *(see p114)*. 🔥 📷 ♿ **W** luxor.com

With its pyramid design, Luxor is undoubtedly the most unique and recognizable hotel in Las Vegas. The magnificent entrance is marked by a huge sandstone obelisk and the resort's crowning glory is a ten-story towering replica of the Great Sphinx. Built in 1993, the 350-ft- (106-m-) high pyramid is covered in dark glass. Its apex features a 42.3-

An impressive replica of the Great Sphinx at the entrance of Luxor

Colorful towers of the medieval fantasy castle at Excalibur

billion-candlepower beacon – the world's strongest – emitting a shaft of light that reaches more than 10 miles (16 km) high into space each night. Inside, the pyramid's atrium is the largest open atrium in the world. There are no supporting columns to block the view as guests travel in "inclinators" to their rooms. The guest rooms of the hotel are built into the pyramid's sloping walls and are reached by "inclinators" – elevators that rise at a 39-degree angle.

Among the hotel's many attractions is **BODIES: The Exhibition**. This showcases real specimens of the human body including 13 whole bodies and more than 260 organs and body parts, giving visitors a detailed, three-dimensional look at the human form – something rarely seen outside the medical profession. Another exhibition, **Titanic: The Artifact Exhibition**, gives visitors an insight into life aboard the doomed ship.

Luxor is also home to the Cirque du Soleil production, **Criss Angel MINDFREAK LIVE!**, a haunting exploration inside the mind of Criss Angel, an entertainer whose spectacular illusions have awarded him "Magician of the Century." The Blue Man Group *(see p138)*, whose sensational shows combine music, comedy, and multimedia are in residence at the hotel.

BODIES: The Exhibition
Luxor. **Open** 10am–10pm daily. 🔥 ♿

Titanic: The Artifact Exhibition
Luxor. **Open** 10am–10pm daily. 🔥 ♿

Criss Angel MINDFREAK LIVE!
Luxor. **Open** 7pm & 9:30pm (Pre show: 6:30pm & 9pm) Wed–Sun. 🔥 ♿

❹ Excalibur

3850 Las Vegas Blvd S. **Map** 3 B–C4. **Tel** (702) 597-7777; (877) 750-5464. **Open** 24 hours *(see p114)*. 🔥 ♿ **W** excalibur.com

Built to resemble a medieval castle, Excalibur's entrance features white towers, turrets, and a 265-ft- (81-m-) high bell tower that stands guard over the moat. Inside, the medieval theme is further reflected in the cobblestone foyer and rock-walled atrium with a three-story-high fountain. The massive registration desk is flanked by suits of armor, and decorated with medieval chandeliers.

One of the Strip's larger hotels, Excalibur caters mostly to families and is usually packed. At the 100,000-sq ft (9,300-sq m) casino, the action is usually fast, frenzied, and fairly noisy.

The Octane bar on the Castle Walk level is the perfect place for a drink before dinner or a show. The bartenders and waiters perform high-energy dance routines throughout the evening.

The level below the casino has Fun Dungeon, a "fun zone" for kids, with a video arcade, midway games, a Dairy Queen and entertaining rides.

❺ The Orleans

4500 W Tropicana Ave. **Map** 3 A4.
Tel (702) 365-7111; (800) 675-3267.
Open 24 hours *(see p115).* ♿ ✎
W orleanscasino.com

This Cajun-themed hotel and casino opened in 1996 and was initially a clone of its more popular cousin, Gold Coast. However, since then its popularity with local gamblers has flourished, and the property has undergone expansion three times.

In 2004, The Orleans completed a third hotel tower that increased the resort's room count to 1,886. The casino was also expanded and now covers an area of about 135,000 sq ft (12,542 sq m). Among the facilities on offer, visitors can try their luck on over 2,600 slot machines or take their place at one of 35 tables in the Poker Room.

Like the other "locals-oriented" resorts in town, The Orleans offers a variety of attractions for the Vegas resident. Among them are an 18-screen movie theater and 70-lane bowling alley. The hotel also features an 850-seat headliner showroom that often

The sensational Big Apple roller coaster at New York-New York

hosts rock stars from the 1960s and 1970s, as well as seven restaurants and seven fast food eateries that serve an eclectic range of cuisines. There is also an 8,500-seat arena, which is home to the Las Vegas Legends (a professional indoor soccer team), and hosts various concerts and events taking place throughout the year.

The glittering neon sign of The Orleans

❻ New York-New York

3790 Las Vegas Blvd S. **Map** 3 C4.
Tel (702) 740-6969; (866) 815-4365.
Open 24 hours *(see p116).* ♿ ✎
W newyorknewyork.com

This hotel's re-creation of the Manhattan skyline dominates the Tropicana Avenue corner of the Strip – no mean feat in a street of such impressive facades.

is entered from the Strip via a replica of Brooklyn Bridge, which is one-fifth the size of the original.

Adding to the Manhattan flavor are versions of many popular New York eateries. Set among Greenwich Village brownstones is a wide selection of cafés, restaurants, and bars offering a choice of live music from swing and jazz to Motown and rock.

At the core of the hotel's towers are replicas of some of New York City's most famous landmarks, such as the New York Public Library, the Empire State, Chrysler, and Seagram Buildings, and a 150-ft- (46-m-) high Statue of Liberty. Roaring around the complex is the thrilling **Big Apple** – a Coney Island-style roller coaster – that twists and dives at speeds of 67 mph (108 kph) and passes through the casino itself. Every detail of the hotel's interior is designed to reflect a part of New York City, from the 1930s-style wood-paneled lobby to the areas around the casino floor, which feature many of the city's most famous landmarks, including Times Square. This striking casino

❼ Monte Carlo

3770 Las Vegas Blvd S. **Map** 3 B–C4.
Tel (702) 730-7777; (888) 529-4828.
Open 24 hours *(see p116).* ♿ ✎
W montecarlo.com

European refinement and Vegas glitz come together in a unique blend at Monte Carlo. The architecture features stately columns, Renaissance-style statues, and cascading fountains, yet it resists lapsing into over-stated Baroque.

Amenities include a shopping mall, wedding chapel, and spa.

The top floor of the resort is occupied by a hotel within a hotel. The exclusive boutique HOTEL32 has 50 rooms and penthouse suites, which are accessible only by an express elevator. All guests are offered a personal butler service and have access to a private lounge with panoramic views of the Strip.

The resort is set to undergo renovation and, by the end of 2018, it will be rebranded into two different hotels - The Park MGM and The NoMad Las Vegas.

Palm trees combine with stately columns at the Monte Carlo

Showcase Mall, featuring M&M's World

❽ Showcase Mall

3785 Las Vegas Blvd S. **Map** 3 C4.
Tel (702) 597-3117. **Open** varies for
each attraction. ♿ ✍

This neon-clad building, which
showcases an unmissable 100-
ft- (33-m-) high neon Coca-Cola
bottle, is an excellent place to
take children and also offers
enough to satisfy adults who
need a break from the casinos.

The main attraction here is
M&M's World, a four-floor monument to the famous colorful
candies. It may be little more
than a promotional exhibit for
the company's products, but it
does provide fun elements and
plentiful chocolate samples on
the M&M's Tour. Visitors can also
customize their own M&Ms with
their name, special messages, or
an array of Vegas icons such as
the "Welcome to Las Vegas" sign.

Connected to M&M's World
is **Everything Coca-Cola**, home
to the world's largest Coke
bottle, which stands 100 feet
(30 m) tall. The store features
shelves filled with thousands
of souvenir Coca-Cola branded
items, from stuffed polar bears
to signs and clothing. For a
savory experience, head upstairs
and try the Around the World
soda selection, with tastes of
16 Coca-Cola drinks from
around the globe.

There are also reasonably
priced restaurants and cafés
throughout the mall, and an
eight-screen United Artists
movie theater.

🎪 **M&M's World**
Showcase Mall. **Tel** (702) 740-2504;
(800) 848-3606. **Open** 9am–midnight
daily. ♿

🎪 **Everything Coca-Cola**
Showcase Mall. **Tel** (702) 270-5952.
Open 10am–11pm daily. ♿

❾ MGM Grand

3799 Las Vegas Blvd S. **Map** 3 C4.
Tel (702) 891-1111; (800) 929-1111.
Open 24 hours *(see p116)*. ♿ 🎫 ✍
🆆 mgmgrand.com

The emerald-green MGM Grand
building is fronted by a 45-ft-
(15-m-) tall bronze lion used
as the symbol of the MGM
Hollywood film studio. The
original MGM hotel was built in
the 1970s farther down the Strip
on the site of the present Bally's
hotel *(see p53)*, and was named
after the 1930s film, *Grand Hotel*,
which starred Joan Crawford
and Greta Garbo.

Today, the MGM Grand has a
massive 5,044 rooms and is home
to a huge casino, which sprawls
over 170,000 sq ft (15,794 sq m),
and is bigger than the playing
field at Yankee Stadium.

Proclaiming itself as
"Maximum Vegas," MGM Grand
has an exhilarating variety of
bars and restaurants including
fine dining at L'Atelier de Joël
Robuchon, and Centrifuge, a
bustling bar with good pop
music and fun live entertainment.
MGM Grand is also home to a
luxurious spa and salon.

One of the resorts biggest
attractions is the blockbuster
exhibition **CSI: The Experience**.
Inspired by the popular TV
series, visitors are asked to
investigate a series of fictional
crimes, guided by real-life
forensic scientists and videos
featuring cast members from
the show.

The Grand Garden Arena is a
16,800-seat venue famous for
hosting special events, and
mega-concerts for big names
such as the Rolling Stones, U2,
Paul McCartney, and Alicia Keys,
as well as major sports events
and world championship boxing.
The 740-seat Hollywood Theater
attracts many top entertainers,
including David Copperfield,
Jo Koy, and Tom Jones. At night,
Hakkasan, a massive five-level
nightclub and restaurant complex,
hosts world-renowned DJs
Tiësto, Calvin Harris, Hardwell
and Steve Aoki.

🔬 **CSI: The Experience**
MGM Grand. **Open** 9am–9pm
daily. ♿

Get sleuthing at CSI: The Experience

The luxury pool club at Tropicana Las Vegas

⑩ Tropicana Las Vegas

3801 Las Vegas Blvd S. **Map** 3 C4.
Tel (702) 739-2222; (800) 634-4000.
Open 24 hours *(see p116).* ♿ ✏
w troplv.com

A $180-million renovation has transformed the Tropicana with a South Beach-themed decor, featuring white floors, furniture, and columns.

A delightful 5-acre (2-ha) water park Is home to three pools, three spas, and a water slide. Waterfalls and exotic foliage provide a habitat for flamingoes, black swans, and parrots. In addition to the main casino, the pool provides swim-up blackjack tables that have a waterproof surface and money dryers. The vast pool area includes a restaurant and a luxury pool club, which transforms into a nightclub in the evening.

Nightly entertainment includes the Laugh Factory comedy club, and "Band of Magicians", a supergroup of magicians from around the world.

⑪ UNLV Barrick Museum

4505 S Maryland Pkwy, University of Nevada, Las Vegas. **Map** 4 E4. **Tel** (702) 895-3381. **Open** 9am–5pm Mon–Fri (to 8pm Thu), midday–5pm Sat. **Closed** public hols. ♿
w barrickmuseum.unlv.edu

Located at the University of Nevada, Las Vegas *(see pp88–9),* this museum showcases exhibits relating to the state's flora and fauna, and some anthropological displays. The Southwestern collection features mammals and fossils from the Mojave Desert *(see p107).* The highlight is the collection of Native American and Meso-American artifacts, Guatemalan textiles, and Mexican dance masks. The museum also displays several works by students and faculty staff, as well as traveling exhibitions. In front of the museum is the Xeric Garden, which displays drought-tolerant indigenous plants and uses efficient irrigation methods to create an attractive desert landscape. Shaded benches provide a peaceful refuge steps away from the college quad.

Exhibit at UNLV Barrick Museum

⑫ Hard Rock Hotel & Casino

4455 Paradise Rd. **Map** 4 D4.
Tel (702) 693-5000; (800) 473-7625.
Open 24 hours *(see p117).* ♿ ✏
w hardrockhotel.com

As the name suggests, the rock 'n' roll theme reigns supreme at this hotel. The theme extends well beyond just the resort's decor, as the Hard Rock Hotel & Casino presents itself as a shrine to rock and its unforgettable superstars.

The circular-shaped casino showcases various priceless treasures, such as Elton John's piano, Elvis Presley's jumpsuit, and a gold-plated, 32-saxophone chandelier. The casino also features several museum-like displays of rock memorabilia, which includes Beatles collectibles, vintage records, guitars, drum sets, and much more. Reflecting a Southern California influence, the hotel's pool area has a sandy beach lagoon, gardens, and a row of tent cabanas. Whirlpools and spas are also available here. Moreover, the hotel's 4,000-seat venue, the Joint *(see p140),* is an excellent place to experience a rock concert.

The resort underwent an expansion in 2009, including the opening of 860 guest rooms, restaurants, a health club and spa, and retail outlets.

The rock 'n' roll-themed exterior of Hard Rock Hotel & Casino

A remarkably meticulous re-creation of the Eiffel Tower, Paris Las Vegas

⑬ Planet Hollywood Resort & Casino

3667 Las Vegas Blvd S. **Map** 3 C3–4.
Tel (702) 785-5555; (877) 333-9474.
Open 24 hours *(see p116)*. ♿ ⬚
ⓦ planethollywoodresort.com

This resort, at the center of the Strip, features over 100,000 sq ft (9,300 sq m) of gaming, fine dining, lounges, nightclubs, a full-service spa and celebrity-themed suites. It is also home to the pop icon Britney Spears' *Piece of Me* show. Some of the frequently spotted celebrities who perform here include Jennifer Lopez, Lionel Richie, and Frankie Moreno.

The Crazy Shirts shop logo from Miracle Mile

A major attraction of the resort is the **Miracle Mile** shopping center *(see p129)*. Over 170 shops and 15 restaurants can be found in this modern "experimental" shopping center, which contains an interactive directional system to help shoppers get around the huge complex, a multi-million-dollar water feature with a free show on the hour, and state-of-the-art video imagery.

The AXIS theater at the hotel *(see p140)* is currently one of the best venues in town for shows and concerts. Murray "Celebrity Magician" is part of the nightly entertainment on offer here.

⑭ Paris Las Vegas

3655 Las Vegas Blvd S. **Map** 3 C3.
Tel (702) 946-7000. **Open** 24 hours *(see p116)*. ♿ ⬚ ⬚
ⓦ parislasvegas.com

Paris Las Vegas welcomes its guests into a miniature version of France's City of Lights. The resort showcases replicas of famous Paris landmarks, such as the Louvre, Hôtel de Ville, Opera House, Arc de Triomphe, and a 50-story-high **Eiffel Tower**.

The authenticity extends to parking valets yelling "*allez-allez*" to one another and the casino employees spouting phrases such as "*bonjour*" and "*comment allez-vous?*" to guests who are often amused, if not surprised, to hear French expressions from a Pacific Rim bellhop. The architectural details of the casino meticulously re-create Parisian street life, including cast-iron street lamps, and everything is set beneath a fabulous painted sky.

Cobblestone streets wind along the edge of the casino and are filled with shops selling an array of expensive French goods, including clothes, wine, gourmet cheese, and chocolate. You can even buy Eiffel Tower memorabilia here.

The resort also boasts five lounges, a spa, and two wedding chapels.

⑮ Bellagio

See pp50–51.

⑯ The Cosmopolitan of Las Vegas

3708 Las Vegas Blvd S. **Map** 3 B–C4.
Tel (702) 698-7000; (877) 551-7778.
Open 24 hours. ♿ ⬚
ⓦ cosmopolitanlasvegas.com

Sandwiched between the grand Bellagio *(see pp50–51)* and the CityCenter complex *(see p49)*, The Cosmopolitan of Las Vegas opened in December 2010 at a cost of $3.9 billion. It offers 2,995 rooms with luxurious urban-inspired interiors, decadent bathrooms, and sliding glass doors opening onto large terraces.

Guests can enjoy the 100,000-sq ft (9,290-sq m) casino, 18 restaurants, including the Italian-themed D.O.C.G. Enoteca, the Marquee Nightclub with its multi-million dollar sound system, several bars, and three pool areas. During the warmer months, the Dayclub offers cabanas with individual infinity pools, as well as three-story bungalow lofts, complete with their own private spa, and a top-floor party deck.

A desert oasis-inspired spa and hammam with silver, night-sky ceilings covers 44,000 sq ft (4,088 sq m). It offers a full range of treatments and incorporates a serenity lounge, monsoon cave, steam room, and a giant heated stone slab to relax on.

A glitzy bar, one of several at The Cosmopolitan of Las Vegas

⑰ CityCenter and ARIA

CityCenter opened in 2010 as a city within a city, designed to have all the commodities for daily life. Located on 67 acres (271,000 sq m) in the heart of the Strip, it encompasses a casino, hotels (including ARIA Hotel & Casino), spas, a retail center, a residential community, and an art gallery – all within walking distance. The center was built with sustainability in mind, with such features as natural lighting, an on-site natural gas co-generation plant, a large-scale recycling operation, and a limousine fleet powered by clean-burning compressed natural gas. A complimentary tram service links Bellagio, Monte Carlo, and CityCenter.

VISITORS' CHECKLIST

Practical Information
CityCenter: 3740 Las Vegas Blvd S.
Map 3 B4. **Tel** (702) 590-9230.
Open 24 hours. 🦽 ▦ ∥ ▤
📷 🅿 🅆 citycenter.com
ARIA Hotel & Casino: 3730 Las
Vegas Blvd S. **Map** 3 B4. **Tel** (866)
359-7111. 🅆 arialasvegas.com

Transport
🚆 Bally's Station; free tram
at Crystals.

ARIA Hotel & Casino
The hotel boasts 4,004 high-tech guest rooms and suites with floor-to-ceiling windows offering panoramic views of the fabulous Las Vegas skyline.

BARDOT Brasserie
One of 16 restaurants at ARIA, Michael Mina's popular BARDOT Brasserie serves French cuisine.

CityCenter and ARIA
Designed by eight of the world's foremost architects, the distinctive architecture of the complex features glass towers and curvilinear steel, crescent shapes, and patterned glass skins. The aim was for CityCenter to be physically different from other hotels on the Strip.

Crystals at CityCenter
This vast retail and entertainment district offers visitors the ultimate combination of couture, cuisine, and entertainment.

Mastro's Ocean Club
Located within the Crystals center, Mastro's Ocean Club is inside an 80-ft- (24-m-) high sculptural Tree House. Guests can enjoy Mastro's famous three-tiered, iced Seafood Tower.

⑮ Bellagio

The crown jewel of the South Strip, the luxurious Bellagio resort opened in 1998 at a cost of $1.6 billion. The goal of Steve Wynn, who conceived this monument to leisure, was to create a hotel "that would exemplify absolute quality while emphasizing romance and elegance." Facing a large pristine lake, the resort has been built to resemble an idyllic village on the shores of Italy's Lake Como. Inside, beautiful carpets and delicate Carrara marble mosaics adorn the floors. Bellagio is also home to Cirque du Soleil's mesmerizing and awe-inspiring water spectacular, "O".

Cirque du Soleil's "O"
Swimmers perform flawlessly choreographed musical acts at this water-based show.

Bellagio Gallery of Fine Art
As the Strip's only art venue to hold exhibitions, this gallery hosts temporary shows of paintings, sculptures, and other masterpieces by internationally acclaimed artists such as Claude Monet.

The Conservatory
This massive greenhouse has picturesque floral displays, exquisitely arranged in theatrical presentations. The colors and themes of these natural displays change from season to season.

↑
Entrance

★ The Lobby
The ceiling of the hotel's lobby is adorned with a dazzling display of colorful and vibrant glass flowers in the sculpture, *Fiori di Como*, by world-renowned glass artist Dale Chihuly.

★ Front Facade
The classical elegance of Italian architecture comes to life with ocher- and terracotta-colored Mediterranean-style buildings and cobblestone pathways that overlook an expansive lake.

★ Via Bellagio
This upscale shopping promenade is a glass-enclosed version of Beverly Hills' famed Rodeo Drive, and presents a vast selection of designer shops and boutiques, such as Hermès, Prada, Giorgio Armani, Tiffany, Chanel, Dior, and Gucci *(see p129).*

Restaurants Facing the Lake
Spectacular views and a romantic ambience are combined with a range of cuisines at some of the city's best eateries, including Todd English's Olives.

★ Fountains of Bellagio
Each evening the lake features a magnificent ballet of dancing fountains choreographed to music and lights. More than 1,000 streams of water shoot up to 250 ft (76 m) in the air accompanied by music by Luciano Pavarotti, Andrea Bocelli, Frank Sinatra, and Lionel Ritchie.

People outside the T-Mobile Arena, west of the Las Vegas Strip

⓲ T-Mobile Arena

3780 Las Vegas Blvd South. **Map** 3 B4.
Tel (702) 692-1600. **Open** for events
only. W **t-mobilearena.com**

Opened in 2016, the T-Mobile
Arena is the largest indoor arena
in Las Vegas. Situated just west
of the Strip, the venue hosted
more than 100 world-class
sporting events and concerts in
its opening season, including
performances by The Killers and
Barbra Streisand.

The arena is architecturally
advanced. The 20,000 steep
seats can be adjusted to provide
the best views for each show. The
multi-level space is ringed with
eateries and bars. Hyde Lounge,
the nightclub on the top floor,
allows patrons to party before,
during, and after an event.

⓳ Palms Casino Resort

4321 W Flamingo Rd. **Map** 3 A3.
Tel (702) 942-7777. **Open** 24 hours
(see p117). 🚷 💦 W **palms.com**

The amenities on offer here
have made the resort a favorite
of many partygoers who are
attracted by the Palms' vibrant
nightlife scene.

One of the hotel's most
popular nightclubs, Ghostbar,
has 14-ft (4.25-m) floor-to-
ceiling windows, which offer
spectacular views of the city.
A balcony with a glass panel in
the floor also allows partygoers
a dizzying look down to the
resort's pool below.

In addition to its nightlife, the
resort boasts a Michelin-starred
restaurant, a luxury spa, and a
range of plush suites that have
played host to a number of
Hollywood celebrities.

⓴ Rio

3700 W Flamingo Rd. **Map** 3 B3.
Tel (702) 777-7777; (800) 752-9746.
Open 24 hours. 🚷 💦
W **riolasvegas.com**

The Brazilian theme runs strong
at this upbeat and fast-paced
all-suite hotel. Located just about
half a mile west of the Strip, this
flamboyant hotel is easily identified by the red-and-purple neon
accented towers.

The Mardi Gras atmosphere is
nowhere more evident than at
the Masquerade Village – a
dining, shopping, gambling,
and entertainment complex.
Thrill seekers will appreciate the
VooDoo Zip Line on the 51st
story of Rio's Masquerade Tower.
Riders are transported at speeds
up to 35 mph (56 km/h) to the
Ipanema tower and back, while
enjoying panoramic views.

One of the major attractions
at this hotel is the annual **World
Series of Poker** competition,
which takes place in June and
July (see p33) and attracts
thousands of applicants. The Rio
also plays host to regular shows
by Penn & Teller, a popular
comedy illusionist duo.

🎢 VooDoo Zip Line
Rio. **Open** 11am–11pm daily. Under
21s not allowed after 7:30pm 💦

㉑ Caesars Palace

3570 Las Vegas Blvd S. **Map** 3 B3.
Tel (702) 731-7110; (800) 634-6661.
Open 24 hours (see p116). 🚷 💦
W **caesarspalace.com**

The grandeur that once defined
Ancient Rome now exists at
Caesars Palace. Marble statues,
fountains, imported cypress trees,
and toga-clad cocktail waitresses
realize the theme of Roman
opulence. The hotel's Roman
Plaza hosts a number of shops
and The Spanish Steps Bar.

Outside the palatial entrance
and to the right of the fountain is
the Brahma Shrine, a replica of a
popular Buddhist site in Thailand,
where visitors can pray and leave
offerings of fruit and flowers.

This classic Vegas casino was
the first themed hotel on the
Strip and soon established a
reputation for attracting top
artists. The tradition continues
in the **Colosseum** (see p140),
with visiting artists such as
Elton John, Mariah Carey,
Celene Dion, and Rod Stewart.

The hotel now houses three
casinos, four lounges, and the
5-acre (2-ha) Garden of the
Gods – a landscaped area with
fountains, three swimming pools,
and an outdoor wedding chapel.
The Qua Baths and Spa include
Roman-style baths, waterfalls,
a fitness center, and an arctic
ice room. In the refurbished
casinos, Olympian wall-art,
coffered ceilings, and light decor
create an elegant atmosphere.

The Forum Shops (see p128)
at Caesars Palace offers more

The exclusive Forum Shops,
Caesars Palace

than 160 designer shops and chic eateries. Replicas of the exquisite Trevi and Triton Fountains in Rome adorn a sweeping plaza, which has a large reflective pool at its center.

㉒ The Cromwell

The Cromwell Las Vegas 3595 Las Vegas Blvd S. **Map** 3 C3. **Tel** (702) 777-3777. **Open** 24 hours *(see p116).*
W thecromwell.com

The Cromwell opened its doors to the public in May 2014. A luxury boutique hotel, it places an emphasis on small details such as free coffee and tea machines on every floor, and hair-straighteners in each room.

The hotel's sole restaurant is GIADA, the first restaurant by Food Network television personality Giada de Laurentiis. GIADA features Italian recipes from the chef's cookbooks, and views of Caesars Palace and the Bellagio fountains.

The hotel also houses a casino and a popular nightclub situated on the 11th-floor rooftop pool deck.

㉓ Flamingo Las Vegas

3555 Las Vegas Blvd S. **Map** 3 C3. **Tel** (702) 733-3111; (800) 732-2111. **Open** 24 hours *(see p114).*
W flamingolasvegas.com

The bright pink-and-orange neon feather sign of the Flamingo's facade is the archetypal Las Vegas icon. Most are unaware that this sign was never a part of the original 1946 hotel and was added much later. Nothing remains of the first Flamingo: the last vestiges of this building, including notorious mobster Bugsy Siegel's *(see p28)* private suite, were bulldozed in 1996. A pillar and a plaque in the garden pay tribute to the mobster.

In the 1990s, a $130-million renovation created one of the most elegant pool areas in Vegas. Set among landscaped gardens, two Olympic-sized pools, veiled by palm trees, are flanked by islands that provide a home to

Brilliantly illuminated pink-and-orange feather sign, Flamingo Las Vegas

pink flamingoes. The hotel also has a kids' pool, two Jacuzzis, and a water slide that leads to three additional pools.

㉔ The LINQ Hotel & Casino

3545 Las Vegas Blvd S. **Map** 3 C3. **Tel** (800) 522-4700. **Open** 24 hours *(see p116).* W thelinq.com

The centerpiece to the LINQ is the 550-feet **High Roller**, which has been certified by Guinness as the world's tallest observation wheel. It offers stunning views of the Las Vegas skyline, particularly at sunset. Leading to the wheel is the LINQ Promenade, an open-air entertainment walkway.

Perhaps the LINQ's most unique attraction is the huge vintage car showroom within the hotel's self-parking garage. More than 250 classic automobiles are on display. The collection includes vehicles once driven by Marilyn Monroe and President John F. Kennedy.

View from the High Roller – each of its 28 cabins holds up to 40 people

The resort is also home to a large casino, a wedding chapel, a number of celebrity chef restaurants, and a tropics themed poolside area offering daybeds and luxury air-conditioned cabanas.

🎡 High Roller
The LINQ. **Open** 11:30am–2am daily.

㉕ Bally's

3645 Las Vegas Blvd S. **Map** 3 C3. **Tel** (702) 739-4111. **Open** 24 hours *(see p116).* W ballyslasvegas.com

Bally's was originally built as the MGM Grand in 1973. In 1980, the hotel was the site of a terrible fire and, in 1986, Bally Gaming Corporation bought the property and named it Bally's.

The resort's 2,814 rooms are among the largest in the city, and are mostly decorated with upscale contemporary furniture.

The Colorful Plaza is a space-age entryway of neon columns, palm trees, and cascading fountains. It also has four, 200-ft (61-m) long, moving sidewalks.

One of Vegas's legendary artists, Wayne Newton, performs here, singing crowd favorites such as his hit, "Danke Schoen".

Another highlight is the resort's spa – a full-service health club with state-of-the-art fitness equipment, whirlpool spas, steam and sauna rooms, and hydrotherapy tubs.

The hotel also has a good collection of shops and a large outdoor pool area. A monorail links the hotel with MGM Grand.

NORTH STRIP

At one time, the northern end of the Strip was known for its aging and often "working-class" casinos. Hotels such as the Sahara (now closed), and Circus Circus were popular with travel agents and tour operators, but never held the star billing of the elite resorts south of Flamingo Road. That all changed with the opening of The Venetian (1999), Wynn Las Vegas (2005), The Palazzo (2008), Encore (2009) and the SLS (2014). These incredible mega-resorts leveled the field with their southern counterparts, and set the standard for not just future developments, but also for older resorts that underwent large-scale modifications and renovations. North Strip also hosts the city's premier shopping complex, the Fashion Show Mall. Expansion of the area has made this mall the jewel of Vegas's shopping promenades and one of its most visited destinations.

Sights at a Glance

See also Street Finder maps 3 & 4

◀ View of the Cloud, a futuristic steel canopy at the Fashion Show Mall

For keys to symbols see back flap

A View of North Strip

The first casino resort to open on the Las Vegas Strip in 1941 was the El Rancho Vegas Hotel & Casino, which was located on the northern section of the Strip, on the corner of Sahara Avenue. A building boom followed in the 1950s, resulting in a swathe of resorts. The Sands, Desert Inn, Sahara, and Stardust hotels began the process that has transformed the Strip into a high-rise adult theme park. Much of the North Strip has been redeveloped and is now unrecognizable from earlier incarnations – thanks to million-dollar rebuilding programs.

The Palazzo and The Venetian

Today, resorts such as The Venetian, SLS, and The Mirage have established the Strip's reputation for upscale quality, and almost nothing remains of the spit-and-sawdust atmosphere the city once had.

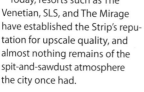

❺ Treasure Island – TI
Treasure Island lures passers-by with its lagoon and popular Señor Frog's restaurant.

❼ Walk of Stars
One hundred stars bearing the names of celebrities are embedded in the sidewalk.

❹ The Mirage
Both stylish and ornate, this resort's beautiful, Strip-facing gardens feature a striking, "erupting" volcano.

❻ Fashion Show Mall
Currently the largest shopping center in Vegas, this mall has more than 250 stores, an entertainment complex, and a food court.

SPRING MOUNTAIN RD

LAS VEGAS BLVD

SANDS AVE

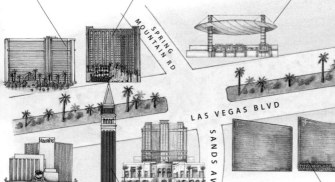

❶ Harrah's
A colorful mural adorns the facade of this resort. The hotel also hosts the Carnaval Court – a carnival-themed entertainment, dining, and shopping complex.

❸ The Palazzo
This stylish hotel-casino opened in 2008, and features its own theater and 60 luxury boutiques.

❷ ★ The Venetian
Acclaimed as one of the world's most luxurious hotels, The Venetian has mock canals flowing through its shopping area.

❾ ❿ ★ Wynn Las Vegas
This opulent hotel with a striking entrance sits alongside its equally luxurious sister hotel, Wynn Encore.

⓯ Stratosphere
An observation deck at the top of this hotel's 1,149-ft (350-m) tower offers fine views. There are thrill rides too, including the Big Shot *(see p65)*.

Locator Map
See Street Finder maps 3 & 4

0 meters		300
0 yards		300

⓬ ★ Circus Circus
Lucky the Clown beckons visitors to this resort, which offers circus acts and traditional carnival games on the mezzanine floor above the casino.

W. SAHARA AVE

THE STRIP

⓮ SLS Las Vegas
Las Vegas's newest resort, situated at the former location of the iconic Sahara, opened in 2014 after a $415 million renovation.

❽ Guardian Angel Cathedral
Located on Desert Inn Road, this chapel has elegant marble floors and imposing flying-buttress support columns.

The facade of Harrah's, a large casino and hotel complex

❶ Harrah's

3475 Las Vegas Blvd S. **Map** 3 C3.
Tel (702) 369-5000. **Open** 24 hours
(see p116). ♿ 🚭 🌐 **harrahs.com**

Once the world's largest Holiday Inn, Harrah's is now a property of Harrah's Entertainment Inc., which has owned and operated the 2,579-room resort since 1983. However, it was only in 1992 that the name was changed in order to enhance the corporation's image in the gaming industry. Until the mid-1990s, the hotel followed a riverboat theme but this was scrapped in 1997 in favor of a European carnival theme that features an entertainment and shopping complex – Carnaval Court – strolling performers, and colorful exterior murals.

The casino, which always seems to be in a state of renovation, meanders over nearly 100,000 sq ft (9,290 sq m), and is often crowded and noisy.

A race and sports book is also available for betting purposes.

The hotel's entertainment offerings are anchored by Menopause The Musical and concerts by The Righteous Brothers, the duo of Bill Medley and Bucky Heard.

❷ The Venetian

See pp60–61.

❸ The Palazzo

3325 Las Vegas Blvd S. **Map** 3 C3.
Tel (702) 607-7777. **Open** 24 hours.
♿ 🚭 🌐 **palazzolasvegas.com**

Following a celebratory opening in 2008, The Palazzo aims to achieve unparalleled luxury and contemporary chic on the Las Vegas Strip. This resort-hotel-casino combines sophisticated design with home comforts. Together with The Venetian *(see pp60–61),* and Sands Expo and Convention Center, The Palazzo helps create the largest hotel and convention complex in the world.

❹ The Mirage

3400 Las Vegas Blvd S. **Map** 3 C3.
Tel (702) 791-7111; (800) 627-6667.
Open 24 hours *(see p117).* ♿ 🎫
🌐 **mirage.com**

Perhaps more than any other hotel, The Mirage revolutionized the Strip when it opened in 1989, drawing visitors with attractions other than just the casino.

The exterior grounds introduce the complex's South Sea Island theme with tropical gardens, a blue lagoon, and waterfalls. However, the star of the show is a huge volcano that erupts at fixed hours in the night.

Inside, there is an atrium filled with exotic plants and, behind the main desk, a 20,000-gallon (90,000-liter) aquarium is filled with brightly colored fish. The hotel also hosts **Siegfried & Roy's Secret Garden and Dolphin Habitat**. This facility is home to several rare breeds and a family of common bottlenose dolphins. The lush, landscaped area allows a close look at rare or endangered white tigers, lions, and leopards, and is designed to resemble their natural habitat. The 2.5 million-gallon (9.5 million-liter) Dolphin Habitat provides a wonderful, spacious home for the dolphins.

🎭 **Siegfried & Roy's Secret Garden and Dolphin Habitat**
The Mirage. **Open** Call (702) 791-7188 for opening hours and pricing.
🎫 ♿

❺ Treasure Island – TI

3300 Las Vegas Blvd S. **Map** 3 C2.
Tel (702) 894-7111; (800) 944-7444.
Open 24 hours *(see p117).* ♿ 🚭
🌐 **treasureisland.com**

Located next to The Mirage, Treasure Island offers contemporary style, a high-energy atmosphere, and superb service. Its stunning facilities include nine restaurants, seven bars, a salon, outdoor pool, as well as a cabana.

The hotel's old pirate theme has been completely revamped. The cove now boasts a blue-water lagoon that fronts the Strip and is surrounded by high rock cliffs, shrubs, and palm trees.

Nightlife includes *Mystère (see p136),* a Cirque du Soleil production, which is performed in a specially customized showroom. This stunning contemporary circus is a surrealistic celebration of music, dance, spellbinding

Waterfall by day, volcano by night – the impressive entrance at The Mirage

acrobatics and gymnastics, mime, and comedy.

Treasure Island's other attractions include Marvel's Avengers S.T.A.T.I.O.N. (Scientific Training and Tactical Intelligence Operative Network), an engaging and educational experience for visitors to discover more about The Avengers. There's also Wild West-themed Gilley's Saloon (see p143) and Señor Frog's, a Vegas branch of this raucous, party atmosphere restaurant and bar.

❻ Fashion Show Mall

3200 Las Vegas Blvd S. **Map** 3 C2. **Tel** (702) 781-3777. **Open** varies. ♿ ♻ ⓦ **thefashionshow.com**

This sprawling multi-level shopping mall (see p128) is spread over 2 million sq ft (185,806 sq m) and is the largest on the Strip. Known as one of Las Vegas's premier shopping destinations, the Fashion Show Mall features more than 250 shops and boutiques, and is anchored by several major department stores, such as Macy's, Saks Fifth Avenue, Dillard's, Neiman Marcus, Forever 21, and Nordstrom. The mall also has fine art galleries, restaurants, cafés, and a food court.

Part of the latest expansion includes a Great Hall that has an 80-ft- (24-m-) long catwalk and is often the venue for fashion

Stylish and modernist lobby of the Fashion Show Mall

The altar of the Guardian Angel Cathedral

shows and demonstrations. One of the newest attractions here is a huge mushroom-like steel canopy called the Cloud. This provides shade for visitors in the day and serves as an image projection screen at night, broadcasting special events, exhibitions, and shows taking place inside the mall.

❼ Walk of Stars

Map 3 C2. **Open** 24 hours.

Following in the footsteps of Hollywood's Walk of Fame, Las Vegas christened its own Walk of Stars along the famed Strip in 2004. Located on the sidewalks between Sahara Avenue and Russell Road, the Walk honors people who have achieved prominence in a variety of fields such as entertainment, sports, and the military. Each star is embedded in a 3-ft- (0.9-m-) square slab of polished granite weighing 350 lb (159 kg), and is inlayed with the recipient's name and their area of specialty. The first inductee was Wayne Newton, whose granite star and plaque was placed in the sidewalk close to where the New Frontier hotel once stood, where Newton performed for 15 years. Other names that have been nominated for the Las Vegas honor include members of the Rat Pack (see pp22–3), Siegfried & Roy, and Liberace (see p29). Eventually, the Walk of Stars could host as many as 3,000 stars.

❽ Guardian Angel Cathedral

336 Cathedral Way. **Map** 3 C2. **Tel** (702) 735-5241. **Open** 7am–3pm Mon–Fri, 10am–7pm Sat, 7:30am–6pm Sun. ♿

Of the many churches in Las Vegas, the one with the largest percentage of visitors is the Guardian Angel Cathedral. One of its most famous worshippers was Danny Thomas, a successful comedian and entertainer, whose charitable donations helped furnish the church.

Located just east of the Strip near Desert Inn Road, the huge A-frame church was built in 1963 and is paved with beautiful marble floors and has flying-buttress support columns. An unusual feature of the sanctuary is the stained-glass window, which depicts a harlequin hovering over a hotel and a pair of dice at the foot of a cross.

Nevertheless, services are conventional with several services of Mass celebrated on weekends along with two daily ones during the week. Tourists often drop casino vouchers into the collection plate, and an employee is periodically sent to redeem the vouchers.

Visiting Catholics may be wed here, though there is no such thing as a "quickie" Catholic wedding – formal marriage preparation must take place in the local parish, with the papers then forwarded to the Diocese of Las Vegas.

❷ The Venetian

One of Las Vegas's most spectacular mega-resorts, The Venetian is a meticulous re-creation of the grandeur and beauty of Venice. Much of the architecture includes nearly exact reproductions of well-known landmarks, such as St. Mark's Square, the Doge's Palace, Rialto Bridge, and a 315-ft- (96-m-) tall Campanile Tower, which overlook the waters of the Grand Canal – complete with authentic wooden gondolas and singing gondoliers. The fantasy continues inside where vast areas of lavish marble flooring, ceilings painted with frescoes, statues, and replicas of famous Venetian paintings are found.

★ **Casino**
The interior of the 120,000 sq-ft (11,000 sq-m) casino is full of Italianate architectural details.

The Grand Canal
This graceful waterway winds its way through shops, boutiques, and restaurants as it sparkles beneath faux Adriatic skies, painted and lit to replicate dusk at all times of the day and night.

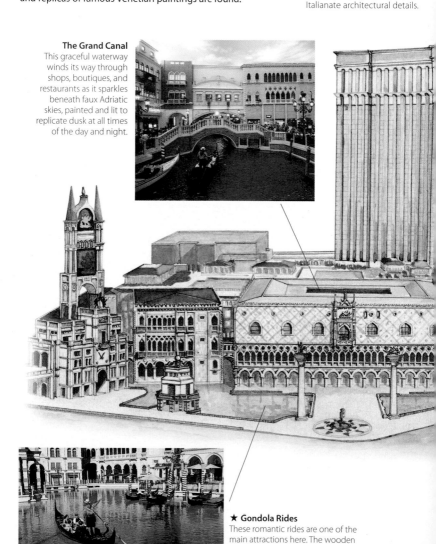

★ **Gondola Rides**
These romantic rides are one of the main attractions here. The wooden gondolas are authentic, and the singing gondoliers charge for a ride.

Entrance from the Strip
Graceful bridges, brick piazzas, a serpentine canal, and faithful renditions of classical and stylish Italian architecture enthrall those passing by along the Strip.

VISITORS' CHECKLIST

Practical Information
3355 Las Vegas Blvd S.
Map 3 C3. **Tel** (702) 414-1000;
(888) 283-6423. **Open** 24 hours.

ⓦ venetian.com

Transport
🚌 RTC bus The Deuce.
🚃 Harrah's Station.

KEY

① **The Rialto Bridge** is a strikingly accurate version of Venice's Ponte di Rialto, the city's oldest bridge. The people-mover sidewalks, however, are a strictly Las Vegas touch.

② **The Campanile Tower** is another excellent replica of a Venetian monument and serves as an entrance to the resort's Grand Canal Shoppes.

★ **Madame Tussauds**
This branch of London's renowned waxworks museum features many Las Vegas legends, including Frank Sinatra.

The Lobby
The stunning lobby is decorated with polished marble and glimmering lamps, under a domed ceiling of exquisite gilt and hand-painted frescoes framed in 24-carat gold.

❷ Wynn Las Vegas

The opening of Wynn Las Vegas in 2005 saw the addition of one of the city's most dramatic casino-resorts to the Strip. The hotel complex is the first element of what will eventually become the ultimate city resort. A stage of development was completed in December 2008 at the opening of Encore, Wynn's new resort. Wynn's luxurious surroundings – a marble-walled casino, award-winning restaurants, dazzling nightspots and entertainment, and an elegant shopping promenade – are open to the public. The spa is available to non-guests during the week and all Strip guests can play on the golf course.

Curved bronze-glass facade of the 50-story hotel tower

Decor and Design

Whereas most Strip hotels are designed to show off their attractions, Wynn Las Vegas was fashioned to hide them. The stunning bronze-glass facade of the hotel's gigantic 60-story **tower** and part of the forest-clad mountain are all passers-by see from Las Vegas Boulevard. The fact that its treasures are not on display adds to the resort's reputation for exclusivity and for being the most expensive in town.

Once inside, the extent of Wynn's opulent design and the quality of the workmanship and materials becomes apparent. From the main entrance, visitors arrive at the **Atrium** where they can stroll along its tree-lined walkways tiled with brightly colored floral mosaics and where globes of silk flowers adorn the trees. At the center of the resort is its architectural highlight: the shimmering **Lake of Dreams** and its magnificent backdrop, the **man-made mountain**. Covered with more than 1,500 trees, the 140-ft- (43-m-) high mountain towers over the lake while curtains of water cascade down its dramatic waterfall. Together they form an amphitheater lined with restaurants and shops, a unique setting for the theatrical performances held here at night.

Unlike the decor in other Las Vegas casino-hotels, which are unified by a theme, Wynn is decorated in a casual chic style. The bedrooms have floor to ceiling windows offering stunning views of the Las Vegas skyline.

Gambling and Entertainment

Although its gaming space totals 111,000 sq ft (10,000 sq m), Wynn's **casino** feels intimate. It comprises ten areas, including Baccarat, High Limit, Poker, Private Gaming, Race and Sports Book, plus four gaming rooms containing slot machines and table games. The casino is designed around comfort and the latest technology and there are daily poker tournaments.

The resort features two entertainment venues including the specially designed Wynn Theater, where **Le Rêve** (see p139), a live aquatic production of aerial acrobatics, gymnastics and dazzling technological effects, is performed. The stage is surrounded by a pool of water

Spectacular light show projected onto the waterfall at the Lake of Dreams

out of which rise the actors and sets. As the theater is in the round, all seats have great, uninterrupted views of the spectacular show.

Wynn's other stage, the **Encore Theater**, is home to an impressive variety of headline, international performers.

One of the most exciting spots to view a performance on the Lake of Dreams is from one of the **Parasol Up/Down** bars with a cocktail. The nightly productions feature 4,000 color-changing lights that project images onto the natural screen created by a wall of water.

Dining and Nightlife

Celebrity chefs at Wynn, unlike those at most big-name establishments, are on the premises. A market-driven dinner menu at **The Country Club** offers classic steakhouse fare with innovative touches. At **Costa di Mare** the finest seafood is flown in daily from Europe. For a romantic experience, diners can eat in their own private lakeside cabana. At elegant Japanese restaurant **Mizumi**, floor-to-ceiling windows provide a view of the tranquil pagoda, with an eco-garden, waterfall and koi fish pond. **Intrigue** (see p142) is located beneath Mizumi. This

Metallic spheres on the lake in front of Costa di Mare

stunningly stylish 14,000-sq-ft (1301-sq-m) nightclub has as its centerpiece a 94-ft (29-m) waterfall, which descends into a lagoon. With its glass-enclosed patio which allows spectacular views throughout the year to the venue's remarkable pyrotechnics show, Intrigue is an alluring, if pricey night out.

Luxury Shopping

The glass, brass, and chrome storefronts along the **Wynn Esplanade** (see p129) glitter with the golden names of the luxury trade – Chanel, Cartier, Christian Dior, Alexander McQueen, Louis Vuitton, Moncler, and Prada. There are also two exclusive Steve Wynn stores: Wynn & Co. Watches and Wynn collection. The latter

VISITORS' CHECKLIST

Practical Information
3131 Las Vegas Blvd S. **Map** 3 C2.
Tel (702) 770-7000; (888) 320-7123. **Open** 24 hours.
♿ 🚻 ♻ 🖥 📷 🅿
Ⓦ wynnlasvegas.com

Transport
🚌 RTC bus The Deuce.
🚆 Harrah's Station.

sells a thoughtfully curated selection of fashionable clothes, bags, shoes, and accessories for men and women.

Enthusiasts who are fascinated with timekeeping will be amazed at the Rolex store, where they can browse through the world's largest selection of Rolex timepieces and be a part of the one-of-a-kind "Rolex Experience," an exhibit of historic timepieces dating back to 1905.

The high-end Prada store at the Wynn Esplanade

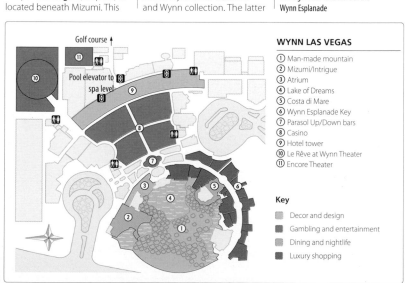

WYNN LAS VEGAS

① Man-made mountain
② Mizumi/Intrigue
③ Atrium
④ Lake of Dreams
⑤ Costa di Mare
⑥ Wynn Esplanade Key
⑦ Parasol Up/Down bars
⑧ Casino
⑨ Hotel tower
⑩ Le Rêve at Wynn Theater
⑪ Encore Theater

Key
☐ Decor and design
☐ Gambling and entertainment
☐ Dining and nightlife
☐ Luxury shopping

The prestigious Wynn Encore resort

⑩ Wynn Encore

3131 Las Vegas Blvd S. **Map** 3 C2.
Tel (702) 770-7100; (877) 321-9966.
Open 24 hours *(see p117)*. 🚹 📶
ⓦ wynnlasvegas.com

Standing side-by-side with its sister property Wynn Las Vegas, and on the site of the old Desert Inn, is Steve Wynn's luxurious Encore. Originally planned as an expansion of Wynn Las Vegas, Encore turned into a resort in its own right. Although the hotel has 2,034 spacious suites, it retains an intimate, residential atmosphere. Unusual for a Las Vegas hotel, Encore manages to incorporate a great deal of natural light into its public spaces by using skylights and atria. This open feel is enhanced by sprawling pools, which can be viewed from vantage points throughout the property, lush foliage, and a butterfly design scheme.

The spacious rooms and suites at Encore combine sophisticated, timeless decor with high-tech features such as an all-in-one remote that allows you to operate the lights, air-conditioning, TV, and drapes. Wynn Dream Beds provide the ultimate in sleep comfort, while luxurious bathrooms feature soaking tubs and flat-screen TVs. Floor-to-ceiling glass windows offer fantastic views.

Encore offers all the amenties of Wynn Las Vegas, as well as five restaurants (including a

Frank Sinatra-themed steakhouse), seven bars, the über-chic XS and Surrender nightclubs *(see pp142–3)*, and a collection of designer boutiques at The Esplanade retail space. Within the Encore Esplanade is The Wynn Theater, which is shared by both Wynn Las Vegas and Encore. The theater hosts the breathtaking *Le Rêve (see p62)*.

Encore's Spa and Salon offers a tranquil sanctuary in which to relax and recharge. There are separate men's and women's areas with steam rooms, saunas, hot and cold plunge pools, and showers, as well as a full range of spa treatments.

⑪ Westgate Las Vegas

3000 Paradise Rd. **Map** 4 D2.
Tel (702) 732-5111; (800) 732-7117.
Open 24 hours *(see p115)*. 🚹 📶
ⓦ westgatelasvegasresort.com

Elvis Presley is the star most associated with this hotel, originally the International Hotel, appearing here for a record 837 performances, all of which were sold out. Today, visitors can pay tribute to the King at his lifesize statue just inside the entrance.

The hotel's proximity to the Las Vegas Convention Center makes it popular with business people. The convenience of a walkway through the property and a Las Vegas Monorail station afford conventioneers easy and quick access. The Westgate also offers more than 200,000 sq ft (18,600 sq m) of versatile meeting space.

Luxurious surroundings, a plush 95,000-sq-ft (8,826-sq-m) casino, and the SuperBook, the world's largest race and sports book with over 400 seats with 32-inch LED touch screens and USB ports available at each seat, and 29 giant screens, draw others to the resort too.

A $100 million renovation in 2008 added the 3rd-floor rooftop pool with private cabanas, and a spa, while the fitness center

The decorated ceiling outside the Wynn Theater at Wynn Encore

Players trying their luck at the casino of SLS Las Vegas

includes championship tennis courts. Jason Tenner performs the award-winning Prince tribute show, Purple Reign at this hotel.

Of the ten restaurants, a highlight is Benihana, a Japanese exhibition-style eatery with lush gardens.

⑫ Circus Circus

See pp66–7.

⑬ Lucky Dragon Hotel & Casino

300 W Sahara Ave. **Map** 3 C2. **Open** 24 hours *(see p114).* ♿ 🚭
🅦 luckydragonlv.com

Reflecting its purely Asian theme, the Lucky Dragon is the first hotel and casino in Las Vegas to have a completely Asian atmosphere, ranging from its decor to the food. This boutique hotel has 204 rooms including 23 suites, a sprawling 27,500-sq-ft (2,555-sq-m) gaming area where guests can play popular Asian games such as Baccarat and Pai Gow, three bars and lounges. The staff and other employees are proficient in Cantonese, Mandarin, and other Asian dialects, as well as English. The five restaurants - Dragon's Alley, Pearl Ocean, Phoenix, Bao Now, and Cha Garden serve authentic Asian cuisine. The outdoor and indoor tea garden serves an extensive selection of traditional and high-end teas from all over Asia. The spa has different treatment rooms offering relaxing massages, reflexology and acupuncture.

⑭ SLS Las Vegas

2535 Las Vegas Blvd S. **Map** 4 D1. **Tel** (702) 737-2111 **Open** 24 hours *(see p116).* 🚭 🅦 slshotels.com/lasvegas.

The site of the iconic Sahara Hotel has been given new life with the opening of SLS in 2014. The building was completely transformed, and its 1,600 guest rooms and suites are now located in three distinct towers with amenities that include 55-inch HD TVs and luxury showers. There's a full-service business center with more than 30,000 square feet (2790 sq m) of meeting space, a 50,000-sq-ft (4645-sq-m) casino, rooftop pool, and Foxtail nightclub. Restaurants by world-renowned chefs include Bazaar Meat by Jose Andreas, Katsuya by Starck (run by Master Sushi Chef Katsuya Uechi), and Cleo by Danny Elmaleh.

⑮ Stratosphere

2000 Las Vegas Blvd S. **Map** 4 D1. **Tel** (702) 380-7777; (800) 998 6937. **Open** 24 hours *(see p114).* ♿ 🚭
🅦 stratospherehotel.com

Somewhat isolated at the north end of the Strip, away from the main attractions, this resort hotel boasts the 1,149-ft- (350-m-) high **Stratosphere Tower** – a Las Vegas landmark and the tallest building west of the Mississippi River. The summit has indoor and outdoor observation decks (including the Top of the World restaurant), which offer unparalleled views of the city and the surrounding terrain. The tower's elevators whisk visitors to the top, where there is a choice of four exciting – not to say alarming – rides: the **Big Shot**, which shoots visitors 160 ft (49 m) up in the air; the **X Scream**, an open vehicle that resembles a huge seesaw and swings riders over the tower's edge; the Sky Jump, a free fall dive off the 108th floor of the Stratosphere Tower; and **Insanity**, which dangles daredevils over the tower's edge with the help of cables.

The casino at Stratosphere is spread over an expansive area of 100,000 sq ft (9,500 sq m), and includes both a poker room and a keno lounge.

🎡 **Big Shot, X Scream, Sky Jump, and Insanity**
Stratosphere. **Open** 10–1am Sun–Thu, 10–2am Fri & Sat. 🚭 ♿ for observation deck only.

Stratosphere Tower, a prominent landmark at the north end of the Strip

Riders being spun around on Chaos in Adventuredome

⓬ Circus Circus

2800 Las Vegas Blvd S. **Map** 3 C2.
Tel (702) 734-0410; (800) 634-3450.
Open 24 hours *(see p114)*. 🚻 ♿
w circuscircus.com

Located at the north end of the Strip, this circus-themed casino opened in 1968 as a complete family destination offering a unique combination of gambling and children's entertainment. Hotel accommodations were first offered in 1972. When Circus Circus was purchased by businessman William Bennett in 1974, the site expanded, and has continued to do so, with the addition of several hotel towers. Today, the hotel is known for the wide variety of attractions it offers for adults and children alike, and is still a very popular stop for the whole family.

A large colorful clown marquee fronts this hotel, which has three casinos spread over 100,000 sq ft (9,500 m). The main casino resembles a circus tent with a pink-and-white big top. The floor above the casino hosts the Carnival Midway, which features a video arcade, fair games, and free circus acts, as well as trapeze artists and other aerialists flying high above the heads of the gamblers below. At the rear of the hotel is the Adventuredome theme park, housed in a pink canopy. It features 25 thrilling rides and attractions to suit guests of all ages.

Circus Circus: Adventuredome

The largest indoor theme park in the country, Adventuredome is spread over a massive area and has enough rides and attractions to keep visitors fully engaged for an entire afternoon. While some rides are gentle and ideally suited for younger children, the park also has several exciting rides, including thrilling roller coasters, a gut-wrenching sling shot, and a pirate ship swing. A carnival midway and many smaller attractions, such as bumper cars, rock- and net-climbing, and miniature golf, are also available.

Pacific Rim Motion Movie Experience
A favorite with children and adults, this is an intense film experience with heart-pounding action and ground-shaking special effects. The story line is one of monstrous sea creatures threatening mankind, and the Earth being saved by massive fighting robots.

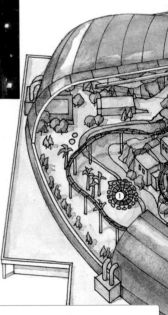

Circus Circus Casino

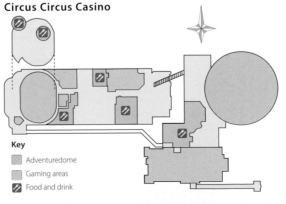

Key

- Adventuredome
- Gaming areas
- Food and drink

★ Sling Shot
This exciting and spine-chilling tower ride shoots its passengers 100-ft (30-m) up along its pole at an incredible force of acceleration, and then hurls them back down again.

VISITORS' CHECKLIST

Practical Information
Circus Circus. **Map** 3 C2.
Tel (702) 794-3939.
Open daily, hours vary. 🚼 ♿
🆆 adventuredome.com

Xtreme Zone
Enjoy the physical challenge of rock climbing and rappeling up and down on this formidable mountain face.

②

③

★ Canyon Blaster
This is the country's largest indoor double-loop, double-corkscrew roller coaster. Carrying up to 28 passengers, the ride reaches speeds of 55 mph (88.5 km/h) as it makes several sudden, hair-raising vertical drops, twists, and turns.

KEY

① **Chaos** is a circular ride that spins and twirls its passengers, moving backward, counterclockwise, and upside down at varying speeds.

② The **Batman Lazer Challenge** involves racing through a maze of lasers to reach the finish line either by dodging or breaking beams, depending on the mission.

③ **Disk'O** is an exhilarating ride that spins and rocks with upbeat disco music. Passengers face outwards on a pedestal seat with arms and legs free while moving at 22 mph (35 km/h).

El Loco
This roller coaster reaches a top speed of 45 mph (72 km/h) during its 72-second ride, and includes a nail-biting vertical drop.

DOWNTOWN & FREMONT STREET

The city of Las Vegas and its now flourishing gambling industry grew up around Fremont Street in the early 1900s. This is where the first casinos and their colorful neon signs were originally located. Although the area has undergone a vast transformation since then, some vestiges of its heritage can still be seen. The Golden Gate Hotel, for instance, has stood at the corner of Fremont and Main Street since 1906, and illuminated landmarks, such as Vegas Vic, a cowboy, continue to light up the night sky. More recent attractions on this street, also known as "Glitter Gulch", include the amazing light-and-sound shows of the Fremont Street Experience. While an enhancement program has brought new restaurants, bars, and clubs to the area, downtown still offers unpretentious dining, lodging, and entertainment at affordable prices compared to those on the Strip.

Sights at a Glance

Hotels and Casinos
1 Golden Gate Hotel
2 Plaza Hotel & Casino
3 California Hotel
4 Main Street Station
5 Golden Nugget
6 Four Queens
7 Fremont Hotel
8 The D Las Vegas
12 El Cortez

Entertainment
9 Fremont Street Experience
10 Downtown Grand Las Vegas
11 Fremont East District

Museums and Galleries
13 Downtown Container Park

14 The Arts Factory and the 18b Arts District
15 Discovery Children's Museum
16 Las Vegas Natural History Museum
17 Old Las Vegas Mormon Fort
18 Neon Museum
19 Mob Museum

See also Street Finder maps 1 & 2

0 meters 500
0 yards 500

Restaurants p123
1 Andiamo Streakhouse
2 Binion's Ranch Steakhouse
3 Carson Kitchen
4 La Comida
5 MTO Café
6 Pizza Rock

◀ Old Vegas sign, downtown

For keys to symbols see back flap

Around Fremont Street

Originally known as "Glitter Gulch", Fremont Street formed the heart of Las Vegas when the city was established in 1905. This is where the first casinos were founded, complete with stylish neon signs. Today, the area has outgrown its frontier heritage, but still boasts the best collection of neon lighting. The main attractions here are the shows at the Fremont Street Experience and the Slotzilla Zip Line. Plus there are dozens of shops and restaurants, and the Fremont East Entertainment District between Las Vegas Boulevard North and Eighth Street.

The exterior of Main Street Station

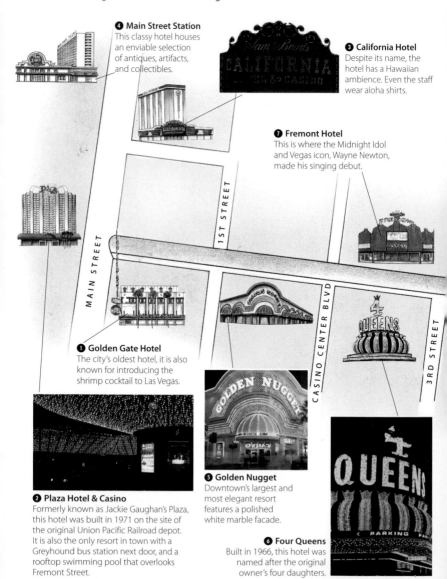

❹ Main Street Station
This classy hotel houses an enviable selection of antiques, artifacts, and collectibles.

❸ California Hotel
Despite its name, the hotel has a Hawaiian ambience. Even the staff wear aloha shirts.

❼ Fremont Hotel
This is where the Midnight Idol and Vegas icon, Wayne Newton, made his singing debut.

❶ Golden Gate Hotel
The city's oldest hotel, it is also known for introducing the shrimp cocktail to Las Vegas.

❺ Golden Nugget
Downtown's largest and most elegant resort features a polished white marble facade.

❷ Plaza Hotel & Casino
Formerly known as Jackie Gaughan's Plaza, this hotel was built in 1971 on the site of the original Union Pacific Railroad depot. It is also the only resort in town with a Greyhound bus station next door, and a rooftop swimming pool that overlooks Fremont Street.

❻ Four Queens
Built in 1966, this hotel was named after the original owner's four daughters.

9 Fremont Street Experience
This open-air canopy generates a spectacular light-and-sound show nightly, and protects pedestrians from the harsh sun during the day.

11 Fremont East District
A $5.5-million streetscape effort is part of a plan to revitalize the downtown area, including the Neonopolis complex.

Locator Map
See Street Finder maps 1 & 2

0 meters		300
0 yards		300

10 El Cortez
With a multi-million dollar upgrade in 2008, El Cortez led the Downtown Vegas renaissance, however it still retains some of its 1950s architecture.

4TH STREET

FREMONT STREET

LAS VEGAS BLVD

6TH STREET

Fremont East continues →

8 The D Las Vegas
Formerly Fitzgeralds, the D Las Vegas offers several restaurants, a pool, and a two-level casino.

Las Vegas Neon

The neon sign remains the dominant icon of Las Vegas, despite the fact that many of the new themed mega-resorts and shopping centers here have opted for a more understated look. Neon is a gas discovered by British chemist Sir William Ramsey in 1898. But it was a French inventor, Georges Claude, who, in 1910, found that when an electric current passed through a glass tube of neon, it emitted a powerful, shimmering light. In the 1940s and 50s, the craft of neon sign making was elevated to the status of an art in Vegas. The sidewalks near and around Neonopolis are home to an interesting collection of historic neon signs.

Glittering sign of
Sassy Sally

❶ Golden Gate Hotel

1 Fremont St. **Map** 2 D3. **Tel** (702) 385-1906. **Open** 24 hours *(see p114)*.
🚹 🆆 goldengatecasino.com

Located at the head of the Fremont Street Experience, Golden Gate was built in 1906 and is the city's oldest and smallest hotel. It was originally known as Hotel Nevada and later as Sal Sagev. The hotel also has the distinction of introducing Las Vegas to the shrimp cocktail, brought over from San Francisco by the hotel's owner in the 1950s. While Golden Gate has been expanded and modernized over the years, the casino and public areas retain a feeling of 19th-century San Francisco. Visitors can still get a great shrimp cocktail served in a tulip glass with a wedge of lemon. However, Golden Gate's 122 rooms have come a long way since the days of horse-drawn carriages, and are furnished with most modern amenities. The casino has about 500 slot and video poker machines, plus the usual table games.

❷ Plaza Hotel & Casino

1 Main St. **Map** 2 D3. **Tel** (702) 386-2110. **Open** 24 hours *(see p114)*. 🚹 🆆 plazahotelcasino.com

Established on land once owned by the railroad, the Plaza has a Greyhound bus station next door. Located at the head of Fremont Street, the hotel was opened in 1971 by renowned hotelier Jackie Gaughan who sold it in 2004 to the Barrick Corporation.

The Plaza is mostly noted for its cascading neon waterfall along the facade of its tower. The hotel's 1,003 rooms and suites are spacious, comfortable, and airy. The decor is pleasant, featuring walnut veneer, and colorful patterns in the draperies and bedspreads.

Other amenities include a sports deck with a pool, renovated in 2016, which is

The massive sign of California Hotel, as seen from the Strip

often used as a venue for pool parties and other outdoor events during the summer months. This pool has a blackjack gaming pit, bar, food truck, jacuzzi, and cabana rentals. The hotel also hosts many eateries that offer a variety of cuisines from across the globe, as well as popular chains such as Subway and McDonald's.

California's staff in Hawaiian shirts

❸ California Hotel

12 Ogden Ave. **Map** 2 D3. **Tel** (702) 385-1222. **Open** 24 hours *(see p114)*.
🚹 🆔 🆆 thecal.com

Despite its hip Hollywood implications, the California Hotel abounds with a tropical flavor and the aloha spirit. A part of the Boyd Gaming family of resorts, this 781-room hotel has been a mecca for the Hawaiian tourist since it was built in 1975 – about 70 per cent of the clientele are Hawaiians availing the resort's special tour packages. In keeping with the theme, the hotel staff wear colorful aloha shirts, the restaurants offer Polynesian and Asian specialties, and the bars serve tropical drinks. Even California Hotel's casino, which is decorated with crystal chandeliers, etched glass, and Italian marble, has slot and video poker machines with Hawaiian names and themes. It also has a live keno lounge and a sports book.

As part of an expansion in 1996, a pedestrian walkway, which connects California Hotel with the Main Street Station resort, was constructed over Main Street.

❹ Main Street Station

200 N Main St. **Map** 2 D3. **Tel** (702) 387-1896. **Open** 24 hours. 🚹 🆔 🆆 mainstreetcasino.com

Although this hotel originally opened in 1991, it closed after a few months because of severe financial problems. Thereafter, Main Street Station was purchased by Boyd Gaming and, since then, has emerged as one of downtown Las Vegas's classiest destinations.

The architecture suggests 1890s New Orleans with its brick promenade, magnolia trees, wrought-iron fences, and Victorian street lamps from

Slot machines lined up in the casino of Main Street Station

pre-World War I Brussels. Inside, the hotel makes liberal use of hardwood and tile floors, gas lamps, brass fixtures, and enough antiques to fill a Southern mansion.

The hotel's lobby contains authentic hardwood railroad benches and bronze, dropped-dome chandeliers from the El Presidente Hotel in Buenos Aires. The stained-glass window greeting casino visitors is from singer Lillian Russell's Pennsylvania mansion, and the carved mahogany cabinetry behind the registration desk came from a Kentucky apothecary. The hotel also showcases President Theodore Roosevelt's Pullman railroad car, a fireplace from Scotland's Preswick Castle, US army scout and showman Buffalo Bill Cody's private rail car, and a section of the Berlin Wall. It is also the only downtown resort with a brewpub and RV Park *(see p117).*

❺ Golden Nugget

129 E Fremont St. **Map** 2 D3. **Tel** (702) 385-7111. **Open** 24 hours *(see p114).*
♿ 🅿 🔲 goldennugget.com/lasvegas

With its facade of polished white marble and gold trim, Golden Nugget stands out as a jewel among downtown hostelries. It has a brightly lit sign composed of thousands of lights. Inside, the hotel hosts the world's largest gold nugget, weighing an incredible 61 lb (27 kg). The hotel's elegant lobby has white marble floors and columns, etched glass panels, gold accessories, and richly colored Oriental rugs. The white marble and gold trim-themed decor is also evident throughout the common areas. The hotel's guest rooms are among the most luxurious in town with plush cream-colored carpeting and wall coverings.

Facilities include an expanded poker room and a $30-million pool complex with The Tank as its centerpiece. This pool contains an enclosed aquarium, allowing guests the opportunity to

Marble floors in the lobby at the Golden Nugget

practically swim side by side with more than 300 sharks, rays, and other marine life, and to take an exhilarating ride through the shark tank on a three-story-high secured slide. The hotel also offers tours of The Tank with staff marine biologists. Away from the sharks (and kids) is The Hideout, a secluded infinity pool with plush poolside cabanas for the over 21s only.

A table game at the Four Queens hotel's casino

❻ Four Queens

202 Fremont St. **Map** 2 D3. **Tel** (702) 385-4011. **Open** 24 hours *(see p114).*
♿ 🔲 fourqueens.com

Reflecting a New Orleans motif, Four Queens is the Grand Old Dame of downtown Las Vegas. Built in 1966, the hotel was named in honor of the original owner's four daughters, and has one of the best arrays of lights on the street.

The Four Queen's decor suggests the French Quarter with its carved wood registration desk, brass trim, gilt mirrors, and hurricane-lamp chandeliers. The hotel has 690 rooms which were re-modeled in 2008. They are brightly furnished and feature luxurious tan carpets, and dark polished wood furniture.

The chandeliered casino and keno lounge has plenty of action, with an array of the most sought-after table games and slot and video poker machines that visitors to Las Vegas would expect.

❼ Fremont Hotel

200 Fremont St. **Map** 2 D3. **Tel** (702) 385-3232. **Open** 24 hours *(see p114).* ⬧ **w** fremontcasino.com

This renowned casino was built in 1956 and was downtown's first high-rise hotel. Fremont Hotel was also the first to have a fully carpeted casino at a time when all other establishments had sawdust-covered floors. Moreover, it was here that the famous Las Vegas headliner, Wayne Newton, made his singing debut.

Today, the hotel's block-long neon sign helps light up the dazzling Fremont Street Experience. The hotel is often described as the heart of Fremont Street and is definitely close to all the action in the area. Across the street is its sister resort, the tropical-themed California Hotel *(see p72).*

The sprawling casino is always busy as gamblers flit from machine to machine – there are more than 1,000 slot and video poker machines to choose from. And, during the football season, Fremont Hotel's race and sports book is one of downtown's busiest.

❽ The D Las Vegas

301 Fremont St. **Map** 2 D3. **Tel** (702) 388-2400. **Open** 24 hours. ⬧ **w** thed.com

The 34-story tower at this 638-room resort is located next to the Fremont Street Experience and offers an excellent vantage point to see the light shows that take place there each evening.

The bold facade of The D Las Vegas

The "D" in the resort's name stands for downtown and also refers to the nickname of the resort's owner, Derek Stevens.

The hotel has a universal appeal and knows how to attract a younger audience. Rooms are modern and fitted out with flatscreen televisions, high-speed wireless Internet access, and iPod docking stations.

The table games at the casino stand out due to the Dancing Dealers dressed in fringed bikinis, who perform and deal after 6 pm in the party pit, located at the center of the casino floor.

The D offers a selection of dining options ranging from an on-site McDonald's to the upscale restaurant Andiamo Steakhouse. The *Marriage Can Be Murder* dinner show is a popular and regular feature.

❾ Fremont Street Experience

Map 2 D3. **Open** Light shows: hourly 6pm–midnight daily (from 8pm–1am in summer). ⬧ 🚲 **w** vegas experience.com

Fremont Street has been at the heart of Las Vegas since it was established in 1905. When gambling was legalized in Nevada in 1931, this is where the first casinos were located. The street became known as "Glitter Gulch" when neon lighting became available, as stylish illuminated signs lit up the night sky.

In the 1980s and 1990s Fremont Street suffered in competition from more lavish attractions on the Strip and became a run-down city center, generally avoided by

Adventure seekers at the SlotZilla Zip Line in the Fremont Street Experience

tourists. In 1994, an ambitious $70-million project to revitalize the area was initiated. A vast steel canopy now covers five blocks of the street, onto which is displayed the spectacular Fremont Street light-and-sound shows, which are collectively known as Viva Vision. The canopy's ceiling showcases high-resolution images presented by more than 12 million synchronized LED modules with concert-quality sound controlled by 10 computers. The street is pedestrianized and visitors can stroll from casino to casino, stopping to snack and shop at kiosks on the way. Some of the famous 1950s and 1960s neon signs gave way to the new show, but many of the dazzling facades belonging to some of the oldest and best-loved casinos remain.

The newest attraction to Fremont Street is the SlotZilla Zip Line, a 12-story slot-machine-inspired zip line that transports riders from 77 ft (23.5 m) across half the length of the promenade.

The colorful, neon-lit facade of the Neonopolis entertainment center

❿ Downtown Grand Las Vegas

206 N 3rd St. **Map** 2 D3. **Tel** (702) 719-5100. **Open** 24 hours (see p114). 🖉
w downtowngrand.com

On the site of the former Lady Luck Hotel & Casino, this hotel is the centerpiece of Downtown3rd, a new entertainment development in the downtown area. The hotel opened in 2013 and has the convenience of being steps from the Mob Museum, the Fremont Street Experience, and Fremont East Entertainment District. The hotel's two towers, the 17-story Casino Tower and 25-story Grand Tower, are joined by an elevated walkway and are decorated in a stylish, contemporary manner throughout. All rooms have modern amenities, including flatscreen HD TVs. Perhaps the biggest draw to the hotel is its rooftop pool retreat, which boasts a fire pit, restaurant, cabanas, picnic tables, and a stage where concerts are hosted on weekends.

⓫ Fremont East District

Map 2 E3. ♿ 🖉

The Fremont East District extends along Fremont Street from Las Vegas Boulevard to 8th Street. The area had fallen on hard times, but improvements have been made by a $5.5-million streetscape renovation plan featuring wide sidewalks, lighted gateways, and neon signs from the 1950s and 1960s.

The area boasts an eclectic mix of cafés, bars, and nightclubs, including Beauty Bar, Downtown Cocktail Room (see p142), The Griffin, and Atomic Liquors.

At the gateway to the district, Neonopolis is an open-air, multi-level dining, shopping, and entertainment complex. Eateries such as Denny's, Heart Attack Grill, and Banger Brewing, a brewery with a tasting room have recently opened there. Hennessey's Tavern and the Mickie Finnz Fish House & Bar are located just across the street from the complex.

The spectacular light-and-sound show at the Fremont Street Experience

El Cortez, one of the few hotels to retain parts of its original architecture

⑫ El Cortez

600 E Fremont St. **Map** 2 E3. **Tel** (702) 385-5200. **Open** 24 hours *(see p114)*. ♿ **W** elcortezhotelcasino.com

One of Las Vegas's most recognized landmarks, the El Cortez Hotel & Casino was built in 1941 and is the oldest continually operating casino in town. Leading the Fremont East rejuvenation, El Cortez upgraded the exterior in 2005 at a cost of $20 million. In 2009, 64 El Cortez Cabana Suites were opened in the former Ogden Hotel. However, it still retains some of its original architecture.

The hotel's original guest rooms with their hardwood floors and tile baths are still intact and are reached via a creaky staircase just off the casino floor. For more modern accommodation, there is a 14-story, 300-room tower with pleasant rooms.

The hotel was once owned by Bugsy Siegel *(see p28)* who sold it when he needed to raise cash to build his famous Flamingo hotel on the Strip. Jackie Gaughan, another former owner, was one of Las Vegas's true pioneers. He owned several other hotels and casinos in downtown Las Vegas, including The Plaza, Vegas Club, Western Hotel, and Gold Spike, all of which he sold in 2004.

Today, El Cortez caters mostly to budget travelers, senior citizens, and slot machine players who enjoy playing in the ambience of an "old Las Vegas" style casino. Video poker and video keno are two of the most popular games in the sprawling casino, which is crammed with rows of machines of every type and for differing bets. El Cortez also has a race and sports book.

⑬ Downtown Container Park

707 Fremont St. **Map** 2 E3. **Tel** (702) 637-4244. **Open** Retail: 11am–9pm Mon–Thu, 10am–10pm Fri & Sat, 10am–8pm Sun. Food & Beverage: 11am–11pm Mon–Thu, 10am–1am Fri & Sat, 10am–11pm Sun. **W** downtowncontainerpark.com

Opened in late 2013 and located at the corner of Fremont and 7th Street, this unique sustainable shopping and dining attraction is a collection of small businesses set within more than two dozen 250-sq-ft (76-sq-m) repurposed shipping containers and 41 modular metal cubes. A center courtyard contains a giant treehouse playground with a 33-ft- (10-m-) tall slide, stage, and a colossal fire-breathing praying mantis. No under 21s permitted after 9pm.

⑭ The Arts Factory and 18b Arts District

101–109 E Charleston Blvd. **Map** 1 C4. **Tel** (702) 383-3133. **Open** daily, varies for each gallery. ♿ **W** 18b.com **W** theartsfactory.com

Located just about a mile (1.6 km) south of Fremont Street, is the 18b Arts District.

The name of this area refers to the 18 blocks originally designated as the Las Vegas Arts District. The District has now expanded to cover a much wider area and features an eclectic mixture of of galleries, unique stores, bars, and restaurants. Places of particular interest include Art Square – three remodeled 1950s buildings and an outdoor art garden – and Antique Alley, which has more than 20 independent antique and vintage stores, including a warehouse full of antiques with monthly auctions, a costume design shop, and several vintage clothing stores.

One of the biggest draws to the 18b Arts District is the Arts Factory, a diverse collection of local artists who have set up shop in a long strip of storefront buildings. Included in the mix are artists, graphic designers, architects, photographers, interior designers, and other craftspeople who enjoy the creative energy of working under one roof.

⑮ Discovery Children's Museum

360 Promenade Pl. **Map** 2 E2. **Tel** (702) 382-5437. **Open** Jun–early Sep: 10am–5pm Mon–Sat, noon–5pm Sun; early Sep–May: 9am–4pm Tue–Fri, 10am–5pm Sat, noon–5pm Sun, & most school holidays. **Closed** major hols. ♿ **W** discoverykidslv.org

This excellent museum, located in Symphony Park, is devoted to interactive exhibits that are fun for both adults and kids.

Inside the Discovery Children's Museum

◄ The Fremont Street Experience

It encompasses nine themed exhibition halls, which explore all manner of topics, including electricity, flight, the movement and power of water, magnets, machines, and art. Most exhibits are aimed at children attending elementary school, but there is plenty to keep all ages amused. Older kids will love The Summit, a 13-level climbing structure, while children under five will have hours of fun in Toddler Town, a padded play area.

⑯ Las Vegas Natural History Museum

900 Las Vegas Blvd N. **Map** 2 E2. **Tel** (702) 384-3466. **Open** 9am–4pm daily. **Closed** Thanksgiving, Dec 25. 🅿 ♿ 🆆 lvnhm.org

This museum attracts families with its appealing, large range of exhibits. Dioramas re-create the African savanna and display a variety of wildlife from majestic leopards to African antelopes. The Wild Nevada Gallery displays fantastic flora and fauna from the Mojave Desert. Animatronic dinosaurs include a 35-ft- (10.5-m-) long Tyrannosaurus rex, while the marine exhibit has live sharks and stingrays in a 3,000-gallon tank. In the hands-on discovery room visitors can dig for fossils and explore the five senses. The museum also has an exhibition on Egypt, following the generous donation of replica Tutankhamen artifacts, including the Golden Thrown, by Luxor (see p44).

A wagon outside the Old Las Vegas Mormon Fort

⑰ Old Las Vegas Mormon Fort

500 E Washington Blvd. **Map** 2 E2. **Tel** (702) 486-3511. **Open** 8am–4:30pm Tue–Sat. **Closed** public hols. ♿ ♿ 🆆 parks.nv.gov/parks/old-las-vegas-mormon-fort

The small soft-pink adobe building is all that remains of the Mormon Fort. The oldest building in Las Vegas, the fort dates back to 1855, when the first group of Mormon settlers arrived in the area (see p20). It became part of a ranch in the 1880s, run by Las Vegas pioneer Helen Stewart. The City of Las Vegas bought the site in 1971, and restoration work has been ongoing since.

Today, visitors enter a reconstruction of the original adobe house with its simply furnished interior much as it would have been under Mormon occupation.

⑱ Neon Museum

770 N. Las Vegas Blvd. **Map** 2 E2. **Tel** (702) 387-6366. **Open** 9am–9pm daily; summer: from 8–10am & until 8–9pm. 🗗 🆆 neonmuseum.org

This museum offers an hour-long guided tour of a collection of more than 150 neon signs dating from the 1930s. The signs, taken from old casinos and other businesses, are displayed over 6 acres. The visitors' center is inside the historic La Concha Motel lobby, a distinctive example of mid-century modern design that was originally constructed in 1961. The building was saved from demolition in 2005 and moved to its current location in 2006.

⑲ Mob Museum

300 Stewart Ave. **Map** 2 D3. **Tel** (702) 229-2734. **Open** 9am–9pm daily. 🆆 themobmuseum.org

Located in the old federal building that was the site of the Kefauver Committee hearings on organized crime held on November 15, 1950, this museum details the history of organized crime in the United States. Throughout the three-story building, multimedia displays show how the law enforcement agencies battled to end the mob's rule in Las Vegas. Exhibits include the wall from Chicago's 1929 St Valentine's Day Massacre, and belongings of gangsters such as Al Capone, Charles "Lucky" Luciano, Bugsy Siegel and more.

An animatronic Tyrannosaurus rex in roaring form at the Las Vegas Natural History Museum

FARTHER AFIELD

Beyond the neon glow of the downtown district and the monetary lure of the Strip casinos, lies a land of diversity filled with scenic and historical treasures. Canyons, mountains, deserts, and some of the most magnificent wilderness that the US has to offer can be seen in almost every direction just beyond Vegas's bright lights, and present a sharp contrast to the artificial wonders of the city. A short drive away are the lush, alpine forests and snow-laden peaks of Mount Charleston, the steep gullies, bristlecone canyons, and red sandstone escarpments of Red Rock Canyon and Valley of Fire State Park, and the expansive shoreline and scenic blue splendor of Lake Mead. For admirers of contemporary architecture, the modern day marvel of Hoover Dam is a must-see. Hailed as an engineering victory, the dam offers splendid views of the surrounding badlands from the top of its visitor center, and is a highly popular tourist destination. Situated a comfortable distance southeast of Las Vegas are two inviting and well-planned cities – Henderson and Boulder City – each with its own distinct character. Most of these side trips can be enjoyed in just a few hours or as a day excursion, and all offer a chance to renew body and spirit.

Sights at a Glance

Areas of Natural Beauty
1 Red Rock Canyon Tour p82
2 Spring Mountain Ranch State Park
4 Mount Charleston
5 Valley of Fire State Park
6 Lake Mead National Recreation Area

Historic Cities
7 Boulder City
8 Henderson

Landmarks
9 Hoover Dam p85

Entertainment
3 Bonnie Springs Ranch/Old Nevada

Key
- Central Las Vegas
- National highway
- Major road
- Minor road
- Railroad
- State line

0 kilometers   20
0 miles   20

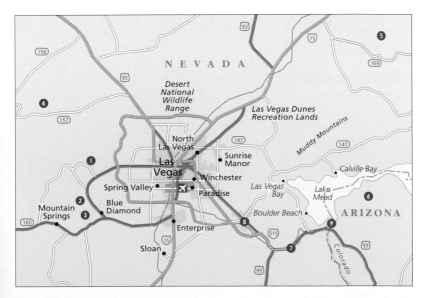

◀ The Hoover Dam

For keys to symbols *see back flap*

➊ Red Rock Canyon Tour

The centerpiece of Red Rock Canyon is a yellow and red sandstone escarpment incised with numerous deep canyons formed by years of erosion. These spectacular rock formations are the geological result of the Keystone Thrust fault, where the earth's tectonic plates collided with such force that one rock plate was thrust over another. Perennial and seasonal springs encourage lush vegetation in relatively shaded places in contrast with the arid desert floor.

Tips for Drivers

Tour length: 13 miles (21 km).
Getting there: 17 miles (27 km) west on Charleston Blvd (Hwy 159) from Las Vegas.
When to go: The Scenic Loop Drive opens daily at 6am. Closing hours: 7pm Mar & Oct; 8pm Apr–Sep; 5pm Nov–Feb. The weather is good all year, except for flash floods.

③ Keystone Thrust
This fracture in the earth's crust details the sharp contrast between the older gray limestone and the younger red sandstone. The rock formations show where the "thrust" of the tectonic plates took place.

④ Willow Springs
Located just past the halfway point on the drive, this is an idyllic picnic spot. It is also a good place to see ancient rock carvings.

② Calico Hills
The two Calico Vista points here offer great panoramic views of the striking and flame-colored sandstone bluffs.

⑤ Ice Box Canyon
This popular trail features huge vertical cliffs and three waterfalls that cool this area all year.

⑥ Pine Creek Canyon
This canyon is home to some of the best trails in Red Rock. Rows of ponderosa pine trees and a meandering clear stream add to the tranquil beauty of the area.

⑦ Red Rock Overlook
Although not part of the Scenic Loop, this vantage point offers excellent views over the canyon.

① Visitor Center
Set against a backdrop of sandstone cliffs, the center provides maps and information on the geology, wildlife, and history of the region.

Key

— Tour route
- - Hiking trail
— Highway

0 kilometers 2
0 miles 2

❷ Spring Mountain Ranch State Park

6375 Nevada Hwy 159, Blue Diamond, NV. **Tel** (702) 875-4141. **W** parks.nv.gov/parks/spring-mountain-ranch-state-park

Less than a mile north of Bonnie Springs, this state park was once a stop on the Old Spanish Trail *(see p19)* historic trade route and contains some of the oldest buildings in Southern Nevada, dating back to the 1860s or earlier. Guided tours are available upon request and take visitors to the historic blacksmith shop, Wilson cemetery, sandstone cabin, bunkhouse and main ranch house, which was once owned by Howard Hughes. Various trails lead to Lake Harriet, a creek, and an ash grove planted in the 1930s. A stage is home to the popular "Super Summer Theatre" musical theater series that runs every May through September.

❸ Bonnie Springs Ranch/Old Nevada

16395 Bonnie Springs Rd, Blue Diamond, Nevada. **Tel** (702) 875-4191. **Open** summer: 10:30am–6pm daily; winter: 10:30am–5pm daily. **W** bonniesprings.com

Bonnie Springs Ranch and Old Nevada are located a short distance from Red Rock Canyon. Built in 1843 as a cattle ranch and watering hole for wagon trains on their way to California, Bonnie Springs now has a petting zoo, duck pond, aviary, and riding stables.

Pine, aspen, and fir cover the peaks of Mount Charleston

Next door, Old Nevada is a full-scale restoration of an old Western mining town. The buildings include a candy shop, a shooting gallery, a saloon where melodramas are performed, and a chapel. Fake gunfights are held in the street, and a miniature train takes visitors through the desert.

❹ Mount Charleston

Tel (702) 515-5400 (Forest Service). Las Vegas. **W** fs.fed.us

Rising out of the **Toiyabe National Forest** at the considerable height of 11,918 ft (3,632 m), Mount Charleston is covered with pine, aspen, mountain mahogany, and fir. About 45 miles (72 km) northwest of Las Vegas, it is part of the Spring Mountain Recreation Area, and offers refuge from the city's summer heat with a variety of hiking trails and picnic areas. In winter, snowboarding and skiing are popular *(see p147)*.

Among the many hikes available are the 11-mile (18-km) North Loop Trail and the 9-mile (14-km) South Loop Trail. Easier walks are also marked, such as a one-hour hike up Cathedral Rock.

❺ Valley of Fire State Park

Tel (702) 397-2088. Las Vegas. partial. **W** parks.nv.gov/parks/valley-of-fire-state-park

This spectacularly scenic state park has a remote, desert location some 60 miles (97 km) northeast of Las Vegas. Its name derives from the striking red sandstone formations. There are four well-maintained trails across this wilderness, which take in several fine prehistoric Ancestral Puebloan rock carvings. The best time to visit is spring or fall.

Nearby Overton lies along the Muddy River. Ancestral Puebloan people settled here in around 300 BC but left 1,500 years later, perhaps because of a long drought *(see p19)*. Archaeologists have unearthed hundreds of prehistoric artifacts. Overton's **Lost City Museum**, just outside the town, has a large collection.

🏛 Lost City Museum
721 S Moapa Valley Blvd, Overton. **Tel** (702) 397-2193. **Open** 8:30am–4:30pm daily. **Closed** Jan 1, Thanksgiving, Dec 25. **W** museums.nevadaculture.org/lcm

Red sandstone formations, Valley of Fire State Park

❻ Lake Mead National Recreation Area

US 93 W of Las Vegas. **Tel** (702) 293-8906; Alan Bible Visitor Center (702) 293-8990. 🚌 Las Vegas. **Open** 9am–4:30pm daily. **Closed** Jan 1, Thanksgiving, Dec 25. 🅿️ ♿ limited. ⚠️ 🅆 nps.gov/lame

After the completion of the Hoover Dam, the waters of the Colorado River filled the deep canyons that once towered above the river to create a huge reservoir. This lake, with its 700 miles (1,130 km) of shoreline, boasts forests and flower-rich meadows, and is the centerpiece of Lake Mead National Recreation Area, a remarkably expansive tract of land. The focus is on water sports, especially sailing, waterskiing, boating, and fishing. Striped bass and rainbow trout are popular catches. There are also several campgrounds and marinas.

The lake and its main marina are easily accessed through Boulder City. However, a more scenic route is available via the Lakeshore and Northshore Drives along the lake's northern finger. These

Power boating on Lake Mead

vistas offer panoramic views of Lake Mead with the desert and mountains for a backdrop.

Speedboats moored on either side of a jetty on Lake Mead

The serene setting of Green Valley Ranch Resort, Henderson

❼ Boulder City

US 93 SE of Las Vegas. ⛰️ 15,000. ✈️ 🚌 🅆 bouldercity.com

Just eight miles (13 km) west of the colossal Hoover Dam, Boulder City was built as a model community to house the dam's construction workers. With its neat yards and suburban streets, it is one of Nevada's most attractive and well-ordered towns. Its Christian founders banned casinos, and there are none here even today. Several of its original 1930s buildings remain, including the restored 1933 Boulder Dam Hotel, which now houses the **Hoover Dam Museum**. On display here are posters, memorabilia, photographs, films, and other exhibits that provide an insight into the dam and the people who built it.

While visiting the dam itself, take in the surrounding grandeur from the **Mike O'Callaghan–Pat Tillman Memorial Bridge**. Built 880 ft (270 m) above the Colorado River, this huge pedestrian walkway is a worthy companion to the dam.

🏛️ **Hoover Dam Museum**
Boulder Dam Hotel,1305 Arizona St, Boulder City. **Tel** (702) 294-1988. **Open** 10am–5pm daily. **Closed** Jan 1, Thanksgiving, Dec 25. 🅿️ ♿ 🅆 bcmha.org

🏛️ **Mike O'Callaghan-Pat Tillman Memorial Bridge**
Hoover Dam Bypass, Boulder City. **Open** dawn–dusk ♿

❽ Henderson

US 93 SE of Las Vegas. ⛰️ 291,000. ✈️ 🚌 ℹ️ Henderson Convention Center and Visitors Bureau (702) 267-2171. 🅆 cityofhenderson.com

Often mistaken as a suburb of Las Vegas, Henderson is an incorporated city that is now the state's second largest. It is home to one of Southern Nevada's most upscale planned communities, Green Valley, where championship golf courses intermingle with million-dollar estates and villas. The city has also developed a gaming industry of its own, which is split between the blue-collar casinos downtown, and the more fashionable resorts such as the **Green Valley Ranch Resort** (see p117), which features Mediterranean architecture and some great dining options.

One of the main attractions in Henderson is the **Ethel M Chocolates** factory. The "M" stands for Mars, as in Mars Bars, who are the makers of candies such as Milky Way, Snickers, Twix, and M&Ms, as well as Ethel M Chocolates, which are now produced exclusively in Las Vegas. Free tours are available to view the gourmet chocolates being created. For $10, classes are held on chocolate making and the history of Ethel M.

Green Valley Ranch Resort
2300 Paseo Verde Pkwy, Henderson. **Tel** (702) 617-7777. **Open** 24 hours. ♿ 🅆 greenvalleyranch.sclv.com

Ethel M Chocolates
2 Cactus Garden Dr, Henderson. **Tel** (702) 433-2655. **Open** 8:30am–6pm. ♿ 📷 🅆 ethelm.com

❾ Hoover Dam

Originally known as the Boulder Dam, the Hoover Dam project began in 1931 and was completed in 1935, ahead of schedule and under budget. Hailed as an engineering victory, this massive concrete structure stands 54 stories tall, has a 600-ft- (183-m-) thick base, and controls the flow of the Colorado River. Today, the dam provides this desert region with a reliable supply of water and electricity and is a major tourist attraction. Due to security restrictions, the only way to tour the dam is through the visitor center. Certain vehicles are restricted from driving over the dam.

VISITORS' CHECKLIST

Practical Information
US Hwy 95 S past Boulder City.
🛈 Hoover Dam Visitor Center
(702) 494-2517; (866) 730-9097.
Open 9am–5pm (4pm winter).
Closed Thanksgiving, Dec 25.
🖼 gallery, exhibitions. ♿ 📷
Ⓦ usbr.gov/lc/hooverdam

The Colorado River, flowing along its 1,400-mile (2,253-km) journey from the Rocky Mountains to the Gulf of Mexico, is the source of all power generated by the dam.

Intake Towers
These four, 400-ft (122-m) tall towers, two on either side of the dam, control water flow through the electric turbines.

★ Visitor Center
This three-level center features audiovisual and theater presentations as well as multimedia exhibits that explain the processes involved in building the dam.

Art Deco Details
Large cast-concrete panels on the entrance towers, as well as the dam's design and craftsmanship, reflect Art Deco elements in the architecture.

★ Hydroelectric Power Generators
The dam's 17 turbine-driven generators supply electricity to the states of California, Nevada, and Arizona.

TWO GUIDED WALKS AND A DRIVE

Las Vegas is a fascinating and diverse city with many layers that can both charm and intrigue those who venture to explore it. In the pages that follow, two guided walks and a drive have been chosen to capture a distinct view of a neo-Southwestern city, where brightly lit, ultra-modern casinos exist alongside unexpected, yet vivid vestiges reminiscent of the town's frontier heritage.

Breaking from the flamboyance of the Strip, the first walk offers a different view of the main area of the city. The university campus is a sanctuary for the arts, culture, literature, and history of Southern Nevada, and teems with youthful and intellectual vibrancy. The second walk introduces Las Vegas's famous

"themed" resorts that meticulously re-create the architectural beauty of man-made sights and landmarks from all around the world. En route you can gaze at the Eiffel Tower, walk across the Brooklyn Bridge, and admire the opulent grandeur of the Roman Colosseum.

Finally, a scenic drive takes visitors beyond the neon and through several generations of the city's neighborhoods. It covers the downtown residential district where the city was born and the midtown estates where the community's founding fathers used to live.

Remember that Las Vegas is situated in a desert, so wear appropriate clothing, sensible shoes, and sunscreen, and carry drinking water.

CHOOSING A WALK OR A DRIVE

This map shows the location of the two guided walks and the drive in relation to the main sightseeing areas of Las Vegas.

Key

• • • Walk/Drive route

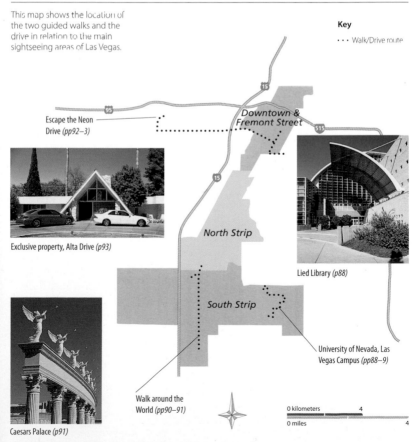

Escape the Neon Drive (pp92–3)

Exclusive property, Alta Drive (p93)

Downtown & Fremont Street

North Strip

Lied Library (p88)

South Strip

University of Nevada, Las Vegas Campus (pp88–9)

Walk around the World (pp90–91)

Caesars Palace (p91)

0 kilometers 4
0 miles 4

◀ A gondola ride through the canals of The Venetian

A 90-Minute Walk around the University of Nevada, Las Vegas Campus (UNLV)

This walk offers a stimulating glimpse into the University of Nevada, Las Vegas, which serves as the intellectual and cultural center of the city. Each year, UNLV's performing arts venues showcase ballets, operas, theatrical productions, and classical musical concerts by world-renowned artists. In addition, the university features fine arts galleries, museums, and an extensive library – its collection of casino memorabilia is the most comprehensive in the state of Nevada. The surrounding area offers various off-campus diversions that provide a respite from university life.

Front facade of the Lied Library ②

Thomas & Mack Center to the Lied Library

At the southwest end of the UNLV campus, located just off Swenson Street is the Thomas & Mack Center ①. This 18,000-seat sports and entertainment arena is home to the school's Runnin' Rebels basketball team. It is also the site of various community events, such as the annual National Finals Rodeo (see p34), the Mountain West Conference basketball tournaments, rock shows, Disney musicals on ice, and more. The adjoining 3,000-seat Cox Pavilion, added to the center in 2001, is the venue for UNLV's volleyball and women's basketball games. From Thomas & Mack, walk about two blocks north along Gym Road to Lied Library ② for a must-see visit to its Special Collections section. Thousands of maps, manuscripts, periodicals, drawings, and pictures document the history, art, and culture of Las Vegas.

Barrick Museum ③

A good place to start is the public reading room, stocked with volumes dating back to the 18th century and earlier. You can also head for the oral history room that has audio- and videotapes of interviews and documentaries on famous Las Vegans. The library has a wide selection of gaming memorabilia as well.

UNLV Barrick Museum to Donna Beam Gallery

From the library, walk across Gym Road to the UNLV -Barrick Museum ③ (see p47). Exhibits here focus on the area's flora and fauna. There is also a fine collection of Native American and Meso-American cultural artifacts, such as textiles and dance masks. The museum also chronicles the history of ancient peoples such as the Anasazi and the Hopi Indians. Situated at the entrance to the museum is the Xeric Garden ④, which

Entrance to the massive sports arena, Thomas & Mark Center ①

features an attractive landscape of indigenous plant life, paved pathways, and striated sandstone boulders. Continue east until Brussels Street and then head north to the Donna Beam Fine Art Gallery ⑤. Located in the Alta Ham Fine Arts Building, the gallery showcases an eclectic collection of artworks by a number of critically acclaimed contemporary artists, as well as by students and faculty members of the university's Department of Art. The ever-changing exhibitions include those organized by professional touring artists, and by renowned art companies, such as Crayola Crayon Inc., National Council on Education for the Ceramic Arts, and American College Theater Festival.

Nuclear bomb, Atomic Testing Museum ⑦

Flashlight Sculpture to the Atomic Testing Museum

The Fine Arts building and Donna Beam Gallery are just a few steps from the Performing Arts Center, which houses the Artemus Ham Concert Hall and the Judy Bayley Theater – two of UNLV's most prominent entertainment venues for various cultural shows. On the plaza between these two venues, stands a massive sculpture, the 38-ft (11.5-m) tall *Flashlight* ⑥, created by Swedish-born artist Claes Oldenburg. Installed in 1981, the pop art sculpture has become a favorite on campus. I lead east from here till you reach Maryland Parkway, one of the city's oldest boulevards, connecting the area east of downtown with McCarran Airport. The section near UNLV is home to a wide selection of shops, bookstores, coffee houses, restaurants, and bars, and is always crowded with students. Walk north on Maryland and turn east on Cottage Grove Avenue. At the north end of the UNLV

Flashlight sculpture ⑥

campus is the Desert Research Institute (DRI), home to the Atomic Testing Museum ⑦. Some of the most notable displays here are the Nevada Test Site's *(see p24)* vast collection of photographs and memorabilia, a one-fifth-scale model of a test canister used in underground nuclear experiments, and a letter written by eminent scientist Albert Einstein to President Franklin D. Roosevelt. The museum also features interactive multimedia exhibits, the Ground Zero Theater that shows films of actual atomic tests, and works from the Smithsonian Institution.

Tips for Walkers

Starting point: Thomas & Mack Center.
Length: 2 miles (3.2 km).
Getting there: Take the RTC bus no. 201 on Tropicana Avenue heading east from the Strip and get off at Swenson Street. From downtown you can take RTC bus no. 108 south on Paradise Road all the way to the airport, at which point the bus loops and returns via Swenson Street.
Stopping-off points: Maryland Parkway has an array of good eateries serving up a variety of international flavors, including Paymon's Mediterranean Café, which serves excellent Middle Eastern cuisine. Or there's Einstein Bagels for a quick and tasty snack.

MINGO ROAD
MARYLAND CIR
COTTAGE GROVE AVE
MARYLAND PARKWAY
UNIVERSITY ROAD
DOROTHY AVE
TROPICANA AVENUE

0 meters 200
0 yards 20w

Key
••• Tour route

A painting by actor Tony Curtis at the Donna Beam Fine Art Gallery ⑤

A Two-Hour Walk around the World

Nothing characterizes Las Vegas like its imaginatively conceived and exquisitely designed, themed mega-resorts. Lined along the Strip, these opulent hotels pay tribute to some of the most renowned cities and countries in the world through remarkable re-creations of their architectural landscape. This walk allows you to stroll along the streets of Venice, marvel at international landmarks such as the Eiffel Tower, Brooklyn Bridge, and the Egyptian sphinx, and see beautiful Roman sculptures and fountains – all within a few blocks of each other.

Egypt to New York

Begin the walk at the corner of Las Vegas Boulevard and Hacienda Avenue to see one of the city's most spectacular resorts – Luxor ① *(see p44)*. The main building consists of a 30 story-high pyramid, encased in dark reflective glass with its entrance guarded by a ten story-high sphinx, flanked by a sandstone obelisk and statues of pharaohs. Two fascinating exhibitions are housed here: Titanic: The Artifact Exhibition and BODIES: The Exhibition. In the latter exhibit, real bodies are displayed, giving a detailed, 3D vision of the human form rarely seen outside of an anatomy lab or morgue.

From Luxor, take a free tram to Excalibur *(see p44)*, where it's just a short walk across the street to New York-New York ② *(see p45)*. A replica of the Statue of Liberty marks the entrance to this hotel. The hotel's towers contain replicas of other famous landmarks, including the Empire State Building

and the Chrysler Building. The casino also duplicates New York icons such as Times Square, and a replica of Coney Island, featuring an arcade with video games.

Stroll past New York-New York towards The Park, a varied blend of restaurants, bars, and live music. It is also home to the T-Mobile Arena, a 20,000-seater

A replica of the Brooklyn Bridge at New York-New York ②

A majestic reproduction of the Great Sphinx, Luxor ①

Key

···· Tour route

— Monorail and tram routes

entertainment venue. When it's time to leave, walk across the Brooklyn Bridge, and head north towards Monte Carlo ③ *(see p45)*.

Monte Carlo to Paris

From the sidewalk, admire the European-style architecture at Monte Carlo, an impressive array of elegant alabaster columns, Renaissance statues, and a gleaming marble lobby. From here you can view the pool area with its lush landscaping, wave pool, and a lazy river. For kids of all ages, Lick on the Street of Dreams is the ultimate candy store. Their vast range includes confectionary classics, modern creations, and souvenir novelties from around the world.

From here, continue walking north along the Strip, and stroll along the new open-air plaza, which contains six unique dining concepts, vibrant community spaces and live entertainment; or head across the road to MGM Grand where you can take the monorail to Bally's, which is just a short stroll away from Paris Las Vegas ④ *(see p48)*. Designed to resemble a mini version of the French capital, this resort has an impressive half-size replica of the iconic Eiffel Tower, as well as copies of other famous French buildings such as l'Opera, Louvre, and Arc de Triomphe.

Lombardy to Venice via Rome

Take the overpass crosswalk across Las Vegas Boulevard to Bellagio ⑤ *(see pp50–51)*. One of the main attractions at this chic hotel, which was inspired by the village of Bellagio near Lake Como, is the 8.5-acre (3.4-ha) lake in front. Each night, the lake comes alive with dancing fountains set to the music of artists ranging from Sinatra to Pavarotti. The hotel's lobby is adorned with a breathtaking glass flowers sculpture. A short walk from the lobby is the Conservatory, a massive atrium

For keys to symbols *see back flap*

Italianate architecture comes to life at Bellagio ⑤

filled with beautiful plants and flowers that change with the seasons. If you have the time, visit the Bellagio Gallery of Fine Art, which showcases rotating exhibitions with original works by artists such as Monet, Renoir, Picasso, van Gogh, Hockney, Warhol, and Lichtenstein. On the way out, stroll along Via Bellagio *(see p129)*, a promenade of upscale shops. Use the overhead sidewalk to make your way across Flamingo Road to Caesars Palace ⑥ *(see p52)*. Marble statues, Roman fountains, imported cypress trees, and toga-clad cocktail waitresses contribute to the resort's opulent and lavish Roman theme. On your way into the casino, note the imposing Colosseum and the Roman aqueducts. From Caesars Palace, it is a comfortable stroll north to

Artistic fountains, Monte Carlo ③

Tips for Walkers

Starting point: Luxor.
Length: 3.5 miles (5.6 km).
Getting there: Take The Deuce from any point along Las Vegas Boulevard. Buses run every 10 minutes; it is a 25–30-minute ride from downtown. Raised walkways allow safe crossing of intersections. The Las Vegas Monorail runs from the Convention Center to MGM Grand. You can also take the free tram from Mandalay Bay to Luxor.
Stopping-off points: All the resort hotels offer a wide variety of eating options. Bally's has a nice cluster of fast-food outlets and an ice cream parlor. Caesars Palace serves a superb buffet, as does Paris Las Vegas, which also has a first-rate bakery. The plaza at Caesars offers great photo opportunities, as do the canals at The Venetian and the sweeping panoramic views from atop Paris's Eiffel Tower.

The Venetian ⑦ *(see pp60–61)*. Graceful bridges, bustling piazzas, and stone walkways meander among replicas of landmarks, including the Doge's Palace, Rialto Bridge, St. Mark's Square, and the 315-ft (96-m) high Campanile Tower – all successfully re-creating the charm of Venice. The casino is tastefully decorated with Italian-style frescoes, gilded ceilings, marble floors, and plush furnishings. Just off the casino floor is the Grand Canal Shoppes *(see p129)*, a shopping arcade built along winding canals, with authentic gondolas and singing gondoliers adding to the flavor.

The grandeur of the Colosseum as seen at night, Caesars Palace ⑥

Escape the Neon Drive

Most visitors are unaware of the many attractions Las Vegas has to offer beyond the bright lights of the Strip. But hidden in the jumbled cityscape, not far from the pulsating excitement of gambling resorts, are various unique, yet generally unknown, sights and symbols that represent the history and culture of Las Vegas. Because the city is spread across a large area, the best way to experience the municipal kaleidoscope is by car. This drive not only takes a trip into Las Vegas's past, but also affords a closer glimpse at the path it took in becoming one of the most modern and fastest growing cities in the world today.

Carvings above the entrance of Las Vegas Academy ⑤

Performers at the Huntridge Theater, Las Vegas ①

Huntridge Theater to Las Vegas Academy

Start a few blocks south of Fremont Street at the junction of Charleston Boulevard and Maryland Parkway. You can't miss the tall, Art Deco facade of the Huntridge Theater ①. Built in the 1940s, Huntridge was once the most popular movie theater in the city. It was also a well-known launch pad for several musical groups, including Foo Fighters, Red Hot Chili Peppers, Smashing Pumpkins, and many more. Unfortunately, this interesting building is no longer open to the public.

Directly across Maryland Parkway is the family-owned Huntridge Pharmacy and Soda Fountain ②, one of the few independent drug stores that hasn't been driven out by pharmaceutical giants such as Walgreens or CVS. The old-fashioned soda fountain serves authentic ice cream treats, along with plenty of pleasant conversation. Drive west on Charleston and turn left on 8th Street, then immediately turn right and continue west to Park

architecture of the 1930s. In the 1950s and 1960s, students would cruise down Fremont Street to malt shops such as the long-gone Blue Onion. Although the academy is still owned by the Clark County School District, it is now used as a performing and visual arts academy.

Avenue. The large white building is Hartland Mansion ③, which was once visited by Elvis Presley.

Drive back on to Charleston, and turn into 7th Street, heading toward Fremont Street. You'll pass through a pleasant neighborhood of modest Tudor-style homes ④, many of which have been converted to offices by local attorneys and accountants.

The building near the intersection of 7th Street and Bridger Avenue is the Las Vegas Academy ⑤, and a great example of the Gothic Revival

Tudor-style house, today a law office ④

Rancho Circle to Springs Preserve

Leaving the Fremont Street neighborhood, drive south to Bonneville Avenue and turn right. Continue about 2 miles (3.2 km) along this route to Rancho Drive, home to two of the most exclusive neighborhoods in the city – Rancho Circle ⑥ and Rancho Bel Air. Since both are gated neighborhoods, one can only peek at the homes from the perimeter. For the best view drive west along Alta Drive. The first home on your right, at the corner, once belonged to Frank Hawkins, a former city councilman and football player for the Oakland Raiders. Continue along Alta, past old money estates that are home to Vegas icons such as Phyllis McGuire of the McGuire Sisters singing trio and the Herbsts, one of the city's richest business families.

Take Alta as far as Valley View and turn right.

Samples of the desert's plant life at Springs Preserve ⑦

For an insight into the desert's plant life, stop at Springs Preserve ⑦. The 180-acre (73-ha) cultural and historic preserve sits on the site of the original Las Vegas Springs, the birthplace of Las Vegas. Attractions here include numerous live Mojave Desert animal exhibits, art galleries, a desert wetland that is the habitat of native plants and animals, 3.65 miles (5.9 km) of hiking trails leading to historical sites, a narrated locomotive ride, animal shows and a botanical desert garden.

The Divine Café overlooks the grounds and is open for lunch on weekdays and for both breakfast and lunch on weekends.

Tips for Walkers

Starting point: Huntridge Theater at the corner of Charleston Boulevard and Maryland Parkway.
Length: 15 miles (24 km).
Getting there: From Fremont Street, drive east to Maryland Parkway and then south to Charleston. You can also drive along Las Vegas Boulevard to Charleston, turn east and drive to Maryland Parkway.
Stopping-off points: The 1930s Gothic Revival architecture at Las Vegas Academy provides an interesting snapshot. The pastoral setting of Lorenzi Park is a nice spot for relaxing or a picnic. The Omelet House, at Rancho and Charleston, serves great burgers.

Nevada State Museum

Las Vegas Springs Preserve is home to the Nevada State Museum and Historical Society. Housed in a beautiful, 70,000-sq-ft (6,500-sq-m) building, it has displays, artifacts, newspaper clippings, and photographs illustrating southern Nevada's history. Visitors can step inside a stalactite cave, watch holographs tell the story of Nevada's miners, and witness an atomic explosion. An enormous Columbian mammoth dominates the complex, as does a full-sized model of a 48-ft (14.6-m) long Ichthyosaur, along with many other archaeological exhibits.

0 meters 800
0 yards 800

Key

••• Tour route

For keys to symbols see back flap

Skeleton of a Columbian mammoth at Nevada State Museum in Springs Preserve

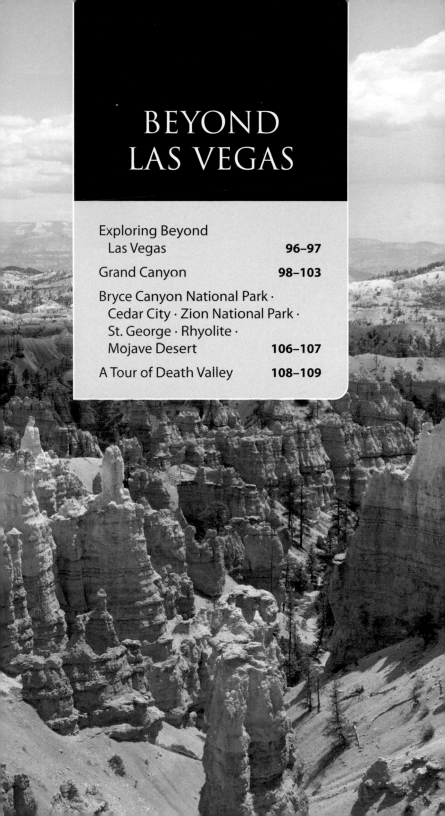

BEYOND
LAS VEGAS

Exploring Beyond Las Vegas

The wilderness areas beyond Nevada's borders are home
to some of the country's most dramatic and fascinating
natural wonders and treasures. Heading west and just
two hours away from Las Vegas is the austere but quietly
breathtaking Death Valley, a giant geological lab containing
salt beds, sand dunes, and multi-tiered hills whose layers
are windows to the history of the Earth. Within a few hours'
drive northeast of Vegas are the soaring peaks, sandstone
crags, and lush rolling meadows of the Zion and Bryce
Canyon National Parks in Southern Utah. And located
east of Las Vegas is the most spectacular marvel of them
all, the Grand Canyon with its awe-inspiring dimensions.
Each of these regions has its own distinct flora and fauna,
with some species found nowhere else on Earth.

Flowers of a Mojave yucca plant,
Mojave Desert

Sights at a Glance

① *Grand Canyon pp98–103*
② Bryce Canyon National Park
③ Cedar City
④ Zion National Park
⑤ St. George
⑥ Rhyolite
⑦ Mojave Desert
⑧ *A Tour of Death Valley pp108–9*

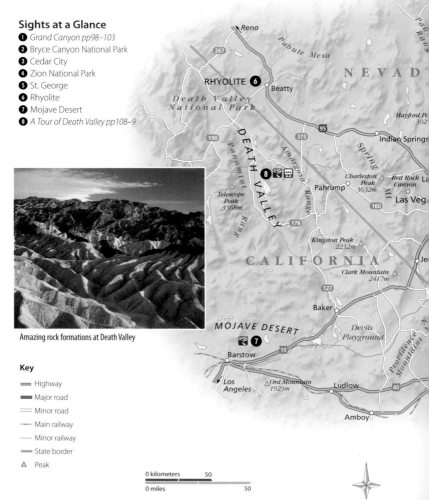

Amazing rock formations at Death Valley

Key

━━ Highway
━━ Major road
══ Minor road
╍╍ Main railway
⋯⋯ Minor railway
━━ State border
△ Peak

0 kilometers   50
0 miles   50

Historic Mormon Rock Church, Cedar City

Getting Around

There are several Las Vegas tour operators that fly regularly to the Grand Canyon. In addition, some commercial airlines fly from McCarran Airport to a few of these areas. The I-15 north from Las Vegas leads to St. George, Cedar City, and Zion and Bryce Canyon National Parks. For Death Valley, drive northwest on US 95, which also accesses the historic towns of Beatty and Rhyolite. To reach the Grand Canyon's South Rim, drive southeast on US 95, then head east on Route 40, and drive north on Route 64 to Grand Canyon Village.

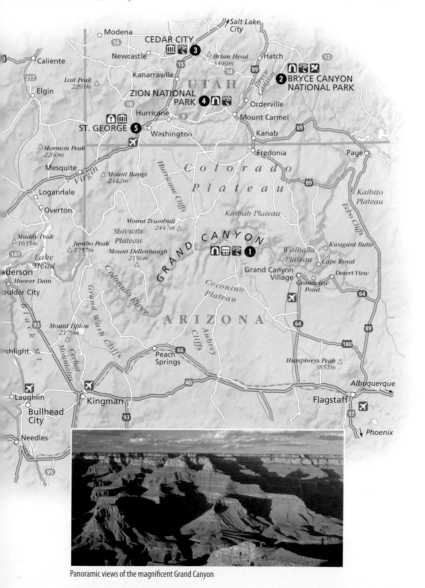

Panoramic views of the magnificent Grand Canyon

For keys to symbols see back flap

❶ Grand Canyon

Grand Canyon is one of the world's great natural wonders and an instantly recognizable symbol of the Southwest. The canyon runs through Grand Canyon National Park *(see pp100–3)*, and is 277 miles (446 km) long, an average of 10 miles (16 km) wide, and around 5,000 ft (1,500 m) deep. It was formed over a period of six million years by the Colorado River, whose waters sliced through the Colorado Plateau, which includes the gorge and most of Northern Arizona and the Four Corners region. The plateau's geological vagaries have defined the river's twisted course, and exposed vast cliffs and pinnacles that are ringed by rocks of different colors, variegated hues of limestone, sandstone, and shale. The canyon is spectacular by any standard, but its beauty is in the colors that the rocks take on – bleached white at midday, but red and ocher at sunset. The South Rim, which is easier to access than the North Rim, is a five-hour drive from Las Vegas.

Mule Trip Convoy
A mule ride is a popular method of exploring the canyon's narrow trails.

Havasu Canyon
The 10-mile (16-km) trail to the beautiful Havasu Falls is a popular hike. The land is owned by the Havasupai tribe, who offer horseback rides and guided tours into the canyon.

Grandview Point
At 7,400 ft (2,250 m), Grandview Point is one of the highest places on the South Rim, the canyon's southern edge. It is one of the stops along Desert View Drive *(see p101)*. The point is thought to be the spot from where the Spanish had their first glimpse of the canyon in 1540.

North Rim
The North Rim receives roughly one-tenth the number of visitors of the South Rim. While less accessible, it is a more peaceful destination offering a sense of unexplored wilderness. It has a range of hikes, such as the North Kaibab Trail, a steep descent down to Phantom Ranch on the canyon floor.

Grand Canyon Skywalk
This horseshoe-shaped glass walkway is suspended 4,000 ft (1,200 m) above the Colorado River. Some 450 tons of steel were used in the construction of this spectacular structure.

Yavapai Point at the South Rim
Situated 5 miles (8 km) north of the canyon's South Entrance, along a stretch of the Rim Trail, is Yavapai Point. Its observation station offers spectacular views of the canyon, and a viewing panel identifies several of the central canyon's landmarks.

Bright Angel Trail
Used by both Native Americans and early settlers, the Bright Angel Trail follows a natural route along one of the canyon's enormous fault lines. It is an appealing option for day hikers because, unlike some other trails in the area, it offers shade and several seasonal water sources.

Grand Canyon National Park

A World Heritage Site, Grand Canyon National Park is located entirely within the state of Arizona. The park covers 1,904 sq miles (4,930 sq km), and is made up of the canyon itself, which starts where the Paria River empties into the Colorado, and stretches from Lees Ferry to Lake Mead *(see p84)*. The area won protective status as a National Monument in 1908 after Theodore Roosevelt visited it in 1903, observing that it should be kept intact for future generations as "… the one great sight which every American … should see." The National Park was created in 1919 and has two main entrances, on the North and South Rims of the canyon. The southern section of the park receives the most visitors and is often congested during the summer season *(see pp102–3)*.

North Rim Entrance Station

Point Sublime

Crystal Creek

Bright Angel Point

Shiva Temple

Isis Temple

Colorado River

Havasu Canyon

Diana Temple

Hopi Point

Yavapai Point

Grand Canyon Village

Hermits Rest

Yaki Point

Grand Canyon Airport

↓ Flagstaff, Williams

Grand Canyon Lodge
Perched above the canyon at Bright Angel Point, the Grand Canyon Lodge has rooms and a number of dining options *(see p103)*.

Hermit Road
A free shuttle bus runs along this route to the Hermits Rest viewpoint during the summer. It is closed to private vehicles from March to November.

Kolb Studio
Built in 1904 by brothers Emery and Ellsworth Kolb, who photographed the canyon extensively, the Kolb Studio is a National Historic Site. It now houses an art gallery and bookstore.

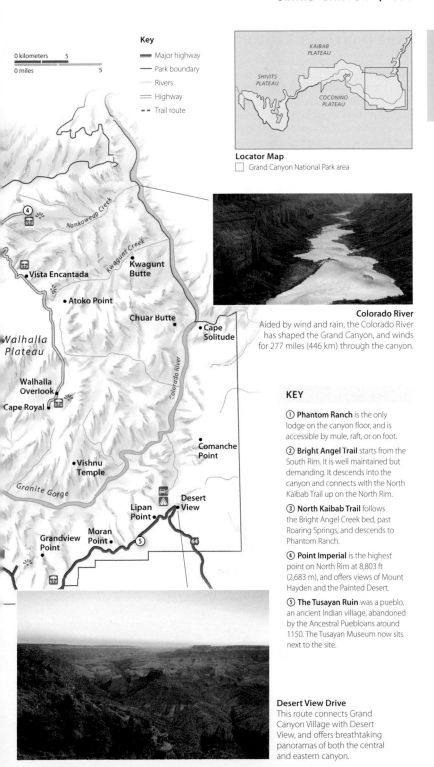

Key

0 kilometers   5
0 miles   5

▬▬ Major highway
—— Park boundary
── Rivers
═══ Highway
– – Trail route

Locator Map
☐ Grand Canyon National Park area

KAIBAB PLATEAU

SHIVITS PLATEAU

COCONINO PLATEAU

Nankoweap Creek

④

Kwagunt Creek

Kwagunt Butte

• Vista Encantada

• Atoko Point

Chuar Butte

• Cape Solitude

Walhalla Plateau

Colorado River

Walhalla Overlook

Cape Royal

Colorado River
Aided by wind and rain, the Colorado River has shaped the Grand Canyon, and winds for 277 miles (446 km) through the canyon.

• Vishnu Temple

Granite Gorge

• Comanche Point

Lipan Point

Desert View

Grandview Point

Moran Point

⑤

64

KEY

① **Phantom Ranch** is the only lodge on the canyon floor, and is accessible by mule, raft, or on foot.

② **Bright Angel Trail** starts from the South Rim. It is well maintained but demanding. It descends into the canyon and connects with the North Kaibab Trail up on the North Rim.

③ **North Kaibab Trail** follows the Bright Angel Creek bed, past Roaring Springs, and descends to Phantom Ranch.

④ **Point Imperial** is the highest point on North Rim at 8,803 ft (2,683 m), and offers views of Mount Hayden and the Painted Desert.

⑤ **The Tusayan Ruin** was a pueblo, an ancient Indian village, abandoned by the Ancestral Puebloans around 1150. The Tusayan Museum now sits next to the site.

Desert View Drive
This route connects Grand Canyon Village with Desert View, and offers breathtaking panoramas of both the central and eastern canyon.

Exploring Grand Canyon National Park

Grand Canyon offers awe-inspiring beauty on a vast scale. The magnificent rock formations with towers, cliffs, steep walls, and buttes recede as far as the eye can see, their bands of colored rock varying in shade as light changes through the day. The park's main roads, Hermit Road and Desert View Drive, both accessible from the South Entrance, overlook the canyon. Grand Canyon Village is located on the South Rim and offers many facilities. Visitors can also enter the park from the north, although this route (Highway 67) is closed during winter. Walking trails along the North and South Rims offer staggering views but, to experience the canyon at its most fascinating, the trails that go down toward the canyon floor should be explored.

The Bright Angel Trail on the South Rim, and the North Kaibab Trail on the North Rim, descend to the canyon floor, and are tough hikes involving an overnight stop.

Adobe pueblo-style architecture of Hopi House, Grand Canyon Village

🏠 Grand Canyon Village

Grand Canyon National Park. **Tel** (928) 638-7888. ♿ partial.

Grand Canyon Village has its roots in the late 19th century. The extensive building of visitor accommodations started after the Santa Fe Railroad opened a branch line here from Williams in 1901, though some hotels had been built in the late 1890s. The Fred Harvey Company constructed a clutch of well-designed, attractive buildings. The most prominent is **El Tovar Hotel**. Opened in 1905, it is named after the Spanish explorers who reached the gorge in 1540. The **Hopi House**, a rendition of a traditional Hopi Indian dwelling, where locals could sell their craftwork as souvenirs, also opened in 1905. It was built by Hopi craftsmen

and designed by Mary E. J. Colter. An ex-schoolteacher and trained architect, Colter drew on Southwestern influences, mixing both Native American and Hispanic styles. She is responsible for many of the historic structures that now grace the South Rim, including the 1914 **Lookout Studio** and **Hermits Rest**, and the rustic 1922 **Phantom Ranch** on the canyon floor.

Today, Grand Canyon Village has a wide range of hotels, restaurants, and stores. It is surprisingly easy to get lost here since the buildings are spread out and discreetly placed

among wooded areas. The village is not only the starting point for most of the mule trips through the canyon, but also the terminus for the Grand Canyon Railway.

South Rim

Most of the Grand Canyon's 4.3 million annual visitors come to the South Rim, since, unlike the North Rim, it is open year-round and is easily accessible along Highway 180/64 from both Flagstaff and Williams. **Hermit Road** and **Desert View Drive** (Highway 64) start at Grand Canyon Village and encompass a selection of the choicest views of the gorge. Hermit Road is closed to private vehicles from March to November each year; free shuttle buses are available. Desert View Drive is open all year.

From the village, Hermit Road meanders along the South Rim, extending for 8 miles (13 km). Its first viewpoint is **Trailview Overlook**, which provides an overview of the canyon and the winding course of the Bright Angel Trail. Moving on, **Maricopa Point** offers especially panoramic views of the canyon but not of Colorado River, which is more apparent from nearby **Hopi Point**. At the end of Hermit Road lies Hermits Rest, where a gift shop, decorated in rustic style, is located in yet another Mary Colter-designed building. The longer Desert View Drive runs in the opposite direction, and covers 26 miles (42 km). It winds for 12 miles (20 km) before reaching **Grandview Point**, where the Spaniards are believed to have

The unique interior of the Hermits Rest gift store which has crafts for sale

Desert View's stone watchtower, on Desert View Drive

had their first glimpse of the canyon in 1540. About 10 miles (16 km) farther on lie the pueblo remains of Tusayan Ruin, where there is a small museum with exhibits on Ancestral Puebloan life. The road continues on to the stunning overlook of Desert View. The watchtower here was Colter's most fanciful creation, its upper floor decorated with early 20th-century Hopi murals.

Just east of Grand Canyon Village is **Yavapai Point** from where it is possible to see Phantom Ranch. This is the only roofed accommodation available on the canyon floor, across the Colorado River.

North Rim

Standing at about 8,000 ft (2,400 m), the North Rim is higher, cooler, and greener than the South Rim, with dense forests of ponderosa pine, aspen, and Douglas fir. Visitors are most likely to spot wildlife such as the mule deer, Kaibab squirrel, and wild turkey on the North Rim.

The Rim can be reached via Highway 67, off Highway 89A, ending at **Grand Canyon Lodge**, where there are visitor services, a campground, a restaurant, a gas station, and a general store. Nearby, there is a National Park Service information center, which offers maps of the area. The North Rim and all its facilities are closed from mid-October to mid-May, when it is often snowed in. The

California Condors

America's largest bird, the California condor, has a wingspan of over 9 ft (2.7 m). Nearly extinct in the 1980s, the last 22 condors were captured for breeding in captivity. In 1996, the first captive-bred birds were released in Northern Arizona. Today, about 70 condors fly over the skies of Arizona. They are frequent guests of the South Rim, though visitors should not approach or attempt to feed them.

A pair of California condors

North Rim is twice as far from the river as the South Rim, and the canyon really stretches out from the overlooks giving a sense of its 10-mile (16-km) width. There are about 30 miles (45 km) of scenic roads along the North Rim, as well as hiking trails to high viewpoints or down to the canyon floor, particularly the **North Kaibab Trail** that links to the South Rim's Bright Angel Trail. The picturesque **Cape Royal Drive** starts north of Grand Canyon Lodge and travels 23 miles (37 km) to Cape Royal on the Walhalla Plateau. From here, several famous buttes and peaks can be seen, including Wotans Throne and Vishnu Temple. There are also several short walking trails around Cape Royal. A 3-mile (5-km) detour leads to **Point Imperial**, the highest point on the canyon rim, while along the way the **Vista Encantada** has delightful views and picnic tables overlooking the gorge.

Bright Angel Trail

This is the most popular of all Grand Canyon hiking trails. The Bright Angel trailhead is at Grand Canyon Village on the South Rim. The trail begins near the **Kolb Studio** at the western end of the village. It then switches dramatically down the side of the canyon for 9 miles (14 km). The trail crosses the river over a suspension bridge, ending a little farther on at Phantom Ranch. There are two resthouses and a fully equipped campground along the way. It is not advisable to attempt the whole trip in one day. Many walk from the South Rim to one of the rest stops and then return up to the Rim. Temperatures at the bottom of the canyon can reach 43°C (110°F) or higher during the summer. Day hikers should, therefore, carry a quart (just over a liter) of water per person per hour for summer hiking. Carrying a first-aid kit is also highly recommended.

Hikers taking a break on the South Rim's Bright Angel Trail

Thor's Hammer hoodoo, Bryce Canyon, shaped by natural forces

❷ Bryce Canyon National Park

Hwy 63 off Hwy 12. **Tel** (435) 834-5322. ✈ Bryce Canyon Airport. 🚌 shuttle service in summer from Bryce Point. **Open** daily. **Closed** Dec 25. 🅿 ♿ 🛍 🏕 ✎ 🏔 w **nps.gov/brca**

A series of deep, cavernous amphitheaters filled with striking, flame-colored rock formations called hoodoos are the hallmark of Bryce Canyon National Park. At a significant altitude, Bryce reaches elevations of 8,000–9,000 ft (2,400–2,700 m), with a scenic road traveling for 18 miles (30 km) along the rim of Paunsaugunt Plateau. The highlights here are the fields of pink, orange, and red spires. The Paiute Indians, once hunters here, described them as "red rocks standing like men in a bowl-shaped recess."

During winter, the panoramic vista of snow-covered rock spires from the Bryce amphitheater is a popular vantage point. The Agua Canyon overlook has views of the layered pink sandstone cliffs of the Paunsaugunt Plateau. One of the park's most famous hoodoos – Thor's Hammer – was formed by wind, ice, and rain. The natural bridge, near the park's highway was formed by the same forces.

❸ Cedar City

🏘 29,000. 🛈 581 N Main St, (435) 586-5124. ✈ 🚌
w **scenicsouthernutah.com**

Founded by Mormons in 1851, this town developed as a center for mining and smelting iron in the latter part of the 19th century. Today, it offers hotels and restaurants within an hour's drive of Zion National Park.

The **Frontier Homestead State Park Museum** pays tribute to the early Mormons, and displays a collection of more than 300 wagons and vehicles, including an original Wells Fargo overland stagecoach. The city's Shakespeare Festival runs annually from June to October and is staged in a replica of London's reconstructed Elizabethan Globe Theatre.

Around 15 miles (24 km) east of the town, along Highway 14, **Cedar Breaks National Monument** features an array of pink and orange limestone cliffs, topped by deep green forest. The monument closes in winter, but remains a popular destination for cross-country skiers.

🏛 Frontier Homestead State Park Museum

635 N Main. **Tel** (435) 586-9290. **Open** Sep–May: 9am–5pm Mon–Sat; Jun–Aug: 9am–6pm daily. **Closed** Jan 1, Thanksgiving, Dec 25. 🅿
w **stateparks.utah.gov/parks/frontier-homestead**

🏛 Cedar Breaks National Monument

Tel (435) 586-0787 ext. 31. **Open** daily. Visitor Center **Open** late May–mid-Oct: 9am–6pm daily. 🅿 w **nps.gov/cebr**

❹ Zion National Park

Hwy 9, near Springdale. 🛈 Zion Canyon Visitor Center (435) 772-3256. **Open** 8am–6pm daily (to 5pm in winter, to 7pm in summer). **Closed** Dec 25. 🅿 ♿ partial. ✎ 🏕 🛍 ✎ 🏔 w **nps.gov/zion**

Zion Canyon lies at the heart of this beautiful national park and is arguably Utah's most famous natural wonder. The canyon was carved by the powerful waters of the Virgin River and then sculpted, widened, and reshaped by wind, rain, and ice. The canyon walls rise up to 2,000 ft (600 m), and form jagged peaks and formations in shades of red and white. One of the best routes in Zion is the Zion–Mt. Carmel highway with splendid views of the canyon and the pastel-colored sandstone of the peaks.

Wild flowers in Zion National Park

The park shuttle is the only way into the canyon from March to October and on weekends in November. The shuttle's stops along the way lead to marked trails for a 16-mile (26-km) hike through the park.

Astonishing scenery on the Zion–Mt. Carmel highway

◀ The Virgin River weaves a scenic trail through Zion National Park

Facade of Brigham Young's winter home in St. George

The Mormons

The church of Jesus Christ of Latter Day Saints was founded by Joseph Smith (1805–44), a farmer from New York State. In 1820 Smith claimed to have had visions of the Angel Moroni. The angel led him to a set of golden tablets, which he translated and published as the *Book of Mormon*. This gave birth to the Mormon faith, which grew rapidly but attracted hostility because of its beliefs and practice of polygamy. In 1839, the Mormons moved to Illinois, where Smith was killed by an angry mob. Brigham Young became the new leader and led members westward. Salt Lake City was founded and the Mormons set up farms in Utah. Today, 62 per cent of Utah's citizens are Mormons.

Brigham Young

❺ St. George

🏞 77,000. 🛈 97 E St, George Blvd. (435) 628-1658. 🚌 🚐 🛈 Visitor Center. **Open** 8am–5pm Mon–Fri. 🌐 sgcity.org

Established by Mormons in 1861, St. George has experienced a population boom as retirees from all over the US discovered its mild climate and tranquil atmosphere. The towering gold spire that can be seen over the city belongs to Utah's first Mormon Temple, finished in 1877. A beloved project of Mormon leader and visionary Brigham Young (1801–77), it remains a key site. Only Mormons are allowed inside the temple, but the Visitor Center, which relates its history, is open to all.

Brigham Young's association with St. George began when he decided to construct a winter home here in 1871. The elegant and spacious **Brigham Young Winter Home Historic Site** is now a museum and has preserved much of its first owner's original furnishings.

Five miles (8 km) northwest of town on Highway 18 lies Snow Canyon State Park. It features hiking trails that lead to volcanic caves and million-year-old lava flows. A paved bike path winds its way through the park and back to St. George.

The Tuacahn Amphitheater, located 9.5 miles (15 km) from St. George, hosts musical theater performances during the summer and concerts thoroughout the year, which are very popular.

🏛 **Brigham Young Winter Home Historic Site**
67 W 200 N. **Tel** (435) 673-2517. **Open** 9am–dusk. 🅿

❻ Rhyolite

Off Hwy 374, 4 miles W from Beatty. 🛈 Beatty Chamber of Commerce, 119 E Main St, (775) 553-2424.

This once prosperous community is located about 120 miles (193 km) northwest of Las Vegas and was founded in 1905. The presence of rich gold mines fueled a growth that made Rhyolite one of Nevada's most thriving cities within just a couple of years. At its peak in 1908, the city had 6,000 people, three railroads, four local newspapers, four banks, an opera house, board of trade, and a telephone exchange. However,

Ruins of a building in the ghost town of Rhyolite, Nevada

when the ore ran out, the mills began to shut down and people started to leave. By 1920 the city was nearly empty. Today, Rhyolite is primarily known for its historic ruins. One of its most famous and unique attractions is the bottle house, which was built in 1906 and is made of about 20,000–50,000 discarded liquor and medicine bottles held together by adobe mud.

❼ Mojave Desert

Barstow. 🚐 🛈 681 N First Ave, (760) 256-8617. 🌐 barstowchamber.com

Lying at an altitude of 2,000 ft (600 m), the Mojave or High Desert was the gateway to California for traders in the 19th century. Barstow, the largest town, is a stopover between Los Angeles and Las Vegas. In the 1870s, gold and silver were discovered in this area, and towns such as Calico sprang up. However, when the mines became exhausted, they were soon abandoned and turned into ghost towns. Many of Calico's buildings are still intact, and visitors can ride in an actual mine train.

To the west, Edwards Air Force Base is famous for its space shuttle landings. The Kelso Dunes, in the Mojave National Preserve, can reach up to 650 ft (200 m) high, while the Mitchell Caverns have limestone formations. Northern Mojave is dominated by the Death Valley National Park *(see pp108–9)*.

❽ A Tour of Death Valley

The native Americans called the valley Tomesha, "the land where the ground is on fire" – an apt name for the site of the highest recorded temperature in the United States: 57°C (134°F) in the shade, in July 1913. Death Valley stretches for some 140 miles (225 km) north to south and was once an insurmountable barrier to miners and emigrants. The valley and surrounding area were declared a National Park in 1994. Unfortunately, many parts of Death Valley are closed to visitors due to flood damage. It is likely to re-open in 2019. However, this remains the California desert at its harshest and most awe-inspiring.

⑧ Scotty's Castle
This incongruous Moorish-style castle was commissioned by Albert Johnson at a cost of $2.4 million. However, the public believed it belonged to Walter Scott, an eccentric prospector. The house remained unfinished after Johnson lost his money in the Wall Street Crash of 1929. In 1970 the building was bought by the National Park Service. The castle is closed due to flood damage and will reopen in 2019.

⑦ Ubehebe Crater
This is one of a dozen volcanic craters in the Mojave area. The Crater is 3,000 years old and is more than 900 yds (800 m) wide and 500 ft (150 m) deep. However due to recent storm damage the crater is now inaccessible.

North Hwy
Death Valley Wash
Titus Canyon Rd
San Dune
Panamint Springs
190

Death Valley Scotty

Walter Scott, would-be miner, beloved charlatan, and sometime performer in Buffalo Bill's Wild West Show, enjoyed telling guests at his house about his wealth that lay in a secret gold mine. That "mine" was his friend Albert Johnson, a Chicago insurance executive, who not only paid for the castle where Scott lived but all his bills as well. "He repays me in laughs," said Johnson. Built in the 1920s by European craftsmen and local Native American labor, the castle represents a mixture of architectural styles and has a Moorish feel. Although Scott died in 1954, the edifice is still known as Scotty's Castle.

⑥ Stovepipe Wells
Founded in 1926, Stovepipe Wells Village was the valley's first tourist resort. According to legend, a lumberjack traveling west struck water here and stayed. An old stovepipe, similar to the ones that were then used to form the walls of wells, marks the site.

Key
▬▬ Tour route
═══ Other roads

Grandiose Scotty's Castle

② Zabriskie Point

Made famous by Antonioni's 1970 film of the same name, Zabriskie Point offers views of the multicolored mud hills of Golden Canyon. The spot was named after a former general manager of the borax operations in Death Valley.

① Furnace Creek

The springs here are one of the few freshwater sources in the desert. They are thought to have saved the lives of hundreds of gold prospectors crossing the desert on their way to the Sierra foothills. The Death Valley Museum and Visitor Center features exhibits detailing the area's history.

③ Dante's View

At 5,475 ft (1,650 m), the view takes in the entire valley floor and is best seen in the morning. The name of the viewpoint was inspired by Dante's *Inferno*. In the distance is Telescope Peak in the Panamint Range.

Tips for Drivers

Tour length: 236 miles (380 km).

When to go: The best time to visit is October to April, when temperatures average 18°C (65°F). May to September, when the ground temperature can be extremely hot, should be avoided. Try for an early start, especially if you are planning to take any hikes. Always wear a hat and use plenty of sunblock.

Precautions: Check the weather forecast before you leave and always carry water, a map, a first aid and snake-bite kit, a cell phone, a jack, and a spare tire. Remain near your vehicle if you break down. If you plan to travel in remote areas, inform someone of where you are going and when you plan to return. The area is not suitable for rock climbing. Do not feed wild animals or reach into burrows or holes.

Stopping-off points: Furnace Creek Ranch, Furnace Creek Inn, Stovepipe Wells Village, and Panamint Springs are the only lodging and eating places in the park. Shoshone, Amarqosa, and Tecopa, outside the park, also have motels.

Emergency: Phone park rangers on 911 or (760) 786-2331.

w nps.gov/deva

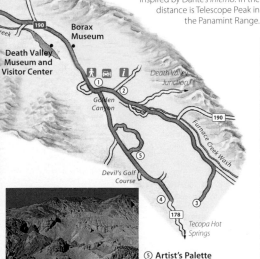

Death Valley Museum and Visitor Center

Borax Museum

374

190

Golden Canyon

Death Valley Junction

190

Furnace Creek Wash

Devil's Golf Course

178

Tecopa Hot Springs

④ Badwater

Badwater is the lowest point in the western hemisphere. It lies 282 ft (85 m) below sea level and is one of the world's hottest places. The water is not poisonous, but it is unpalatable, filled with sodium chloride and sulfates. Visitors should note that the southern end of Badwater road is closed due to flood damage.

0 km   10
0 miles   10

⑤ Artist's Palette

These multicolored hills were created by mineral deposits and volcanic ash. The colors are at their most intense in the late afternoon sun.

TRAVELERS' NEEDS

WHERE TO STAY

Recognized as one of the most popular tourist destinations in the US, Las Vegas has over 150,000 hotel rooms – more than any other American city. Visitors can choose from an extensive range of accommodation that caters to every budget and taste. From fantasy-inspired mega-resorts to basic motels, Las Vegas has it all. The larger resorts include attractions such as casinos, restaurants, nightclubs, theme parks, convention centers, and shopping promenades. There are also non-gaming hotels designed with the family or business traveler in mind. Outdoor enthusiasts can access any of the many RV parks or campgrounds in the nearby Mt. Charleston and Red Rock areas. The accommodation listings on pages 114–17 feature a selection of the very best places to stay in Las Vegas, and cover a variety of different areas and price ranges.

An elegant room at The Venetian *(see p117)*

Hotel Classifications

Las Vegas hotels are known for their quality accommodation and range of amenities, which can be extensive. Travelers can use the diamond rating system of the American Automobile Association (AAA) *(see p180)* as a guideline. Every type of accommodation, from the one-diamond motel to the five-diamond resort hotel, is rated for service, cleanliness, and facilities offered.

Resorts and Casino-Hotels

Most of the opulent resorts in Las Vegas are located along the Strip or downtown. Some recreate world landmarks, such as the Eiffel Tower at Paris Las Vegas *(see p48)*, the Grand Canal at The Venetian *(see pp60–61)*, and the Manhattan skyline at New York-New York *(see p45)*, while others feature dramatic special effects, like the erupting volcano at The Mirage *(see p58)* and the illuminated Fountains show at the Bellagio *(see pp50–51)*. The larger resorts offer an array of amenities, tempting guests with spas, shopping malls, fine restaurants, and star-quality entertainment. Older Strip hotels, such as Flamingo *(see p53)*, have been remodelled in an attempt to modernize, while successfully retaining a pre-corporate charm that harks back to old Las Vegas.

The downtown casino-hotels also provide lavish accommodations. With the arts and entertainment district nearby, these often place an emphasis on culture and highlight a different side of the city.

Locals Casino Hotels

There are more than a dozen hotels scattered throughout the Vegas Valley, mostly in residential areas, catering to both local people and tourists. Advantages include drastically reduced rates and excellent amenities, such as casinos, multi-screen movie theaters, bowling alleys, skating rinks, concert halls, shopping malls, child care and, moderately priced restaurants.

Chain Hotels and Motels

In addition to the unique gaming resorts, Las Vegas is home to a range of national chain hotels and motels, all of which provide efficient service in comfortable surroundings at reasonable prices. The most popular chains include **Holiday Inn**, **Best Western**, **Ramada**, and the **Marriott**. Visitors will also find good value at suite hotels such as **Residence Inns**, **Courtyard, Hyatt Place, Budget Suites**, and **Embassy Suites**, which offer separate living rooms and attached kitchenettes for a little more than the cost of a basic hotel room. Motels usually provide rooms that are accessible from the parking lot and are often the only option in farther afield destinations, such as **Hoover Dam** and **Boulder City**.

Guests enjoying the pool at Flamingo Las Vegas *(see p114)*

◀ Ornate decor in the lobby at The Venetian *(see p117)*

Fresh modern decor at the Bellagio *(see p116)*

Hotel Rates

No matter where you stay in Vegas, hotel prices are among the country's best, generally 10–20 per cent below those of other resort and convention cities. Rates are higher on weekends, so check the prices for a Sunday through Thursday stay. Rooms at downtown hotels are typically 25–50 per cent lower than their Strip counterparts.

Rates can vary drastically from week to week and can be considerably higher during major conventions and holiday weekends. It is best to be flexible with your dates when making a reservation, and to plan as far ahead as possible.

Hidden Extras

Room rates in Las Vegas hotels are usually quoted exclusive of sales and a county-wide tax, which adds 12 per cent to the price of the room with 2 per cent extra for properties within the Fremont Street Experience and 1 per cent for all other downtown properties. Several places also tack on resort fees, which typically add $5–28 per night to your bill. The rates are usually for double occupancy, exclusive of children or additional persons. Most hotels charge about $30–50 for extra persons in the room, though children under the age of 12 can usually stay free.

Reward Programs

All of the casino hotels offer reward clubs that are free to join. Points built up when gambling, dining at restaurants, or staying at hotels, can then be redeemed for cash or credit on restaurant or hotel bills.

Additionally, most offer discounts on the resorts' restaurants. Some hotel groups offer memberships that apply across several resorts, such as M Life with 16 properties within the MGM Resorts family and Total Rewards with 10 resorts within the Caesars Entertainment group.

Campgrounds and RV Parks

Camping in state and national parks is allowed in spaces designated for that use. While most of these parks follow a first come, first served policy, other campgrounds require reservations. Check with the **National Forest Service** for camping information at Mount Charleston, Lake Mead, and Red Rock Canyon. Facilities can range from extremely basic to those with running water and limited electricity.

Recreational vehicles have many ports of call in the city. These include hotels, such as **Sam's Town KOA RV Park** and **Main Street Station RV Park**. Most of the parks offer competitive rates with full connection to electricity, laundry facilities, flush toilets, showers, convenience stores, swimming pools and even free shuttles to downtown or the Strip. They also accept pets. Advance reservations are advised.

Recommended Hotels

The choices in this guide cover a wide range of hotels offering almost every amenity imaginable. Location is a major consideration and the most popular areas for visitors to Las Vegas are the South Strip and North Strip. In both

cases rates are higher, so the budget-minded might prefer to look to the non-gaming chain hotels away from the hustle and bustle; the downtown area for simpler resorts; and the locals casinos throughout the city. Hotels considered outstanding representatives of each area are highlighted as a "DK Choice". These hotels offer excellent service, opulent decor, and a huge range of amenities, or something entirely unique.

Where to Stay

Budget

South Strip

Excalibur $
3850 Las Vegas Blvd S
Tel *(702) 597-7777*   **Map** 3 B4
🆆 excalibur.com
The medieval-themed hotel comes complete with a castle, drawbridge, and moat. Don't miss the action-packed *Tournament of Kings* dinner show.

Flamingo Las Vegas $
3555 Las Vegas Blvd S
Tel *(702) 733-3111*   **Map** 3 C3
🆆 flamingolasvegas.com
This iconic resort was one of the Strip's very first casino-hotels. Though its splendor has somewhat faded, the rooms offer spectacular views of The High Roller and the onsite wildlife and water park.

Luxor $
3900 Las Vegas Blvd S
Tel *(702) 262-4000*   **Map** 3 B5
🆆 luxor.com
A vast glass pyramid and a replica of the Sphinx is all that remain of the former Egyptian theme. The hotel has modern rooms and is also home to the popular Titanic and BODIES exhibits. A free tram connects the resort to Mandalay Bay and Excalibur.

North Strip

Circus Circus $
2880 Las Vegas Blvd S
Tel *(702) 734-0410*   **Map** 3 C2
🆆 circuscircus.com
The young at heart will love the live circus acts, entertainment, and indoor theme park at this friendly and comfortable hotel.

Lucky Dragon $
300 W Sahara Ave   **Map** 3 C2
🆆 luckydragonlv.com
This boutique hotel is the first Asia-inspired hotel and casino in Las Vegas. It features 204 rooms and 24 suites, a spa, an indoor and outdoor tea garden, and five restaurants.

Stratosphere $
2000 Las Vegas Blvd S
Tel *(702) 380-7777*   **Map** 4 D1
🆆 stratospherehotel.com
The hotel is by far the tallest in Las Vegas. Many of the rooms have stunning views of the city. The star attraction is the famous Top of the World restaurant, which revolves 360° every 80 minutes.

Downtown & Fremont Street

California Hotel $
12 Ogden Ave
Tel *(702) 385-1222*   **Map** 2 D3
🆆 thecal.com
This Hawaiian-themed casino-hotel has great customer service and connects to Main Street Station via an overhead walkway.

El Cortez $
600 E Fremont St
Tel *(800) 634-6703*   **Map** 2 E3
🆆 elcortezhotelcasino.com
The longest continuously running casino-hotel in Las Vegas, El Cortez offers comfortable rooms with 1940s-style decor.

Downtown Grand Casino & Hotel $
206 N 3rd St
Tel *(702) 388-2400*   **Map** 2 D3
🆆 downtowngrand.com
This hotel offers well-appointed, contemporary rooms right in the heart of Fremont Street. A fantastic rooftop pool.

Four Queens $
202 E Fremont St
Tel *(702) 385-4011*   **Map** 2 D3
🆆 fourqueens.com
Four Queens is a historic casino-hotel with great service and is located in the center of the Fremont Street Experience.

Fremont Hotel $
200 E Fremont St
Tel *(702) 385-3232*   **Map** 2 D3
🆆 fremontcasino.com
Comfortable and modern rooms, although the ensuites are rather small, are on offer at this 14-story hotel. Staff are friendly and helpful.

The shimmering Golden Nugget, in downtown Las Vegas

Price Guide
Prices are based on one night's stay in high season for a standard double room, inclusive of service charges and taxes.

$	up to $100
$$	$100 to 200
$$$	over $200

Golden Gate Hotel $
1 Fremont St
Tel *(702) 385-1906*   **Map** 2 D3
🆆 goldengatecasino.com
This historic hotel dates back to the birth of Las Vegas in 1906 and sits right on the Fremont Street Experience.

DK Choice

Golden Nugget $
129 E Fremont St
Tel *(702) 385-7111*   **Map** 2 D3
🆆 goldennugget.com
The rooms at this place, the most luxurious of the downtown casino-hotels, resemble those found on the Strip, but at a fairly reduced price. Its pool, dubbed The Tank, is a $30 million complex featuring a tank with sharks and other amazing sea creatures, 15 private cabanas, and a three-story waterslide.

Main Street Station Casino, Brewery & Hotel $
200 N Main St
Tel *(702) 387-1896*   **Map** 2 D3
🆆 mainstreetcasino.com
The decor here harks back to the Victorian period with fully restored train cars and numerous artifacts from the turn of the century.

Plaza Hotel & Casino $
1 Main St
Tel *(702) 386-2110*   **Map** 2 D3
🆆 plazahotelcasino.com
Situated on the site of a historic railway station, this place has glittering views of Fremont Street.

Farther Afield

Alexis Park All Suite Resort $
375 E Harmon Ave
Tel *(702) 796-3300*   **Map** 4 D4
🆆 alexispark.com
This non-gaming hotel offers a relaxed stay with modest rooms and pool facilities.

Artisan Hotel $
1501 W Sahara Ave
Tel *(702) 214-4000*   **Map** 3 C1
🆆 artisanhotel.com
A fun boutique hotel themed around famous artworks, it is great for those in search of a party.

Beyond Las Vegas

Bright Angel Lodge $
9 Village Loop Dr, Grand Canyon
Village, AZ
Tel (928) 638-2631
W grandcanyonlodges.com
This delightful lodge has pretty
log cabins close to the south rim
of the Grand Canyon.

Colorado Belle Hotel & Casino $
2100 S Casino Dr, Laughlin, NV
Tel (702) 298-4000
W coloradobelle.com
Housed in a replica of a paddle-
wheel riverboat, this casino resort
has a very friendly staff.

Circus Circus puts on free shows under the big top

Chains
Farther Afield

**Best Western Mardi Gras
Hotel & Casino** $
3500 Paradise Rd
Tel (702) 731-2020 **Map** 4 D3
W mardigrasinn.com
With modern decor and spacious
rooms, this hotel is close to the
Strip. A good swimming pool.

Super 8 at Ellis Island Casino $
4250 Koval Lane
Tel (702) 794-0888 **Map** 3 C3
W super8vegas.com
This hotel has clean, comfortable
rooms next to a small casino and
brewery. Free airport shuttle.

Embassy Suites $$
3600 Paradise Rd
Tel (702) 893-8000 **Map** 4 D3
W lasvegasembassysuites.com
Enjoy a cooked-to-order
breakfast at this pleasant hotel
near the Convention Center.

Hyatt Place $$
4520 Paradise Rd
Tel (702) 369 3366 **Map** 4 D4
W lasvegas.place.hyatt.com
In a smoke-free establishment,
this hotel offers simply furnished
rooms close to the Strip.

**Residence Inn-
Convention Center** $$
3225 Paradise Rd
Tel (702) 796-9300 **Map** 4 D2
W marriott.com
This Marriott hotel located just
opposite the Las Vegas Convention
Center has huge suites.

Westgate Las Vegas $$
3000 Paradise Rd
Tel (702) 732-5111 **Map** 4 D2
W westgateresorts.com
With immaculate rooms close to
the LV Convention Center, this
hotel is perfect for business trips.

Locals Casinos
Farther Afield

Boulder Station $
4111 Boulder Hwy
Tel (702) 432-7777
W boulderstation.sclv.com
Great food and service are on offer
at this hotel with stained-glass
windows and a quirky exterior.

Cannery Hotel & Casino $
2121 E Craig Rd, North Las Vegas
Tel (702) 507-5700
W cannerycasino.com
This place has bright, modern
decor, excellent food, and a
fantastic swimming-pool area.

Fiesta Henderson $
777 W Lake Mead Pkwy, Henderson
Tel (702) 558-7000
W fiestahenderson.sclv.com
Although the rooms are slightly
dated, this hotel is conveniently
located and has impeccable staff.

Orleans $
4500 W Tropicana Ave
Tel (702) 365-7111 **Map** 3 A4
W orleanscasino.com
A New Orleans theme prevails at
this casino resort located only a
few miles from the Strip.

Palace Station $
2411 W Sahara Ave
Tel (702) 367-2411 **Map** 3 B1
W palacestation.sclv.com
The cozy hotel has comfortable,
modest rooms and friendly staff.
Ideal for budget travelers.

**Sam's Town Hotel &
Gambling Hall** $
5111 Boulder Hwy
Tel (702) 456-7777
W samstownlv.com
This Old Western-themed hotel
features the Mystic Falls Park, a
breathtaking atrium filled with
trees, flowers, and a waterfall.

Silver Sevens Hotel & Casino $
4100 Paradise Rd
Tel (702) 733-7000 **Map** 4 D3
W silversevenscasino.com
The exterior of this hotel resembles
an old Spanish mission town.
Rooms are clean and comfortable.

Silverton Casino Hotel $
3333 Blue Diamond Rd
Tel (702) 263-7777
W silvertoncasino.com
A giant aquarium is the main
draw at this casino resort. Sports
fans will also enjoy the enormous
Bass Pro Shop onsite.

South Point Hotel, Casino & Spa $
9777 Las Vegas Blvd S
Tel (702) 796-7111
W southpointcasino.com
With a huge state-of-the-art
equestrian complex, this hotel
has spacious rooms and facilities.

Suncoast Hotel & Casino $
9090 Alta Dr
Tel (702) 636-7111
W suncoastcasino.com
There's entertainment for families
at this casino resort with a bowling
alley, movie theater, and showroom. Large, clean rooms and
excellent service.

Sunset Station $
1301 W Sunset Rd, Henderson
Tel (702) 547-7777
W sunsetstation.sclv.com
Enjoy cozy bedrooms, a variety
of dining options, and a bowling
alley and multi-screen movie
theater at this off-Strip hotel.

Aliante Casino & Hotel $$
7300 N Aliante Pkwy,
North Las Vegas
Tel (702) 692-7777
W aliantegaming.com
Out on the northern outskirts of
the Vegas Valley, this urban
retreat has a 16-screen movie
theater. Very helpful staff.

For more information on types of hotels see pages 112–13

Luxury
South Strip

DK Choice

ARIA Resort & Casino $$
3730 Las Vegas Blvd S
Tel *(702) 590-7757* **Map** 3 C4
w aria.com
The only hotel in CityCenter with a casino, this fantastic example of modern architecture is just steps away from a wide range of shops and nightclubs. It is home to restaurants by renowned chefs, such as Julian Serrano, Sean McClain, and Michael Mina.

Bally's Las Vegas $$
3645 Las Vegas Blvd S
Tel *(702) 739-4111* **Map** 3 C3
w ballyslasvegas.com
Located in the heart of the Strip, this hotel is within easy walking distance of all the major sights. Comfortable, spacious rooms.

DK Choice

Caesars Palace $$
3570 Las Vegas Blvd S
Tel *(702) 731-7110* **Map** 3 B3
w caesarspalace.com
Built in 1966, Caesars Palace is one of the oldest Vegas resorts, but has kept up to date by modernizing and expanding. It it perhaps most notable for the aptly named Garden of the Gods, featuring eight swimming pools set in palatial surrounds.

The Cromwell $$
3595 Las Vegas Blvd S
Tel *(702) 777-3777* **Map** 3 C3
w thecromwell.com
Sleek modern rooms and excellent service are on offer at this boutique hotel featuring Giada de Laurentiis' first restaurant.

LINQ Hotel & Casino $$
3535 Las Vegas Blvd S
Tel *(800) 351-7400* **Map** 3 C3
w caesars.com/linq
This resort sits at the base of the High Roller observation wheel and the LINQ walkway, lined with dozens of shops and restaurants.

Mandalay Bay $$
3950 Las Vegas Blvd S
Tel *(702) 632-7777* **Map** 3 C5
w mandalaybay.com
Sun-worshippers will love the chance to bask on the artificial beach and watch the waves roll in at this island-themed resort.

DK Choice

MGM Grand $$
3799 Las Vegas Blvd S
Tel *(702) 891-1111* **Map** 3 C4
w mgmgrand.com
With more than 5,000 rooms, a huge shopping promenade, wedding chapel, spa, events center, five-pool complex, and three Jacuzzis, this opulent hotel well and truly lives up to its name. The top three floors of the resort are occupied by SkyLOFTS, a luxurious boutique hotel within the MGM Grand.

Monte Carlo $$
3770 Las Vegas Blvd S
Tel *(702) 730-7777* **Map** 3 C4
w montecarlo.com
This well-presented resort features a pedestrian plaza overlooking the Strip. In 2018, it will become two hotels – NoMad and Park MGM.

New York-New York $$
3790 Las Vegas Blvd S
Tel *(702) 740-6969* **Map** 3 C4
w newyorknewyork.com
Fans of the Big Apple will feel at home here amid a replica Manhattan skyline and NYC-themed restaurants.

Paris Las Vegas $$
3655 Las Vegas Blvd S
Tel *(702) 946-7000* **Map** 3 C3
w parislasvegas.com
Signposted by the Eiffel Tower out front, this Parisian-themed resort replicates the charming cobblestoned streets of Europe's most romantic city.

Planet Hollywood Resort & Casino $$
3667 Las Vegas Blvd S
Tel *(702) 785-5555* **Map** 3 C4
w planethollywoodresort.com
Movie memorabilia abounds at this Hollywood-themed hotel. The popular Miracle Mile shopping complex is onsite.

Tropicana Las Vegas $$
3801 Las Vegas Blvd S
Tel *(702) 739-2222* **Map** 3 C4
w troplv.com
Expect large, elegant rooms at this DoubleTree by Hilton hotel. First opened in 1957, a South Beach theme now prevails.

Vdara $$
2600 W Harmon Ave
Tel *(702) 590-2111* **Map** 3 B4
w vdara.com
This chic, all-suites hotel in City Center, has pieces of fine art showcased all around. An oasis of calm in the bustling heart of the city.

A sumptuously furnished room in the Bellagio

DK Choice

Bellagio $$$
3600 Las Vegas Blvd S
Tel *(702) 693-7111* **Map** 3 B3
w bellagio.com
An art lover's dream, this resort features a fine art gallery, a conservatory with seasonal artistic flower displays, and works of art displayed throughout the property. The lake in front of the hotel is the setting for the famous Fountains of Bellagio show, where jets of water dance to music.

Mandarin Oriental $$$
3752 Las Vegas Blvd S
Tel *(702) 590-8888* **Map** 3 C4
w mandarinoriental.com
Enjoy plush rooms, stunning views and first-rate service at this opulent non-smoking hotel. With no casino, an overwhelming sense of peace and calm pervades.

North Strip
Harrah's $$
3475 Las Vegas Blvd S
Tel *(702) 369-5000* **Map** 3 C3
w caesars.com/harrahs-las-vegas
Just steps from the new LINQ entertainment complex, this fun and friendly hotel features a range of onsite shows, including *Menopause The Musical*. It is perfectly located for visiting most sights on the Strip.

The Mirage $$
3400 Las Vegas Blvd S
Tel *(702) 791-7111* **Map** 3 B3
w mirage.com
An erupting artificial volcano and tiger and dolphin habitat are just some of the attractions in this lively resort. Great food and service.

SLS Las Vegas Hotel & Casino $$
2535 Las Vegas Blvd S
Tel *(702) 737-2111* **Map** 4 D1
W slshotels.com/lasvegas
With excellent restaurants and a pool area, this modern hotel has trendy bars and clubs are great for those who want to dance the night away.

Treasure Island – TI $$
3300 Las Vegas Blvd S
Tel *(702) 894-7111* **Map** 3 C2
W treasureisland.com
Home to Cirque de Soleil's awe-inspiring *Mystère* show, this hotel has fantastic views of the Strip.

DK Choice

Wynn Las Vegas $$
3131 Las Vegas Blvd S
Tel *(702) 770-7100* **Map** 3 C2
W wynnlasvegas.com
This deluxe resort features a 90-foot waterfall, championship golf course, and world-famous restaurants such as SW Steakhouse. Don't miss *Le Rêve*, a mesmerizing aquatic show.

DK Choice

The Venetian $$$
3355 Las Vegas Blvd S
Tel *(702) 414-1000* **Map** 3 C3
W venetian.com
Gondola rides on an artificial canal and replicas of St. Mark's Square and the Rialto Bridge recreate the stunning city of Venice at this luxurious all-suite hotel.

Wynn Encore $$$
3121 Las Vegas Blvd S
Tel *(702) 770-8000* **Map** 3 C2
W wynnlasvegas.com
A sister property to Wynn Las Vegas, the equally luxurious Encore features Asia-inspired decor and top-notch amenities.

Farther Afield

DK Choice

**Green Valley Ranch
Resort & Spa** $$
2300 Paseo Verde Pkwy, Henderson
Tel *(702) 617-7777*
W greenvalleyranch.sclv.com
This elegant resort contains a 10-screen movie theater and expansive landscaped gardens. Just across the road from the hotel is The District, a shopping and dining complex with pretty tree-lined streets.

Hard Rock Hotel & Casino $$
4455 Paradise Rd
Tel *(702) 693-5000* **Map** 4 D4
W hardrockhotel.com
The variety of concert venues at this rock 'n' roll-themed hotel make it a must-stay for music lovers.

**JW Marriott Las Vegas Resort
and Spa** $$
221 N Rampart Blvd
Tel *(702) 869-7777*
W marriott.com
There's a Mediterranean feel to the landscaped gardens and decor at this opulent hotel, also home to a prestigious onsite golf course.

M Resort $$
12300 Las Vegas Blvd S, Henderson
Tel *(702) 797-1000*
W themresort.com
Just south of the Strip, this resort has a top-notch wine cellar and stunning views of the valley.

Palms Casino Resort $$
4321 W Flamingo Rd
Tel *(702) 942-7777* **Map** 3 A3
W palms.com
Expect sleek and stylish rooms at this hotel. Some of the more extravagant suites feature a bowling alley and indoor basketball court.

Red Rock Casino, Resort & Spa $$
11011 W Charleston Blvd
Tel *(702) 797-7777*
W redrock.sclv.com
Enjoy breathtaking views of Red Rock Canyon at this modern and comfortable hotel.

Rumor Boutique Resort $$
455 E Harmon Ave
Tel *(702) 369-5400* **Map** 4 D4
W rumorvegas.com
Located across from the Hard Rock Hotel, this small non-gaming all-suite boutique hotel offers slick, contemporary rooms.

**Trump International
Hotel & Tower** $$
2000 Fashion Show Dr
Tel *(702) 476-7339* **Map** 3 C2
W trumplasvegashotel.com
Huge rooms, plush decor, and stunning views are on offer at this hotel far from the city center.

Beyond Las Vegas

Bryce Canyon Lodge $$
Hwy 63, Bryce Canyon, UT
Tel *(435) 834-5322*
W brycecanyonforever.com
This historic lodge near the canyon rim offers lodge suites, hotel rooms, and cabins.

Zion National Park Lodge $$
1 Zion Canyon Scenic Dr, Springdale, UT
Tel *(435) 772-7700*
W zionlodge.com
Conveniently located for hiking trails, this pleasant lodge offers rooms in Zion National Park.

RV Parks

Downtown & Fremont Street

Main Street RV Park $
200 N Main St
Tel *(702) 387-1896* **Map** 2 D3
W mainstreetcasino.com
Ninety spaces are available at Main Street, the only RV park located at a downtown resort. Amenities include laundry facilities.

Farther Afield

Las Vegas KOA at Sam's Town $
5225 Boulder Hwy
Tel *(702) 454-8055*
W koa.com
Facilities at this pleasant park include full water and electricity connections, easy access for large vehicles, a pool, hot tub, and shuttle service. Pets welcome.

The pool area at Green Valley Ranch, a Mediterranean-inspired luxury resort

For more information on types of hotels *see pages 112–13*

WHERE TO EAT AND DRINK

The consumption of food and drink has always been a cornerstone of Las Vegas's resort industry. Until recently, most casino resort dining rooms were known for the inexpensive food they served – the $10 all-you-can-eat buffets and the 99-cent breakfasts. While some bargains can still be found, resorts now compete to host world-renowned celebrity chefs and restaurateurs, driving up prices accordingly. Las Vegas now rivals the most cosmopolitan of cities for the quality of ingredients and variety of cuisine available, with a roster of the biggest names in the culinary business offering both casual and fine-dining experiences. In addition, the city hosts a vast array of diners, steakhouses, cafés, and snack bars. The restaurants on pages 120–25 have been selected from the best the city can offer across all price ranges.

The imposing entrance to the Joël Robuchon restaurant at MGM Grand *(see p121)*

Eating Hours

Las Vegas really is the city that never sleeps and numerous dining options remain open until midnight or later. Coffee shops in most hotels stay open around the clock and some serve a complete menu throughout the night. The choices at most other restaurants, however, are limited to "regular" breakfast, lunch, and dinner options. Some of the larger resorts have several restaurants. The Venetian, for instance, has 15 fine dining, 24 casual eateries, and 21 snack bars, but most of the fine dining venues are open just for dinner, while several of the casual dining options are open for lunch as well. Las Vegas's popular all-you-can-eat buffets usually offer breakfast, lunch and dinner.

Prices and Tipping

A wide variety of coffee shops, chain restaurants, and the ubiquitous all-you-can-eat buffets offer reasonably priced tasty meals. The city features several fine dining choices as well. Patrons can end up spending $100–150 per person for a three-course meal and a bottle of wine at any of these upscale eateries.

The standard tip is 15–20 per cent of the bill before sales taxes, though tipping should always be based on service. Bartenders and cocktail servers also expect to be tipped for each round of drinks.

Types of Food and Restaurants

Dining establishments in Las Vegas come in a range of shapes and sizes, from small and friendly diners to gourmet restaurants. A variety of restaurants ranging from fine dining to casual eateries can be found in nearly all of the city's top resorts. Practically every major resort offers at least one steakhouse, some with their own butcher. While you might not expect to find outstanding seafood in the desert, many upscale seafood restaurants fly in fresh fish of the highest quality daily. For the budget-minded visitor, an extensive collection of fast-food outlets and pizza chains can be found in all the major resorts throughout the city. The mid-range restaurants include a range of cuisines, such as Italian, Chinese, Japanese, Mexican, and Indian food. Many good restaurants of this type can be found in the resorts or at the shopping malls.

Celebrity chefs head up many of Las Vegas's upscale restaurants, which are usually located in the top luxury hotels. In recent years, several of these TV chefs have also opened casual dining establishments, such as Michael Mina's Pub 1842 at MGM Grand, the Gordon Ramsay Pub at Caesars Palace, and Guy Fieri's Vegas Kitchen & Bar at The LINQ.

The All-You-Can-Eat Buffet

Nearly every hotel in Las Vegas has a buffet and all operate the same way: one price, often as low as $7.99, for all you can eat. The average dinner buffet features about 100 food

Pizza Rock, a popular joint serving award-winning pizzas in a lively setting *(see p123)*

Slick, contemporary decor at the N9NE Steakhouse *(see p124)*

selections that include salads, meat, seafood, vegetables, and an array of desserts. Most offer choices such as Asian, Mexican, and Italian food served at specific stations, or as part of a theme-based buffet highlighting a particular cuisine, usually on different days of the week.

The latest trend is for resorts to compete to serve the most number of items. The Bacchanal Buffet at Caesars Palace, for instance, serves more than 500 different menu items daily, and includes live cooking stations serving made-to-order customized dishes.

Though buffet prices vary greatly depending on the scale of the hotel, they usually average about $12 per person for breakfast to $17 for lunch, and $22 for dinner. Some of the nicer buffets, such as those at the Bellagio or the ARIA, charge more, but the quality of food is better.

In addition to breakfast, lunch, and dinner buffets, most resorts feature weekend champagne brunch buffets for a slightly higher price. If you really want to splurge, the Sterling Sunday Brunch at Bally's lets you feast like royalty on lobster tails, prime meats, sushi, American sturgeon caviar, and fresh-shucked oysters, all served with Perrier-Jouët Champagne. For those that can't get enough of buffets, it's worth purchasing the Buffet of Buffets Pass: a 24-hour all-you-can-eat extravaganza, which is accepted at seven buffets at six resorts.

Vegetarian

While there aren't any strictly vegetarian or vegan eateries in the resorts, most restaurants serve several vegetarian dishes. Casino developer Steve Wynn, who is a vegan, requires all of his restaurants at the Wynn and Encore resorts to feature a vegetarian or vegan menu.

Disabled Facilities

All restaurants in the city are required by law to provide wheelchair access and a ground-level restroom.

Children

Most of the eateries in Las Vegas are child-friendly. Some of the casual dining restaurants feature a kids menu at greatly reduced prices, and the vast majority of the buffets offer reduced prices for children. Most eateries also provide high chairs or booster seats on request.

Dress Codes

Dining is casual throughout Las Vegas, but some of the fine dining venues will suggest business casual attire, which means slacks and no jeans, shorts or T-shirts. Elsewhere, jeans, shorts, and T-shirts are accepted, so you can expect to be seated nearly everywhere.

Recommended Restaurants

The restaurants on the following pages have been chosen to offer something for everyone. Listed by area, they represent a cross section of the city's wide range of dining options and cover a broad spectrum of price points to fit any budget. Included in the mix are big name celebrity chef restaurants in both fine dining and casual dining settings; restaurants featuring gourmet burgers, steak, extensive wine or beer lists, and seafood; gastropubs; all-you-can-eat buffets; and international cuisines such as Chinese, Japanese, French, Italian, and Mexican. Such restaurants can be found in any area of the city, whether in the resort corridor of the Vegas Strip, Downtown area, at locals casinos, or in residential areas throughout the Las Vegas Valley.

The establishments labelled as "DK Choice" have been chosen for one or more area of exceptional quality. This could be outstanding food, a stunning setting, great service, or a combination of these things. These special places come highly recommended and are worth seeking out.

Elegant dining at La Cave Food & Wine Hideaway *(p122)*

Where to Eat and Drink

South Strip

Bobby's Burger Palace   **$**
Casual Dining   **Map** 3 C4
3750 Las Vegas Blvd S
Tel *(702) 598-0191*
This branch of celebrity chef
Bobby Flay's gourmet chain
offers a range of creative burgers
at great value.

Bacchanal Buffet   **$$**
Buffet   **Map** 3 B3
3570 Las Vegas Blvd S
Tel *(702) 731-7928*
The most expansive of any Las
Vegas buffet, this extravagant
feast at Caesars Palace is fit for an
emperor. More than 500 items
served daily.

The Buffet@ARIA   **$$**
Buffet   **Map** 3 C4
3730 Las Vegas Blvd S
Tel *(702) 590-7111*
There's something for everyone
at this buffet. There are 10 stations
with a variety of cuisines, including
Asian, Mediterranean, pasta,
pizza, seafood, and grilled meats.

Burger Bar   **$$**
Casual Dining   **Map** 3 C5
3930 Las Vegas Blvd S
Tel *(702) 632-9364*
Hubert Keller presents his take
on the specialty burger at this
trendy eatery. A choice of
more than 100 craft beers to
accompany your meal.

Carmine's   **$$**
Italian   **Map** 3 C3
3500 Las Vegas Blvd S
Tel *(702) 473-9700*
Epic portions of delicious Italian
classics are served here on huge
platters, family-style. It's best to
go with a large group of people.

D.O.C.G.   **$$**
Italian   **Map** 3 C3
3708 Las Vegas Blvd S
Tel *(702) 698-7920*
Internationally known chef Scott
Conant presents a modern take
on Italian specialties in an artfully
rustic wine bar.

**Emeril's New Orleans
Fish House**   **$$**
Seafood   **Map** 3 C4
3799 Las Vegas Blvd S
Tel *(702) 891-7374*
Emeril Lagasse applies his
signature "New New Orleans" style
of cooking – a modern take on
Louisiana Creole dishes – to a
range of seafood dishes.

Estiatorio Milos   **$$**
Seafood   **Map** 3 C3
3708 Las Vegas Blvd S
Tel *(702) 698-7930*
Greek restaurateur and chef
Costas Spiliadis offers up super-
fresh seafood in a pretty setting
with a stunning view of the
city's skyline.

Gordon Ramsay BurGR   **$$**
Casual Dining   **Map** 3 C4
3667 Las Vegas Blvd S
Tel *(702) 785-5555*
This upscale burger joint focuses
on traditional burgers, fries, and
milkshakes made using the very
best ingredients.

Gordon Ramsay Pub   **$$**
Casual Dining   **Map** 3 C3
3570 Las Vegas Blvd S
Tel *(702) 731-7410*
Gordon Ramsay recreates a
traditional English pub, serving
his take on fish and chips,
shepherd's pie, and sticky toffee
pudding. A wide range of craft
beers are also on offer.

Guy Fieri's Kitchen & Bar   **$$**
Casual Dining   **Map** 3 C3
3535 Las Vegas Blvd S
Tel *(702) 731-3311*
Part of celebrity chef Guy Fieri's
empire, this stylish eatery serves
bold flavors and unique twists
on traditional American dishes.

Holstein's   **$$**
Casual Dining   **Map** 3 C3
3708 Las Vegas Blvd S
Tel *(702) 698-7940*
This gourmet burger restaurant
offers a menu of traditional
American snacks alongside a
wide variety of milkshakes and
craft beers.

Yellowtail's dining room, with elegant
wood and stone decor

> **Price Guide**
> Prices are based on a three-course meal
> for one person, including tax, service
> charges, and half a bottle of house wine.
>
> **$**   up to $35
> **$$** $35 to 75
> **$$$**   over $75

Julian Serrano Restaurant   **$$**
Spanish   **Map** 3 C4
3730 Las Vegas Blvd S
Tel *(702) 590-8520*
Renowned chef Julian Serrano
presents authentic tapas dishes of
his native Spanish fare in sleek,
modern environs. Wash your meal
down with some first-rate Sangria.

Mastro's Ocean Club   **$$**
Seafood   **Map** 3 C4
3720 Las Vegas Blvd S
Tel *(702) 798-7115*
Set in a unique 80-ft (24-m)
wooden lattice sculptural tree,
this restaurant offers an extensive
menu of delectable seafood and
steakhouse dishes.

Rí Rá   **$$**
Casual Dining   **Map** 3 C5
3930 Las Vegas Blvd S
Tel *(702) 632-7771*
Irish pub fare is accompanied by
more than 100 craft beers from
around the globe at this vibrant
nightspot. Live Irish bands
perform every evening.

The Wicked Spoon   **$$**
Buffet   **Map** 3 C3
3708 Las Vegas Blvd S
Tel *(702) 698-7000*
Choose from a variety of food
stations serving turkey, chicken
and prime rib, salads, pastas,
seafood, sushi, and wickedly
good desserts. Portions are small
so you can try a selection.

> ### DK Choice
>
> **Yellowtail Restaurant
> & Lounge**   **$$**
> Japanese   **Map** 3 C3
> *3600 Las Vegas Blvd S*
> **Tel** *702-693-8300*
> Acclaimed chef Akira Back
> delivers traditional and
> contemporary Japanese
> cuisine at this fine dining
> restaurant. An outdoor patio
> contains front row seats for
> Bellagio's fountain show and
> all the major sights on the
> Vegas Strip. Seasonal items
> from the sea are flown in
> daily from all over the world,
> with some served less than
> 72 hours after being caught.

Andre's Monte Carlo $$$
French Map 3 C4
3770 Las Vegas Blvd S
Tel *(702) 798-7151* **Closed** *Mon*
This elegant restaurant serves exquisite seasonal cuisine to Las Vegas's elite. Request a private dining room and order from the tasting menu for the ultimate dining experience. The wine list boasts over 1,500 selections.

DK Choice

Aureole $$$
Fine Dining Map 3 C5
3950 Las Vegas Blvd S
Tel *(702) 632-7401* **Closed** *Sun*
The focal point of this Charlie Palmer restaurant is the four-story wine tower and its wine angels, who fly to retrieve wines from a selection of over 60,000 labels. The progressive American cuisine is prepared by the Parisian-born executive chef Arnaud Masset, who was formerly the executive chef of the Palms.

DK Choice

Giada $$$
Italian Map 3 C3
3595 Las Vegas Blvd S
Tel *(702) 777-3777*
Emmy-Award winning celebrity chef Giada De Laurentiis has opened her first-ever restaurant inside The Cromwell, featuring the recipes from her many cookbooks and TV shows. Warm colors and natural lighting result in a cheery ambience and the restaurant's huge retractable windows offer stunning views of the Fountains of Bellagio and Caesars Palace.

Hakkasan $$$
Cantonese Map 3 C4
3799 Las Vegas Blvd S
Tel *(702) 891-7888*
This multi-level dining and nightclub complex at the MGM Grand serves an extensive menu of modern Cantonese creations. Try the delicious crispy roasted duck with kumquat and mustard sauce.

Jean-Georges Steakhouse $$$
Steakhouse Map 3 C4
3730 Las Vegas Blvd S
Tel *(877) 230-2742*
This steakhouse at ARIA is helmed by world-renowned Chef Jean-Georges Vongerichten, who sources the highest-quality meats from around the world and cooks each dish to perfection.

Indulge in three-Michelin-starred French opulence at Joël Robuchon

Joël Robuchon $$$
French Map 3 C4
3799 Las Vegas Blvd S
Tel *(702) 891-7925*
Dubbed the "chef of the century" by the Gault et Millau guide, Joël Robuchon came out of retirement to open Las Vegas's first and only three-Michelin-starred restaurant. Incredible food in an intimate setting with impeccable service.

Michael Mina Bellagio $$$
Seafood Map 3 B3
3600 Las Vegas Blvd S
Tel *(702) 693-7223* **Closed** *Sun*
This celebrity chef's namesake earned a Michelin star in 2008 and 2009. It overlooks the Bellagio pool and gardens. It offers the freshest seafood, caviar and steaks, and an excellent tasting menu.

DK Choice

Nobu Caesars Palace $$$
Japanese Map 3 B3
3570 Las Vegas Blvd S
Tel *(702) 785-6674*
Chef Nobu Matsuhisa's largest restaurant, located at the world's first Nobu Hotel at Caesars Palace, is the first to offer teppan-yaki in the United States. The dining room serves sushi, sashimi, and toban-yaki offerings such as beef tenderloin enlivened with flamed saké, deglazed yuzu, caramelized onions, and shiitake and enokitake mushrooms.

Old Homestead $$$
Steakhouse Map 3 B3
3570 Las Vegas Blvd S
Tel *(877) 346-4642*
This Vegas branch of the historic New York City steakhouse serves fine cuts of meat complemented by a wine cellar containing 15,000 bottles. The Old-style dining room is decked out in wood and leather.

Prime $$$
Steakhouse Map 3 C3
3600 Las Vegas Blvd S
Tel *(702) 693-8865*
Overlooking the lake at Bellagio, this first-class restaurant serves prime steak, seafood, and lamb accompanied by fabulous sauces. The dining room features paintings by a number of famous artists.

Restaurant Guy Savoy $$$
French Map 3 C3
3570 Las Vegas Blvd S
Tel *(702) 731-7286* **Closed** *Mon & Tue*
Specializing in traditional fare, served with finesse, this two-Michelin-starred restaurant's artichoke and black truffle soup are not to be missed. Flawless service.

RM Seafood $$$
Seafood Map 3 C5
3930 Las Vegas Blvd S
Tel *(702) 632-9300*
This restaurant is celebrated for promoting sustainable fish that is caught and flown in fresh every day. Expertly prepared dishes in chic minimalist surrounds.

Scarpetta $$$
Italian Map 3 C3
3708 Las Vegas Blvd S
Tel *(702) 698-7960*
Internationally renowned chef Scott Conant presents a range of his Italian specialties in an upscale setting overlooking the Bellagio fountains. The wine cellar consists of more than 3,000 labels.

Sterling Brunch $$$
Buffet Map 3 C3
3645 Las Vegas Blvd S
Tel *(702) 967-7999* **Closed** *Mon–Sat*
Las Vegas's most lavish brunch is served only on Sundays. This opulent spread includes sturgeon caviar, unlimited Perrier-Jouët Champagne, lobster, sushi, omelets, and beef tenderloin.

STK   **$$$**
Steakhouse   **Map** 3 C3
3708 Las Vegas Blvd S
Tel *(702) 698-7990*
This chic modern restaurant
serves perfectly cooked prime
cuts. The place transforms into a
high-energy nightclub after
hours and is one of the trendiest
spots on the Boulevard.

Twist by Pierre Gagnaire   **$$$**
French   **Map** 3 C4
3752 Las Vegas Blvd S
Tel *(702) 590 8888*
Set within the Mandarin Oriental
hotel, with stunning views from
its 23rd floor perch, this elegant
restaurant serves classic French
fare with a contemporary edge.

North Strip

B&B Burger & Beer   **$$**
Casual Dining   **Map** 3 C3
3355 Las Vegas Blvd S
Tel *(702) 414-2220*
Celebrity chef Mario Batali runs
this gourmet burger bar.
Creatively flavored shakes and
a well rounded beer selection.

Buddy V's   **$$**
Italian   **Map** 3 C3
3327 Las Vegas Blvd S
Tel *(702) 607-2355*
TLC's *Cake Boss* star Buddy Valastro
serves up home-style cooking in
this restaurant, which features his
family's recipes and photos from
his New Jersey home.

The Buffet   **$$**
Buffet   **Map** 3 C2
3131 Las Vegas Blvd S
Tel *(702) 770-3340*
This buffet at Wynn Las Vegas has
15 live-action cooking stations
featuring freshly grilled meats
and seafood, sushi, salads, and
beautifully presented specialties
such as tandoori chicken.

DK Choice

La Cave Food & Wine
Hideaway   **$$**
Casual Dining   **Map** 3 C2
3131 Las Vegas Blvd S
Tel *(702) 770-7375*
This casual bar resembles a
wine cellar and is tucked away
in a corridor off the casino at
the Wynn Las Vegas, offering a
nice respite from the hectic
gaming area. It serves a menu
of modern American small
plates that is good for sharing,
paired with an extensive range
of wine and beer.

DK Choice

DB Brasserie   **$$**
French   **Map** 3 C3
3355 Las Vegas Blvd S
Tel *(702) 430-1235*
Renowned chef Daniel Boulud
is at the helm of this brasserie
located off of the casino at
The Venetian. The atmosphere
is casual, but the food and
decor are impeccably
presented. The menu consists
of updated classics, such as
onion soup, coq au vin, and
steak frites.

i ♥ burgers   **$$**
Casual Dining   **Map** 3 C2
3325 Las Vegas Blvd S
Tel *(702) 242-2747*
This gourmet burger joint prides
itself on using prime beef raised
without hormones or antibiotics.
Turkey and veggie burgers are
also served, as well as flavored
shakes and craft beer to wash
it all down.

Jardin   **$$**
Steakhouse   **Map** 3 C2
3131 Las Vegas Blvd S
Tel *(702) 770-3463*
Set in a conservatory-like space
overlooking the Encore pool,
Jardin has a classic menu.
In addition to fine steaks and
seafood, an excellent vegan
menu is available. Make room
for one of the decadent desserts.

Lagasse's Stadium   **$$**
Casual Dining   **Map** 3 C2
3325 Las Vegas Blvd S
Tel *(702) 607-2665*
A sports lover's paradise, this
vibrant bar at The Palazzo is
equipped with gigantic TV
screens, a betting station and
Emeril Lagasse's upscale pub food.

LVB Burgers and Bar   **$$**
Casual Dining   **Map** 3 C3
3400 Las Vegas Blvd S
Tel *(702) 792-7888*
This stylish eatery serves a wide
range of different gourmet
burgers including veggie, turkey,
buffalo, and salmon options. A
good range of milkshakes and
beers to accompany your meal.

Maggiano's Little Italy   **$$**
Italian   **Map** 3 C2
3200 Las Vegas Blvd S
Tel *(702) 732-2550*
This chain restaurant, situated on
the second level of the Fashion
Show Mall, serves family-style
Southern Italian favorites of
home-made pastas, prime steaks,
and fresh fish in large portions.

Contemporary decor at La Cave Food &
Wine Hideaway

Public House   **$$**
Casual Dining   **Map** 3 C3
3355 Las Vegas Blvd S
Tel *(702) 407-5310*
Beer lovers will feel really at
home in this gastropub which
serves more than 200 craft
beers to accompany gourmet
American pub fare. Aged whiskeys,
scotches, and bourbons complete
the menu.

Cut   **$$$**
Steakhouse   **Map** 3 C2
3325 Las Vegas Blvd S
Tel *(702) 607-6300*
This refined Wolfgang Puck
restaurant at The Palazzo caters
to true steak connoisseurs. The
menu includes USDA Prime
Nebraska corn-fed, 35-day dry-
aged steaks and true Japanese
100% Wagyu beef. A superb
wine list.

Delmonico Steakhouse   **$$$**
Steakhouse   **Map** 3 C3
3355 Las Vegas Blvd S
Tel *(702) 414-3737*
Located within The Venetian's
Restaurant Row, this Emeril
Lagasse restaurant is renowned
for its finely crafted steaks,
extensive whiskey selection,
and impressive wine list. The
portions are huge and the
service is very attentive.

Fin   **$$$**
Chinese   **Map** 3 C3
3400 Las Vegas Blvd S
Tel *(866) 339-4566***Closed** *Tue & Wed*
Asian-inspired decor and a
relaxing waterfall set the mood
at this stunning venue at The
Mirage. Sample super-fresh fish,
Peking duck, or huge portions
of noodle dishes served family-
style. The staff are happy to
serve classic dishes that aren't
on the menu.

Portofino by Chef Michael LaPlaca

$$$
Italian   Map 3 C3
3400 Las Vegas Blvd S
Tel *(866) 339-4566*   **Closed** *Tue & Wed*
At this place, traditional Italian dishes are given a creative twist. The handmade pastas are a must-try and can be made gluten-free. A great place to go before catching a show at The Mirage.

SW Steakhouse

$$$
Steakhouse   Map 3 C2
3131 Las Vegas Blvd S
Tel *(702) 770-3325*
Named after Steve Wynn's initials, this restaurant is set on a terrace with fantastic views over the Lake of Dreams at the Wynn. A great selection of prime steaks, although a vegan menu is also available.

Table 10

$$$
Fine Dining   Map 3 C3
3327 Las Vegas Blvd S
Tel *(702) 607-6363*
This Emeril Lagasse restaurant at The Palazzo offers upscale versions of American classics. Two flaming rotisseries are used to prepare dishes such as Colorado filet mignon and California halibut. The appetizers are particularly good.

Downtown & Fremont Street

MTO Café

$
Casual Dining   Map 2 D4
500 S Main St
Tel *(702) 380-8229*
This café serves classic breakfast and lunch comfort food made from fresh, locally grown, quality ingredients. The place has a hip, urban atmosphere, with large windows looking out onto Main Street.

Andiamo Steakhouse

$$
Steakhouse   Map 2 D3
301 Fremont St
Tel *(702) 388-2220*
Situated on the 2nd floor at the D Las Vegas, away from the hectic casino, this branch of a chain of Detroit Italian steakhouses serves hormone-free beef, dry-aged for a minimum of 30 days, along with handmade pastas. First-rate service.

Binion's Ranch Steakhouse

$$
Steakhouse   Map 2 D3
128 E Fremont St
Tel *(702) 382-1600*
Set atop the 24-story Binion's Gambling Hall & Hotel, this old school steakhouse with plush Victorian decor is known for dazzling views of the Las Vegas skyline and great food. The fillet steaks, in particular, are perfectly cooked. Friendly, professional waiters and an excellent wine list.

DK Choice

Carson Kitchen

$$
Casual Dining   Map 2 E3
124 S 6th St,, Suite 100
Tel *(702) 473-9523*
Located a block from Fremont Street, this lively downtown neighborhood eatery carries on the legacy of its founder, the late celebrity chef Kerry Simon. The menu changes frequently according to the seasons, but some items are mainstays, such as the bacon jam with baked brie and the cocoa-espresso NY strip with red wine demi.

La Comida

$$
Casual Dining   Map 2 E3
100 S 6th St
Tel *(702) 463-9900*
Just steps from the Fremont Experience, authentic Mexican cuisine is served in this eclectically decorated restaurant with stained-glass windows and wooden pews salvaged from a church. The bar offers over 100 different types of tequila and the margaritas offered here are excellent.

Pizza Rock

$$
Casual Dining   Map 2 D3
201 N 3rd St
Tel *(702) 385-0838*
This place serves award-winning pizzas in a vibrant, contemporary dining room that features, among other props, the cab of a monster truck. Diners are encouraged to make the most of the live DJs until late. Fantastic service and good happy hour deals.

Farther Afield

Café 6

$
Casual Dining   Map 3 B3
4381 W Flamingo Rd
Tel *(702) 944-3292*
Located on the sixth floor of Palms Place, this café has seven gourmet burgers including beef, short rib chicken, and turkey. Vanilla, chocolate or strawberry ice cream shakes are worth trying.

Farm 24/7

$
Casual Dining
7300 N Aliante Pkwy, North Las Vegas
Tel *(702) 692-7777*
The name says it all. This café serves fresh produce sourced from local farms and is open 24 hours, 7 days a week.

Lyfe Kitchen

$
Casual Dining
140 S Green Valley Pkwy # 142, Henderson
Tel *(702) 558-0131*
Located across from Green Valley Ranch Resort, this healthy eatery serves dishes that are designed for vegans and vegetarians, and made using local organic ingredients.

Milo's Cellar

$
Casual Dining
538 Nevada Way, Boulder City
Tel *(702) 293-9540*
Beer and wine aficionados will be happy at this quaint sidewalk café with more than 50 beers and wines by the glass and a selection of salads, soups, and sandwiches.

35 Steaks & Martinis

$$
Steakhouse   Map 4 D4
4455 Paradise Rd
Tel *(702) 693-5500*
The name of this steakhouse is inspired by the number of days it takes to dry age its premium beef. It also reflects the number of different martinis on its menu.

Portofino, for traditional Italian dishes wrought with artisan flair

For more information on types of restaurants *see pages 118–19*

Bonefish Grill $$
Seafood
6527 Las Vegas Blvd S
Tel *(702) 407-0980*
This seafood chain at Town Square offers a wide range of market-fresh fish and wood-grilled specialties at a reasonable price. Its Bang Bang Shrimp is a crowd-pleasing favorite.

Brio Tuscan Grill $$
Italian
6653 Las Vegas Blvd S
Tel *(702) 914-9145*
The upscale Italian chain restaurant serves authentic made-to-order pastas, northern Italian-style grilled and oven-roasted steaks, and fresh fish.

China House $$
Chinese   **Map** 3 B3
4321 W Flamingo Rd
Tel *(702) 990-8888*
This Chinese restaurant features an authentic variety of Szechuan and Cantonese beef, chicken, pork, vegetarian, and seafood dishes, and savoury soups.

Due Forni $$
Italian
3555 S Town Center Dr #105
Tel *(702) 586-6500*
Authentic Neapolitan- and Roman-style pizzas are served straight from the oven at this restaurant. Fresh buffalo mozzarella from Italy, and several American and Italian wines.

DK Choice

Fogo de Chao $$
Steakhouse
360 E Flamingo Rd
Tel (702) 431-4500
This traditional Brazilian churrascaria is decorated with large murals that depict scenes of the gaucho culture and lifestyle. The all-you-can-eat meal includes a trip to the huge salad bar, and a vast choice of different cuts of mesquite-grilled beef, pork, chicken and lamb. Food is delivered to your table by an army of gaucho chefs until you give them the prompt to stop.

Grape Street Wine Bar $$
Casual Dining
7501 W Lake Mead Blvd #120
Tel *(702) 228-9463*
Designed to replicate a wine cellar, this place dishes up Californian bistro-style cuisine with a Mediterranean twist. The extensive wine list gives you the option to take bottles away with you.

Hofbräuhaus Las Vegas $$
German
4510 Paradise Rd
Tel *(702) 853-2337*
An exact replica of the legendary Hofbräuhaus in Munich, this lively beer hall and restaurant features authentic Bavarian food, live bands, and a variety of beers imported from Germany. A fun Oktoberfest-style atmosphere all year round.

DK Choice

Honey Salt $$
Casual Dining
1031 S Rampart Blvd
Tel *(702) 445-6100*
A dynamic husband-and-wife duo offer upscale dining with off-Strip prices in a casual and relaxed setting. The farm-to-table menu is inspired by the couple's own home recipes and uses ingredients from local and regional farmers and fishermen. Try the sea bass served with roasted mushrooms and wilted spinach. An excellent place to enjoy lunch in the area.

DK Choice

Marche Bacchus $$
French
2620 Regatta Dr Ste 106
Tel *(702) 804-8008*
This bistro serves both traditional and contemporary dishes in a tranquil setting with views overlooking Lake Jacqueline. The restaurant doubles as a massive wine shop stocked with more than 950 wines which can be bought at half the price of most restaurants and enjoyed with your meal for a $10 corkage fee.

A romantic view of a sunset over Lake Jacqueline at Marche Bacchus

Marssa Steak and Sushi $$
Japanese
101 Montelago Blvd, Henderson
Tel *(702) 567-6125*   **Closed** *Sun & Mon*
This AAA Four-Diamond award-winning restaurant at the Westin Lake Las Vegas Resort overlooks the lake and serves world-class Japanese cuisine, with a full menu of sushi and sashimi.

McCormick & Schmick's Seafood and Steaks $$
Seafood
335 Hughes Center Dr
Tel *(702) 836-9000*
A wide range of fresh seafood and shellfish are offered at this upscale seafood and steakhouse chain, as well as aged steaks and garden-fresh salads.

N9NE Steakhouse $$
Steakhouse   **Map** 3 B3
4321 W Flamingo Rd
Tel *(866) 942-7770*
Look out for celebrities at this high-energy steakhouse. An array of USDA prime-aged beef selections are on the menu, as well as fresh seafood, and a great wine list.

Royal India Bistro $$
Indian   **Map** 3 B3
3700 W Flamingo Rd
Tel *(702) 777-2277*
Traditional North Indian delicacies are served here, such as king prawn skewers, chicken marinated in yoghurt and spices, freshly baked flatbread known as 'naan', and the tasty sheesh kabob.

Roy's $$
Seafood
620 E Flamingo Rd
Tel *(702) 691-2053*
Quality over quantity is the order of the day at this Hawaiian and Asian fusion restaurant. Delicious seafood creations are presented in a trendy upscale setting.

DK Choice

Sonoma Cellar $$
Steakhouse
1301 W Sunset Rd, Henderson
Tel (702) 547-7777
Set in Sunset Station Hotel & Casino, this classic steakhouse is one of only a handful of restaurants in Las Vegas that still serve Bananas Foster (a nostalgic dessert made from bananas, vanilla ice cream, banana liqueur, and a rum and cinnamon sauce). The steaks are marinated in a tomato base to make them tender and juicy. Accompany your meal with a selection from the award-winning wine list.

Spiedini $$
Italian
221 N Rampart Blvd
Tel *(702) 869-8500*
Famed chef-restaurateur Gustav Mauler oversees this restaurant. The speciality on the Milanese-inspired menu is *ossobuco* (a shank of veal slowly braised in white wine). Several tables overlook the resort's lavish palm trees, gardens, and waterfalls.

Studio B Buffet $$
Buffet
12300 Las Vegas Blvd S, Henderson
Tel *(702) 797-1000*
This live-action cooking studio serves more than 200 different dishes daily. The beer, wine, coffee, cappuccino, and cordials are all included in the price.

Ventano Italian Grill & Seafood $$
Italian
191 S Arroyo Grande Blvd, Henderson
Tel *(702) 944-4848*
A romantic ambience prevails at this pleasant eatery, just a short taxi ride from the centre of Las Vegas. Sit on the terrace for panoramic views of the dazzling lights on the Strip. The menu is loaded with classic Italian dishes, fresh seafood, and an extensive wine list.

Vintner Grill $$
Casual Dining
10100 W Charleston Blvd
Tel *(702) 214-5590*
This elegant New American bistro has French, Italian, and Spanish influences. It has one of the largest selections of cheeses in Las Vegas and an impressive wine list featuring more than 400 options.

Zenshin Asian Restaurant $$
Japanese
9777 Las Vegas Blvd S
Tel *(702) 797-8538*
The centerpiece at this restaurant is its sushi bar, where chefs prepare a variety of sashimi, nigiri, and sushi rolls. They have a fantastic daily happy hour menu from 2 to 6pm.

Kabuto Edomae Sushi $$$
Japanese
5040 W Spring Mountain Rd #4
Tel *(702) 676-1044*
This stylishly yet simply decorated 18-seat sushi house is very similar to some of the places you'll find in Tokyo. It serves authentic Edomae-style dining using fresh fish that is flown in six days a week, most of it from Japan.

Wrangler Steakhouse at Furnace Creek Ranch offers elegant dining in Death Valley

T-Bones Chophouse $$$
Steakhouse
11011 W Charleston Blvd
Tel *(702) 797-7576*
The menu at this Red Rock Resort restaurant is filled with a range of delicious prime steak and seafood options. Diners sit on an alluring patio overlooking the resort's pool and can enjoy a choice of over 7,500 bottles in the superb wine cellar.

DK Choice

Top of the World $$$
Fine Dining   Map 4 D1
2000 Las Vegas Blvd S
Tel *(702) 380-7711*
Set atop the 100-story high Stratosphere Tower, this restaurant revolves 360 degrees every 80 minutes. It would be worth dining here just for the incredible views, but the scenery isn't all this place has going for it. The accomplished chefs also deliver with mouthwatering masterpieces that cover a variety of international cuisines, including steaks, seafood, pastas and vegan specialties. Be sure to book ahead to secure a window seat.

Beyond Las Vegas

Bryce Canyon Dining Room at Bryce Canyon Lodge $
Fine Dining
Hwy 63, Bryce Canyon, UT
Tel *(435) 834-8700*
Breakfast, lunch, and dinner are served at this rustic 180-seat dining room, enhanced by a grand stone fireplace. A salad, soup, and sandwich buffet is served during lunch. The dinner specialties include a delicious buffalo flank steak.

Bright Angel Restaurant at Bright Angel Lodge $$
Casual Dining
9 Village Loop Dr, Grand Canyon Village, AZ Canyon Rim, AZ
Tel *(928) 638-2631*
This family restaurant features diner-style classics such as biscuits and gravy, build-your-own burger, and fajitas. The restaurant decor is accented by stout log columns with colorful mosaics.

The Range Steakhouse $$
Steakhouse
2900 S Casino Dr, Laughlin, NV
Tel *(702) 298-6832*
This chic steakhouse offers filet mignon, NY Strip, rib-eye, prime rib, and a range of seafood dishes such as halibut. The dining room is elegantly decorated and offers superb views of the Colorado River and surrounding Black Mountains.

Red Rock Grill at Zion National Park Lodge $$
Casual Dining
1 Zion Canyon Scenic Dr, Springdale, UT
Tel *(435)-772-7760*
Breakfast, lunch, and dinner are served with entrees such as steaks, burgers, Alaskan salmon, and vegetarian dishes. Large windows overlook the soaring stone walls of the Zion Canyon.

Wrangler Steakhouse at Furnace Creek Ranch $$
Steakhouse
Hwy 190, Death Valley Junction, Death Valley National Park, CA
Tel *(760) 786-3385*
Exquisite steaks, chops, chicken, and seafood dishes are served at this restaurant amid Western-themed decor. Dinner comes with a side from the salad bar and a great buffet selection is offered at breakfast and lunch.

For more information on types of restaurants *see pages 118–19*

SHOPPING IN LAS VEGAS

Las Vegas has consolidated its reputation as a shopper's paradise. Fun and tacky souvenirs are available in small stores along the Strip, whereas jewelry and designer clothes can be found everywhere, from hotel shops to malls. Given the city's hot climate, indoor shopping malls are the norm. All the major resorts have their own covered parades of shops, and some, such as Caesars Palace's Forum Shops, are as flamboyant as the hotels themselves. Several malls in Las Vegas, such as the Strip's Fashion Show Mall, house upscale department stores such as Saks Fifth Avenue and Neiman Marcus. For bargains in adult and children's clothes and shoes, as well as a range of household items, there are three outlet shopping malls, Las Vegas Outlet Center, Fashion Outlets of Las Vegas (south of the Strip), and Las Vegas Premium Outlets (near Downtown). Shopping centrally can be expensive, and for everyday items ordinary malls used by the locals are a short drive away.

The Esplanade at Wynn Las Vegas (see p129) on North Strip

Shopping Hours

Most stores and malls are open seven days a week. Typical business hours are from 9am to 6pm, Monday to Saturday, and 10am to 5pm on Sunday. The closing time for shops located in a mall or promenade usually extends to 9pm, and some stores in hotel shopping arcades open until midnight. Many gas stations, supermarkets, and convenience stores stay open 24 hours a day.

Sales

The Christmas shopping season, which runs from Thanksgiving to January 1, offers some great bargains in the form of promotional deals and discounts. The week after Christmas is probably the best time to buy anything. During this period, several retail outlets reduce prices to move merchandise or make way for the next season's products. Check the local newspapers for advertisements announcing these sales.

Taxes

Sales tax in Las Vegas and the rest of Clark County is 8.15 per cent and is added to the purchase price of all goods, except groceries and prescription drugs, at the time of sale. Sales tax is not refundable to overseas visitors. In addition, international travelers may be required to pay import duties and taxes on their purchases once they reach home.

How to Pay

Most stores accept credit cards including Visa, MasterCard, Discover, and American Express, as well as bank debit cards. Traveler's checks are also acceptable but usually require some form of identification, such as a passport or driver's license. Two-party checks, personal checks drawn on foreign banks, and foreign currency are rarely accepted. Cash is always the best way to pay for small purchases.

Rights and Returns

Be sure you understand the shop's return policy before making an important purchase. The key to obtaining any refund is in the proof of purchase, so keep all sales receipts. It is also important to retain all packaging – original boxes, instructions, and the owner's manuals.

Each store has its own return-and-exchange policy. Most retailers usually give a cash refund or an in-shop credit note, assuming the item being returned has not been altered or damaged. If the purchased item is defective, the store will refund its cost, unless it was sold "as is." Many stores have a time limit within which it will refund your money, typically up to 30 days after the purchase. Goods bought on sale are often not returnable.

Shipping Packages

Most stores will ship goods worldwide, usually for a fee.

Modernist interior of Fashion Show Mall (see p59)

The sprawling outlet of Saks Fifth Avenue, Fashion Show Mall *(see p59)*

Perhaps the best way to send packages is via an international courier such as Federal Express or DHL. Keep copies of shipping forms and airway bills, particularly the tracking numbers, which are instrumental in finding lost packages.

Department Stores

Las Vegas has an excellent mix of department stores, most of them clustered in the shopping malls *(see pp128–9)*. These large retail stores offer a wide variety of merchandise from toys to small appliances, and from apparel to cosmetics.

Sears, **JCPenney**, and **Kohl's** are the least expensive. They all offer complete lines of men's, women's, and children's apparel and shoes, plus jewelry, accessories, and recreational equipment.

Mid-priced department stores include **Dillard's** and **Macy's**

which feature an expansive line of clothing, including designer labels such as Calvin Klein and Tommy Hilfiger.

At the highest end of the department store chains are **Neiman Marcus**, **Saks Fifth Avenue**, and **Nordstrom**, all of which are located at the Fashion Show Mall. In addition to the finest designer label clothing, Neiman and Saks also offer creative, though pricey, home products, gifts, and specialty items. Nordstrom, known for its fashion apparel and shoes, also has an eclectic collection of jewelry.

Shopping Farther Afield

Good shopping options are also available outside Las Vegas. About 10 miles (16 km) east into the adjacent city of Henderson *(see p84)* is the **Galleria at Sunset**. Fountains, pools, and indoor trees make for a pleasant shopping experience. The mall has about 110 stores that include the usual mix of men's and women's clothing, as well as a variety of gift boutiques.

Parking

Most shopping malls and large department stores in Las Vegas offer valet parking as well as free parking in their parking lots. The only area of town that has parking meters is downtown near Fremont Street. However, some parking garages there offer free parking for a few hours with validation.

Entrance to Macy's department store, Las Vegas

DIRECTORY

Department Stores

Dillard's
Meadows Mall.
Tel (702) 870-2039.
Fashion Show Mall.
Map 3 C2. **Tel** (702) 733-2008.
Galleria at Sunset.
Tel (702) 435-6300.

JCPenney
Boulevard Mall.
Tel (702) 735-5131.
Galleria at Sunset.
Tel (702) 451-4545.

Kohl's
8671 W Charleston Blvd.
Map 1 A4.
Tel (702) 387-3191.
30 N Valle Verde Dr, Henderson.
Tel (702) 434-0492.

Macy's
Downtown Summerlin.
Tel (702) 832-1000.
Fashion Show Mall.
Tel (702) 854-6229.
Galleria at Sunset.
Tel (702) 458-7300.

Neiman Marcus
Fashion Show Mall.
Tel (702) 731 3636.

Nordstrom
Fashion Show Mall.
Tel (702) 862-2525.

Saks Fifth Avenue
Fashion Show Mall.
Tel (702) 733-8300.

Sears
Boulevard Mall.
Tel (702) 894-4200.

Malls

Boulevard Mall
3528 S Maryland Pkwy.
W boulevardmall.com

Downtown Summerlin
1980 Festival Plaza Dr.
W downtownsummerlin.com

Fashion Show Mall
3200 Las Vegas Blvd S 600.
W thefashionshow.com

Galleria at Sunset
1300 W Sunset Rd, Henderson.
W galleriaatsunset.com

Town Square
6845 Las Vegas Blvd S.
W mytownsquarelasvegas.com

Shopping Malls and Hotel Shops

Shopping malls in Las Vegas are a quintessential feature of the city, and have achieved the status of must-see attractions in their own right. The city is currently experiencing a shopping boom, and many of the major resorts have jumped on the bandwagon with sumptuous themed malls. Exclusive, elegant, and expensive, these retail destinations not only offer a wide array of products, but are also an entertaining and enjoyable way to explore the city. Although shopping on the Strip is a costly proposition, it is also undeniably an experience worth savoring.

Cloud-shaped canopy, Fashion Show Mall

Fashion Show Mall

Located right across the street from Treasure Island – TI (see p58), the Fashion Show Mall (see p59) is the jewel of the city's shopping malls, and features more than 250 shops on several enclosed levels. The mall covers an area of over 2 million sq ft (185,806 sq m), and is home to six major department stores – Saks Fifth Avenue, Nordstrom, Macy's, Dillard's, and Neiman Marcus – as well as a range of upscale specialty and designer shops such as Brighton Collectibles, Abercrombie & Fitch, Guess, and Coach, to name a few.

In addition, the mall hosts an excellent selection of commercial art galleries. These include the Centaur Art Galleries, which showcase masterpieces by world-renowned artists, such as Salvador Dali and Pablo

Picasso, along with the works of contemporary artists, such as Steve Kaufman and LeRoy Neiman. Stores such as Body Shop and Victoria's Secret cater to the beauty conscious, while Apple and GameStop offer high-tech toys and electronic gizmos to gadget-lovers.

Downtown Summerlin

The city's newest mall is an open-air, fashion, dining and entertainment mecca, conveniently connected by a walkway to the Red Rock Casino, Resort & Spa, and bounded by the 215 Beltway. There are some 125 stores, which cater to a range of budgets and include many popular high street brands.

The mall is home to over 30 dining options, from fast-food outlets to gourmet restaurants. There's also a movie theater with a full bar, and a tranquil pond and two-story fountain at the north end.

Town Square

Just 2 miles (3 km) south of Mandalay Bay and the Strip, this expansive mall houses a large number of popular stores, such as Apple, H&M, Hollister Co., and EXPRESS. Perhaps its biggest attraction is the massive 8,700-sq-ft (2,500-m) GameWorks center (see p164), which features a wide selection of arcade attractions and a bowling alley.

The Shops at Crystals

Located between ARIA and The Cosmopolitan in CityCenter (see p49) on the Strip, Crystals provides a complete experience, with its stunning architecture, gardens, sculptures, art galleries, and high-end restaurants. The shopping mall features several luxury retailers, including Louis Vuitton, Gucci, Prada, and Fendi.

Forum Shops at Caesars

Much more than just another glitzy shopping mall, Forum Shops (see pp52–3) is a major tourist attraction designed along the lines of an ancient Roman street. The mall, which has been expanded three times, has talking statues, dancing fountains, and a trompe l'oeil sky that simulates the change from dawn to dusk. It is also home to the amazing animatronic Fall of Atlantis fountain show, which depicts the Atlantis myth and takes place every hour on the hour. Tourneau Time Dome, the world's largest watch store is worth visiting. For ultra-chic

Roman statues and a painted sky at Forum Shops, Caesars Palace

Shops along the charming streets of Venice, Grand Canal Shoppes

women's wear, head for Versace, Marc Jacobs, and RED Valentino. The Forum Shops also has a wide choice of restaurants and eateries, including a franchise for renowned LA chef Wolfgang Puck's Spago, and the Miami-famed restaurant Joe's Seafood, Prime Steak and Stone Crab.

Grand Canal Shoppes at The Venetian

Of all the hotel shopping malls, the Grand Canal Shoppes (see pp60–61) is the most visually arresting with its Venetian streetscapes, piazza-style promenades, daylight ceiling, and a quarter-mile reproduction of Venice's Grand Canal, complete with a fleet of gondolas, singing gondoliers, waterside cafés, and bridges. The massive complex also features a replica of St. Mark's Square, and seems to be in a constant state of festivity as glassblowers, mask-makers, portrait painters, and street vendors crowd the walkways. Notable shops include bebe for women's fashions, and Sephora for beauty, skin care, make-up, and fragrance.

Miracle Mile at Planet Hollywood Resort & Casino

Designed to evoke the glitz and glamour of Hollywood, this shopping and entertainment district is set in futuristic surrounds, with a multi-million dollar fountain show and state-of-the-art LED video screens (see p48). Visitors can choose from 15 restaurants and 170 stores, including SoHo, Urban Outfitters, and Quiksilver.

Wynn Esplanade

At one of the city's most luxurious resorts (see pp62–3), this exclusive shopping promenade houses in excess of two dozen designer boutiques and jewelry stores in an exquisite retail space. Famous names include Dior, Graff, Louis Vuitton, and Moncler.

Crazy Shirts Forever, Miracle Mile

Via Bellagio

Another exclusive group of shops is found at Bellagio (see pp50–51). Fashion and jewelry collections are on display from high-end designers such as Giorgio Armani, Prada, Chanel, Tiffany & Co., Gucci, and Hermès. The elegant setting is bathed in filtered sunlight from an ornate glass ceiling.

Other Hotel Shops

In addition to the larger shopping promenades, some hotels offer smaller clusters of stores. The **Masquerade Village Shops** at Rio (see p52) invite visitors to stroll down replicas of 200-year-old Tuscan streets and browse among its two-dozen retail stores. Among the more interesting outlets are Fortune Cookie for Asian gifts, and Harley Davidson, who offer a selection of Harley-branded clothing and

toys. **Le Boulevard** at Paris Las Vegas (see p48) is a Francophile's joy and is home to authentic Parisian stores selling French goods including children's clothes, cheese, and chocolate.

The **Tower Shops** at the Stratosphere (see p65) is located one flight up the escalator that leads to the 1,200-ft (366-m) high tower. The 50-plus shops are arranged along a setting inspired by the street scenes of Paris, Hong Kong, and New York.

DIRECTORY

The Malls

Downtown Summerlin
1980 Festival Plaza Dr.
Open 10am–9pm Mon–Sat;
11am–7pm Sun.

Fashion Show Mall
3200 Las Vegas Blvd S. **Map** 3 C2.
Open 10am–9pm Mon–Sat;
11am–7pm Sun.

Town Square
6659 Las Vegas Blvd S.
Open 10am–9:30pm Mon–Thu (to 10pm Fri & Sat); 11am–8pm Sun.

Hotel Shopping

Le Boulevard
Open 10am–11pm Sun–Thu;
10am–midnight Fri–Sat.

Forum Shops at Caesars
Open 10am–11pm Sun–Thu;
10am–midnight Fri–Sat.

Grand Canal Shoppes
Open 10am–11pm Sun–Thu;
10am–midnight Fri–Sat.

Masquerade Village Shop
Open 11am–times vary daily.

Miracle Mile
Open 10am–11pm Sun–Thu;
10am–midnight Fri–Sat.

The Shops at Crystals
Open 10am–11pm Sun–Thu;
10am–noon Fri–Sat.

Tower Shops
Open 10am–11pm Sun–Thu;
10am–midnight Fri–Sat.

Via Bellagio
Open 10am–midnight daily.

Wynn Esplanade
Open 10am–11pm Sun–Thu;
10am–midnight Fri–Sat.

Factory Outlets and Bargain Shopping Centers

Although Las Vegas is considered to be one of the most expensive destinations for shopping in the world, bargain hunters can usually find a range of high-end products at affordable prices in the off-the-Strip outlet malls. Las Vegas Premium Outlets is the largest, and is near Downtown just off I-15. South of the Strip is the Las Vegas Outlet Center and in Primm, on the California border, is Fashion Outlets of Las Vegas. All three are home to a wide variety of stores for all, including several designer outlets, with claims of savings of 20 to 70 per cent below "regular" retail prices. Shoppers can also find great deals at any of the city's pawn shops and stand-alone discount stores, as well as at its massive flea market and swap meet.

Entrance to the massive Las Vegas Outlet Center

Las Vegas Outlet Center

Located a few miles south of the Strip, the Las Vegas Outlet Center has more than 145 stores. Nearly half of all shops sell clothing, including Banana Republic, Calvin Klein, Levis and DKNY. The complex also has a number of jewelry and accessory shops, and a wide selection of stores for toys, sportswear, home furnishings, beauty products, and shoes – all offering discounts of up to 75 per cent.

The Polo Ralph Lauren Factory Store is a popular attraction. Electronics enthusiasts should head to Bose for a selection of turbo-powered speaker systems. Aspiring chefs will enjoy Kitchen Collection, where a wide variety of kitchen items, such as bakeware, cookware, cutlery, gadgets, and high-quality refurbished manufacturers' closeouts, are available at exceptional prices.

In addition to the many shops, the mall has two food courts.

Fashion Outlets of Las Vegas

It's hard to imagine driving to the California border to try on shoes, but Las Vegans are not shy of the 35-minute trip.

The 100-plus outlet stores are a bargain basement for the frugal who nevertheless have an eye for the fineries in life.

The impressive list of shops includes designer stores and famous brands such as Gap, Old Navy, Polo Ralph Lauren, Kate Spade, Williams-Sonoma Marketplace, St. John Company Store, Tommy Hilfiger, NIKE Factory Store, G by Guess, Calvin Klein, Banana Republic, Coach, and Perfumania, to name just a few.

Tranquil fountains create a soothing and relaxing atmosphere. The mall has also been known to attract many pregnant and nursing celebrities shopping for maternity clothes.

The mall offers free Wi-Fi, translation services, stroller rentals for children, and complimentary wheelchairs.

Las Vegas Premium Outlets

The largest outlet center, Las Vegas Premium Outlets, is only five minutes from the Strip and Downtown. Situated in a pleasant outdoor setting, it has 175 designer and name-brand stores. Some of the names found here include Dolce & Gabbana, Lacoste, Michael Kors, Burberry, Kenneth Cole, and Tommy Hilfiger. There are also unusual stores not often found in an outlet mall, such as True Religion, and Ann Taylor.

With so much to choose from, and to make it easier for foot-weary and time-poor shoppers, many of the stores are grouped by style and demographic.

Designer shops line the walkways of Fashion Outlets of Las Vegas

Discount Stores

The nation's major discount stores are well represented in Las Vegas. **Kmart, Target**, and **Wal-Mart** sell virtually anything and everything that can be used at home, work, or school. From clothing and appliances to hardware and cleaning supplies, and from jewelry and computers to DVD players, these stores have it all, usually at prices 10 to 45 per cent lower than other stores. Las Vegas also has two chains of membership discount stores – **Costco** and **Sam's Club**. The membership cost is about $50 a year, but the prices of goods – including grocery, bakery, and meat products – are significantly less than traditional stores. Note that products in these membership stores are often bundled. For instance, a bottle of ketchup might cost less, but you will have to buy three of them to get the savings.

A circus scene on the exterior of Fantastic Indoor Swap Meet, Las Vegas

Pawn shop

Pawn Shops

There are plenty of pawn shops in Vegas, perhaps the result of so many casinos catering to gamblers who frequently turn in their jewelry, watches, cameras, and other valuable items for quick cash. A sharp eye for bargains can often find an inexpensively priced DVD player, guitar, or a computer among other things.

The most well-stocked pawn shops can usually be found downtown, typically on the streets just off Fremont Street. These shops often have a nice mix of diamonds, silverware, watches, tools, and musical instruments. You are also likely to find electronic equipment such as amplifiers, TVs, cell phones, camcorders, and other products. Some even have 24-hour windows for late-night transactions.

The largest operation in town is a chain of pawn shops called **Super Pawn**. These have the usual range of goods, though the stores are usually brighter and not as cramped as some of the downtown pawn shops.

Swap Meets

One of the best places for bargains are swap meets, which are the American equivalent of the European flea markets. **Fantastic Indoor Swap Meet** is the biggest meet in Las Vegas and is held from Friday to Sunday every week. The gigantic indoor mall has about 600 vendors who sell everything, including clothing, electronic equipment, vintage kitchen appliances, tire chains, home-baked bread, power tools, and other knick-knacks. Although there's little to no "trading" taking place, the prices are the lowest.

DIRECTORY

Factory Outlets

Fashion Outlets of Las Vegas
32100 Las Vegas Blvd S, Primm, NV. **Open** 10am–8pm daily. **Tel** (702) 874-1400. W **fashionoutlet lasvegas.com**

Las Vegas Outlet Center
7400 Las Vegas Blvd S. **Open** 9am–9pm Mon–Sat; 9am–8pm Sun. **Tel** (702) 896-5599.
W **premiumoutlets.com**

Las Vegas Premium Outlets
875 S Grand Central Parkway. **Open** 9am–9pm Mon–Sat; 9am–8pm Sun. **Tel** (702) 474-7500.
W **premiumoutlets.com**

Discount Stores

Costco
222 S Martin Luther King Blvd. **Map** 1 C3. **Open** 7am–6pm Mon–Fri; 7am–6pm Sat. **Tel** (702) 384-6247. W **costco.com**

Kmart
Tel (866) 562-7848.
W **kmart.com**

Sam's Club
7175 Spring Mountain Rd. **Open** 10am–8:30pm Mon–Fri; 9am–8:30pm Sat; 10am–6pm Sun.
Tel (702) 253-0072.
8080 W Tropical Pkwy. **Open** 10am–8:30pm Mon–Fri; 9am–8:30pm Sat; 10am–6pm Sun.

Tel (702) 515-7200.
W **samsclub.com**

Target
4001 S Maryland Pkwy. **Map** 4 E3. **Open** 8am–11pm daily. **Tel** (702) 732-2218. W **target.com**

Wal-Mart
Tel (800) 925-6278.
W **walmart.com**

Pawn Shops

Super Pawn
2300 E Charleston Blvd. **Map** 2 F4. **Open** 9am–8pm Mon–Sat, 12–5pm Sun. **Tel** (702) 477-3040.
1040 E Flamingo Road Suite A-6. **Map** 4 E3. **Open** As above. **Tel** (702) 792-3300.

4635 W Flamingo Rd. **Map** 3 A3. **Open** 10am–8:30pm Mon–Sat; noon–8pm Sun. **Tel** (702) 252-7296.
W **superpawn.com**

Swap Meets

Fantastic Indoor Swap Meet
1717 S Decatur Blvd. **Open** 10am–6pm Fri–Sun. **Tel** (702) 877-0087.
W **fantasticindoor swapmeet.com**

Specialty Shops

Beyond traditional shopping venues, Las Vegas holds its own on more eclectic shopping options as well. As one might expect, the city has an extensive selection of stores selling gambling supplies and memorabilia, including books and computer systems for learning casino games. An antiques guild, made up of a small cluster of shops, offers a variety of treasures that range from Victorian jewelry to German clocks, while outlets in the Chinatown Plaza shopping district specialize in Chinese, Korean, and Japanese art, crafts, and curios. Las Vegas also has several stores that sell Southwestern and Native American collectibles and souvenirs.

Gambling product on display at the Gamblers General Store

Gambling Gear

A shopping paradise for both gamblers and memorabilia hunters, **Gamblers General Store** houses one of the most comprehensive collections of gambling supplies in the city. These include full-size crap, blackjack, and roulette tables, folding poker tables, playing cards, dice sets, coin changers, and much more. The store also stocks every type of gambling paraphernalia imaginable, including hundreds of books and videos on gambling, customized poker chips, croupier sticks, green-felt layouts for every type of casino game, and even dice-inlaid toilet seats. A modest collection of vintage slot machines is also available.

Within the General Store, the **Gambler's Book Club** has a huge collection of books on racing, poker, blackjack, casino games, gin rummy, slot machines, and jai alai, to name a few. The store also offers related magazines, special workbooks for tracking teams and recording outcomes, and an admirable selection of archival material. There's even a section of books on compulsive gambling and how to combat and overcome the addiction.

For the serious enthusiasts and collectors a visit to **Spinetti's Home Gaming Supplies** is essential. Here they offer a comprehensive range of home gambling supplies and specialize in customized poker chips and collectible gaming chips, cards, and dice from casinos that are currently open as well as from establishments that are now part of Las Vegas history. Spinetti's has the world's largest selection of chips with thousands to choose from. Any purchase can be packed and shipped worldwide within 24 hours.

Antiques

Las Vegas's biggest selection of antiques is available at **Antique Square**, a complex made up of a dozen assorted shops. The owners of the square, **Nicolas & Osvaldo**, have several rooms lined with cabinets to show off their collection of antiques. A mix of periods, styles, and tastes are reflected in the crystal, china, decorative teacups, clocks, chandeliers, and sterling silver tea sets, spoons, coasters, salt and pepper shakers, and more.

With more than 250 antique clocks in stock, **JJC Clocks & Antiques** is the largest antique clock and repair shop in Nevada, while the **Charleston Antique Mall** is an 18,000-sq-ft (1,672-sq-m) space, where more than 60 dealers offer a wide variety of vintage items, including cuckoo clocks, furniture, clothing, jewelry, signs, artwork, and silver.

Retro Vegas, located in nearby Antique Alley, specializes in items with historical significance from Vegas homes of the past, as well as a wide variety of clocks, ceramics, furniture, glassware, lighting and both modern and vintage art.

Swag Antiques features vintage porcelain signs, sewing machines, board games, wood carnival milk bottles, and vinyl records.

Situated next to the Gold & Silver Pawn Shop, **Lost Vegas** contains collectibles from imploded casinos and souvenirs featuring Las Vegas celebrities. There are also railroad, gasoline, and automobile items, old coins, vintage gambling chips, comic books, and sports memorabilia.

Gifts and Souvenirs

Shopping for souvenirs and gifts is a major activity in Las Vegas. The **Funk House** has a great range of 1950s, 1960s, and 1970s modern antiques, such as glassware, lamps, ceramics, jewelry, toys, and quirky items like an old Coca-Cola vending machine and a vintage airplane pedal car.

The exterior of the Bonanza Gift Shop, crammed with all manner of souvenirs

A must for those who like all things mystical is the **Psychic Eye Book Shop**. As well as a good selection of books on the subject, this shops sells everything from tarot cards, oils, meditation aids, candles, cauldrons, and more. Also available are on-site psychic consultations, although readings can be conducted over the telephone, too.

Bonanza Gift Shop claims to be the world's largest gift shop with products that range from a cheap pair of slot machine earrings to luxury sets of poker chips.

Asian cuisine and merchandise at Chinatown Plaza

Electronics

The largest electronics store in Las Vegas, **Fry's Electronics**, is located on the south end of the Town Square mall. It provides cell phones, communications gear, and much more. High-definition TVs and home theaters, digital cameras, DVDs, and MP3 players are the specialty of stores such as **Best Buy**. The prices at these shops are mostly competitive.

Arts and Crafts

Those looking for collectibles and artifacts should head for the **Gold & Silver Pawn Shop**, run by three generations of the Harrison family, now famous

after its reality show debuted on the History Channel in 2009. It's not uncommon for more than 4,000 people to visit the store each day. Visitors can peruse the varied assortment of collectibles, from small items you can fit in your suitcase, such as rare coins and historical artifacts, rare artworks, antiques, old comic books, and jewelry; to larger pieces, like gas station pumps and jukeboxes. Plan to arrive early, as there is usually a long line to get in, with thousands of fans a day hoping to see the stars of the *Pawn Stars* TV show in action.

For a selection of Asian goods, consider **Chinatown Plaza**. Built in the mid-1990s, this is the city's

first shopping center designed specifically for Asian tenants. Merchants offer jade, gold, and ivory jewelry, exotic herbs and medicines, handcrafted furniture, and Chinese literature, music, and arts. There's a market for live seafood, including fish and crab, fresh vegetables, and an excellent assortment of condiments, spices, and sauces.

Antiquities of Las Vegas is a fabulous source of antiques and collectibles, including autographed items. The store is centrally located on the Strip among the Forum Shops at Caesars Palace. It's a great place to pick up a Las Vegan keepsake such as a neon sign or an autographed guitar.

DIRECTORY

Gambling Gear

Gamblers General Store and Gambler's Book Club
800 S Main St. **Map** 2 D4.
Tel (702) 382-9903, (702) 382-7555.

Spinetti's Home Gaming Supplies
810 S Commerce St. **Map** 4 D1. **Tel** (702) 362-8767.

Antiques

Antique Square
2014–2026 E Charleston Blvd. **Map** 2 E4.

Charleston Antique Mall
560 S Decatur Blvd.
Tel (702) 228-4783.

JJC Clocks & Antiques
1310 S Main St.
Tel (702) 384-8463.

Lost Vegas
625 Las Vegas Blvd S.
Map 2 D4.
Tel (702) 382-1882.

Nicolas & Osvaldo
Antique Square.
Tel (702) 386-0238.

Retro Vegas
1131 S Main St.
Map 1 C4.
Tel (702) 384-2700.

Swag Antiques
630 Las Vegas Blvd S.
Map 2 D4.
Tel (702) 464-3299.

Gifts and Souvenirs

Bonanza Gift Shop
2440 Las Vegas Blvd S.
Map 4 D1.
Tel (702) 385-7359.

Funk House
1228 S Casino Center Blvd. **Map** 1 C5.
Tel (702) 678-6278.

Psychic Eye Book Shop
6848 W Charleston Blvd.
Map 1 A4.
Tel (702) 255-4477.

Electronics

Best Buy
2050 N Rainbow Blvd.
Tel (702) 631-4645.
w bestbuy.com

Fry's Electronics
6845 Las Vegas Blvd S.
Tel (702) 932-1400.
w frys.com

Arts and Crafts

Antiquities of Las Vegas
Forum Shops, 3570 Las Vegas Blvd S. **Map** 3 C3.
Tel (702) 792-2724.

Chinatown Plaza
4255 Spring Mountain Rd.
Map 3 A2.
Tel (702) 221-8448.

Gold & Silver Pawn Shop
713 Las Vegas Blvd S. **Map** 2 D4. **Tel** (702) 530-4959.
w gspawn.com

ENTERTAINMENT IN LAS VEGAS

Las Vegas makes a good claim to be the entertainment capital of the world. From free spectaculars such as the dancing water show at Fountains of Bellagio to lavishly produced theatrical acts, there is a full range of nightlife available. Sinatra and Elvis may be gone but headliners still appear regularly in the city's showrooms, offering a chance to see a star in a surprisingly intimate setting. Most of the major venues can be found in hotels along the Strip and downtown, ranging from small lounges to 1,000-seater showrooms. While visitors can still enjoy the kitsch appeal of a Vegas burlesque show with its scantily clad showgirls, high-quality productions featuring the latest in lighting and special effects are a big draw. Comedy and magic performances are also widely available throughout Las Vegas.

Information

There is no dearth of information on the entertainment scene in Las Vegas. A variety of free publications list all the major productions as well as the latest big acts in town. Magazines and free newspapers such as *Las Vegas Magazine* and *Las Vegas Weekly* can be found at all the major hotels. Even Las Vegas taxis carry free guides to the city, with information on shows and attractions.

The **Las Vegas Convention and Visitors Authority** provides up-to-date showguides, and their website has current listings and reviews on the city's ongoing and upcoming shows and events, as does www.vegas.com.

Magazine kiosk

Buying Tickets

The easiest way to book tickets to the major shows or visiting headliners is to call the venue or hotel directly on their toll-free number. There are also many ticketing websites to choose from. Prices can vary, and range from $30 to $200 per ticket. The ticket may also include drinks, a free program, tips, and in rare cases, even dinner.

Nearly all shows have assigned seating, but it is better to make reservations beforehand. Reservations should always be made in advance, but the length of time varies greatly according to the show's popularity. To see the Cirque du Soleil's *(see p136)* stunning *Mystère* at Treasure Island – TI, you can book up to 90 days in advance, while space for most other shows can be reserved up to 14 days ahead. It is also possible to get tickets on the night of the performance by lining up at the box office an hour or so before showtime, but doing so is not guaranteed to save you money.

Cirque du Soleil act, *Mystère* at Treasure Island – TI *(see pp58–9)*

This is especially true at times when there are no major conventions in town and when it is not a public holiday. Weekdays are usually a better bet than weekends, although most shows have one or two days off during the week.

For sports events, such as world championship boxing, or the big rock and pop concerts frequently held at the impressive MGM Grand Garden and the huge T-Mobile Arena tickets can also be purchased through **Tickets and Tours**, **Ticketmaster**, and other agency outlets.

Discounts for children and senior citizens may be available from the box office. Free tickets to the Garden may be offered to the hotel casino's big winners.

Discount Tickets

The first place to look is in the magazines provided in most hotel rooms. Discount tickets or two-for-one coupons are available for many mid-priced

Blue Man Group performance

Massive volcano outside The Mirage *(see p58)*

shows, but rarely for top-flight productions. You can also find coupons for discounts in "fun books," which are distributed by casinos and tourist centers along the Strip.

Slot club members receive player rewards that can be used as discounts on shows, dining, and other events. Regular casino gamblers can ask a host or supervisor to track their play, and by gambling long enough can qualify for discounts or complimentary passes for shows and meals.

The half-price ticket outlet **Tix4Tonight** has one kiosk in the Hawaiian Marketplace, eight more on the Strip, one at Town Square, and the other in downtown. **Half Price Shows** sells half price tickets up to 60 days in advance and also online. **GoldstarEvents** sell discounted

tickets through the Internet. Many shows offer discounts to Nevada residents.

Free Events

In addition to the numerous ticketed events, Las Vegas offers several free performances and shows as well.

Some of the outdoor events include the amazing special effects of the *Fremont Experience Viva Vision Light Show*, the massive erupting volcano at The Mirage, the beautifully choreographed dancing fountains at Bellagio, and the singing gondoliers as they pole their gondolas along the Grand Canal at The Venetian.

Indoor attractions include the *Big Elvis* show at Harrah's and a tour of M&M's World, which also showcases a 3-D movie.

DIRECTORY

Americans with Disabilities Act (ADA)
W clarkcountybar.org

GoldstarEvents
W GoldstarEvents.com/events

Half Price Shows
W halfpriceshows.com

Las Vegas Convention and Visitors Authority
3150 Paradise Rd. **Map** 4 D4.
Tel (702) 892-0711.
W lasvegas.com

Ticketmaster
W ticketmaster.com

Tickets and Tours
Tel (702) 597-5970.
W ticketsandtours.com

Tix4Tonight
W tix4tonight.com

Facilities for the Disabled

Las Vegas is perhaps the world's most accessible city for people with disabilities. All showrooms, theaters, and concert halls are equipped with ramps for wheelchairs and usually provide special access elevators and entrances as well. Some cultural events hire sign language interpreters for the hearing impaired. Entertainment venues in hotels also offer special facilities for the disabled. For any particular needs, contact the hotel's **Americans with Disabilities Act** – ADA – coordinator. Every major hotel has one. For further information see pp168–9.

The beautifully choreographed dancing fountains at Bellagio *(see pp50–51)*

Casino Shows

There has never been anything subtle about Las Vegas's casino shows. Since their opening day, each resort has tried to create and provide its customers with the most creative and imaginative entertainment possible. Today, much of the city's nightlife revolves around these casinos and their lavish stage productions, celebrity concerts, and comedy clubs. On any given night, visitors can choose from nearly 70 different shows, ranging from star-studded spectaculars such as Britney Spears at Planet Hollywood and Elton John's *The Million Dollar Piano* show at the Colosseum, awesome extravaganzas such as *Mystère* and *"O"* by Cirque du Soleil, spellbinding shows by David Copperfield at the MGM Grand, hilarious comedy acts, and musical tributes to some of the greatest singers of all time.

Performers dressed in creative and colorful costumes, *Mystère*

Cirque du Soleil Shows

This acclaimed French Canadian production company has virtually taken over Las Vegas with five shows currently playing.

KÀ at MGM Grand is one of the least expensive live shows in town and uses a perfect blend of signature Cirque music, fantastic acrobatics, overall aesthetics, and the language of cinema to narrate a mesmerizing story.

The longest-running Cirque show in Las Vegas is ***Mystère*** at Treasure Island – TI. Like other Cirque productions, *Mystère* is an enchanting circus act with a mystical thread running through it. It takes audiences on a metaphorical journey that starts at the beginning of time, symbolized by a powerful opening of Japanese taiko drums supposedly sent from the heavens, and features a riveting mix of music, dance, and stunning athleticism.

It's hard to imagine Cirque du Soleil outdoing itself, but its production of *"O"* at the Bellagio comes close. This spectacular show features swimmers, trapeze artists, and contortionists who navigate an unbelievable stage that transforms from the Arctic Ocean to an African watering hole almost instantaneously. The use of water – as a character and not a theatrical prop – gives fluidity to a show that is like a parade of haunting images with a slightly Fellini-esque quality, and has the feel of climbing inside a painting by surrealist Salvador Dali. Another popular Cirque production is ***Zumanity*** at New York-New York. The show raised eyebrows when it debuted in 2004 because of its sexual overtones – traditional

Cirque aesthetics are sexually charged to create a European-style cabaret theater, often more crude than bawdy. Still, the playful male and female performers who indulge in comic relief produce some memorable moments.

Other popular Cirque productions are ***Criss Angel MINDFREAK LIVE!*** at Luxor *(see p44)*, featuring mind-blowing, original, and revolutionary illusions, with a cast that boasts some of the world's most talented specialty artists; and ***LOVE*** at The Mirage, featuring Beatles' music, acrobats, and dancers.

The latest Cirque show, ***Michael Jackson One*** at Mandalay Bay, takes the audience on a journey through the music of the king of pop.

Musicals and Stage Shows

Traditional musical variety shows are still popular in Las Vegas, even in the face of the more modern Cirque du Soleil productions. The ***Aces of Comedy Series*** at The Mirage features top comedians such as Kathleen Madigan, Ray Romano, Lewis Black, Kevin James, Howie Mandel, Tim Allen, and Jay Leno, who perform at the Terry Fator Theatre.

The Broadway musical ***Million Dollar Quartet*** at Harrah's is reminiscent of the jam sessions of Elvis Presley,

Performers in Cirque du Soleil's *"O"*

Advertisements for shows on the facade of The Venetian

Johnny Cash, Jerry Lee Lewis, and Carl Perkins.

Rock of Ages, at the Rio, is another musical. It is a humorous love story set in the Sunset Strip of 1987 and celebrates 28 rock anthems from the 80s, including "Don't Stop Believin'", "We Built This City," "The Final Countdown," and "I Want To Know What Love Is."

Steve Wynn's ShowStoppers, at Wynn Las Vegas, showcases Broadway hits from over ten musicals, chorus numbers, duets, and solos, performed by a cast of 35 singers and dancers, backed up by a 31-piece full orchestra. The iconic Tony Award-winning renditions include "All That Jazz" and "Cell Block Tango" from *Chicago,* and "Everything's Coming Up Roses" from *Gypsy.*

Another riveting show at the Wynn Las Vegas *(see pp62–3)* is **Le Rêve**, an abstract aquatic masterpiece featuring fabulous costumes, amazing gymnastics, and comedy. It is one of the most popular shows on the Strip and is staged in a magnificent domed aqua theater-in-the-round, so all the seats have great views and no one is more than 40 feet (12 m) from the action. The show's central feature is a circular pond containing nearly a million gallons (4 million liters) of water. The 85 members of the cast perform aerial acrobatics, acts of artistic athleticism, and provocative choreography.

Revues

Presented on a smaller scale, the revues on the Las Vegas Strip are no less entertaining than the larger musical extravaganzas. **Legends in Concert**, at Flamingo Las Vegas, enthralls the audience with amazing musical impersonations of such stars as Whitney Houston, Elvis Presley, Lady Gaga, and Prince.

The Rat Pack is Back plays at the Tuscany with three performers portraying Frank Sinatra, Dean Martin, and Sammy Davis Jr. The intimate show has a laid-back atmosphere, much like the original Rat Pack generated years ago at the Sands.

Sculpture for the *Crazy Girls* show

A bevy of other tribute shows are offered at the resorts, such as **Purple Reign: The Prince Tribute Show** at Westgate Las Vegas, **Australian Bee Gees Show** at Excalibur, **Divas Starring Frank Marino** at The LINQ, **Country Superstars** at Hooters, and **MJ Live** at the Stratosphere Casino Hotel.

Absinthe, the racy adults-only show at Spiegeltent within Caesars Palace's Spiegelworld, transports its audiences to early 20th-century Europe with its acro-cabaret variety show.

World-class artists perform feats of strength, balance, and danger in a brocade emporium.

Adult Entertainment

A few casinos in Las Vegas host topless shows, which are tastefully done and appropriate for mixed audiences. The longest running topless revue is **Crazy Girls,** which plays at Planet Hollywood. The show features eight showgirls who dance to canned music and act out silly skits on a small stage. Excellent solo numbers, rendered by an accomplished singer, and an outrageous male comic MC keep the show from lapsing into banality.

Fantasy at the Luxor has been showcased on the Strip since 2000. The sexy production showcases 15 high-energy numbers set to a variety of today's top music genres. Comic relief from Sean E. Cooper delivers spot-on impressions of some of pop culture's most recognizable personalities.

Pin Up, at the Stratosphere Casino Hotel, starring Playboy 2011 Playmate of the Year Claire Sinclair, features a live band playing music from Frankie Moreno, and is a night of vintage burlesque inspired by the classic pin up calendars from the 1940s, 1950s and 1960s.

Two characters from the spectacular *Le Rêve*, Wynn Las Vegas

Advertisement for *Donny and Marie* at the Flamingo

Variety Shows

Though magicians have become commonplace in Las Vegas, *David Copperfield* remains a big draw. Audiences can see the most successful illusionist in history performing in the intimate space of the Hollywood Theater at the MGM Grand. Mind-boggling magic tricks involve Copperfield seemingly passing through a solid metal sheet, as well as being reduced to mere inches inside a box. The show offers plenty of opportunities for audience participation, since Copperfield calls upon a random helper for almost every illusion.

   Penn and Teller at the Rio offer a different style of magic, one that uses intelligent, often dark humor, to punctuate their illusions.

   Hypnotists have also found a home in Sin City. Audience members can have their minds read by Gerry McCambridge in *The Mentalist*, or volunteer to get hypnotized in *Marc Savard Comedy Hypnosis*, with often hilarious results; both are at Planet Hollywood. The longest-running hypnotist in Vegas is **Anthony Cools**, performing at Paris Las Vegas. A risqué affair, Cools taps into the carnal and subconscious desires of his (willing) subjects plucked from the audience, banishing their inhibitions and thoroughly entertaining the rest of the crowd at the same time.

   Impersonators and impressionists have always had a spot on the Las Vegas stage. **Gordie Brown** performs at the Golden Nugget. His spot-on impressions capture the known quirks of popular entertainers. At The Mirage the headliner, **Terry Fator**, a former winner of *America's Got Talent*, performs a puppet/ventriloquist act, as well as celebrity impersonations.

   Comedians have also entered Las Vegas's main rooms with shows of their own. Some of the comics who have risen to headliner status include **Carrot Top** at Luxor.

   Stand-up comics and comedy clubs are also doing roaring business in the city. The country's best comedians, along with up-and-coming talent, appear nightly at Las Vegas's top comedy clubs, including **Laugh Factory**

Members of the Blue Man Group at Luxor

at Tropicana, **Brad Garret's Comedy Club** at MGM Grand, and **Las Vegas Live Comedy Club** at Planet Hollywood. *Blue Man Group* is a popular show at Luxor, which promotes a party atmosphere. It is unique, funny, and wildly innovative, as three bald blue men take the audience on a multi-sensory journey, featuring theater, percussion, vaudeville and music.

Headliner Shows

Most headline entertainers are content to play Vegas for a weekend or two, but a handful have been able to establish an entire production around their unique talents. Known as Mr Las Vegas, **Wayne Newton** performs at Bally's, drawing on more than 50 years of entertainment experience. At Planet Hollywood, **Britney Spears** and **Jennifer Lopez** split time with alternating performances. **Donny and Marie Osmond**, at the Flamingo, features the brother and sister duo performing a family-friendly variety show that follows the winning formula of their 1970s TV program, incorporating dancing, humor and all of their hit songs, including "Puppy Love," "Paper Roses," and "Soldier of Love." At Caesars Palace, four headliner shows rotate: **Rod Stewart, Celine Dion, Reba, Brooks and Dunn**, and **Elton John**. Each of these iconic musicians perform their hits to sold-out crowds.

Broadway Shows

Broadway shows always face mixed reactions in Las Vegas, evidenced by the limited runs of shows like *Chicago, Rent*, and *Notre Dame de Paris*. Yet, a few will catch the fancy of audiences.

   The Smith Center for the Performing Arts in downtown Las Vegas presents an ongoing *Broadway* series, with hit Broadway shows such as *Wicked, Pippin, Newsies*, and *Annie*.

   The Bronx Wanderers, a retro rock 'n' roll tribute show band, performs at Bally's.

DIRECTORY

Cirque du Soleil Shows

Criss Angel MINDFREAK LIVE!
Luxor. **Map** 3 B5. 7pm & 9:30pm Wed–Sun.
Tel (702) 262-4444.

KÀ
MGM Grand. **Map** 3 C4. 7pm & 9:30pm Sat–Wed.
Tel (702) 891-7777.

LOVE
The Mirage. **Map** 3 B3. 7pm & 9:30pm Thu–Mon.
Tel (702) 792-7777.

Michael Jackson One
Mandalay Bay. **Map** 3 B5. 7pm & 9:30pm Fri–Tue.
Tel (702) 632-7777.

Mystère
Treasure Island – TI. **Map** 3 C2. 7pm & 9:30pm Sat–Wed.
Tel (702) 894-7722

"O"
Bellagio. **Map** 3 B3. 7pm & 9:30pm Wed Sun.
Tel (702) 693-7722.

Zumanity
New York-New York. **Map** 3 C4. 7pm & 9:30pm Fri–Tue. **Tel** (702) 740-6815.

Musicals and Stage Shows

Aces of Comedy
The Mirage. **Map** 3 B3. 10pm Fri & Sat. Show and times vary.
Tel (702) 792-7777.

Million Dollar Quartet
Harrah's. **Map** 3 C3. 7pm Mon & Wed–Fri, 8pm Sun–Fri.
Tel (800) 840-9227.

Le Rêve
Wynn Las Vegas. **Map** 3 C2. 7pm & 9:30pm Fri–Tue. **Tel** (888) 320-7100.

Rock of Ages
Rio. **Map** 3 B3. 7:30pm Tue–Sun.
Tel (855) 234-7469.

Steve Wynn's ShowStoppers
Wynn Las Vegas. **Map** 3 C2. 7:30pm Mon–Thu & Sat, 8pm Fri.
Tel (702) 785-5555

Revues

Absinthe
Caesars Palace. **Map** 3 B3. 8pm & 10pm Wed–Sun.
Tel (877) 723-8836.

Australian Bee Gees Show
Excalibur. **Map** 3 B4. 5pm Sat, 7pm Sun–Thu.
Tel (702) 369 5222.

Country Superstars
Hooters. **Map** 3 C4. 7pm daily. **Tel** (866) 584-6687.

Divas Starring Frank Marino
LINQ Hotel & Casino. **Map** 3 C3. 9:30pm daily.
Tel (702) 731-3311.

Legends in Concert
Flamingo. **Map** 3 C3. 7:30pm & 9:30pm Mon, 4pm & 9:30pm Tue–Thu & Sat, 9:30pm Fri, 7:30pm Sun. **Tel** (702) 369-5222.

MJ Live
Stratosphere. **Map** 4 D1. 7pm daily.
Tel (702) 380-7777.

Purple Reign: The Prince Tribute Show
Westgate Las Vegas. **Map** 3 C3. 9pm Wed–Sat.
Tel (800) 222-5361.

The Rat Pack is Back
Tuscany. **Map** 3 C4. 7:30pm Mon–Sat.
Tel (800) 840-9227.

Adult Entertainment

Crazy Girls
Planet Hollywood. **Map** 3 C4. 9pm Thu–Tue. Guests under 18 will not be admitted.
Tel (702) 794-9433.

Fantasy
Luxor. **Map** 3 B5. 10:30pm daily. Guests under 18 will not be admitted.
Tel (702) 262-4444.

Pin Up
Stratosphere Casino Hotel. **Map** 4 D1. 9:30pm Thu–Mon. Guests under 18 will not be admitted.
Tel (702) 380-7777.

Variety Shows

Anthony Cools
Paris Las Vegas. **Map** 3 C3. 9pm Tue & Thu–Sun.
Tel (702) 946-7000.

Blue Man Group
Luxor. **Map** 3 B5. 7pm & 9:30pm daily
Tel (702) 730-7777.

Brad Garret's Comedy Club
MGM Grand. **Map** 3 C4. 8pm daily.
Tel (702) 891-7777.

Carrot Top
Luxor. **Map** 3 B5. 8pm Wed–Mon.
Tel (702) 262-4400.

David Copperfield
MGM Grand. **Map** 3 C4. 7pm & 9:30pm daily; also 4pm Sat & Sun.
Tel (702) 891-7777.

Gordie Brown
Golden Nugget. **Map** 2 D3. 7:30pm Tue–Thu, Sat & Sun.
Tel (866) 946-5336.

Las Vegas Live Comedy Club
Planet Hollywood. **Map** 3 C4. 9pm daily.
Tel (702) 785-5555.

Laugh Factory
Tropicana. **Map** 3 C4. 8:30pm & 10:30pm daily.
Tel (702) 739-2411.

Marc Savard Comedy Hypnosis
Planet Hollywood. **Map** 3 C4. 10pm Sat–Thu.
Tel (702) 785-5555.

The Mentalist
Planet Hollywood. **Map** 3 C4. 7:30pm Thu–Tue. **Tel** (702) 785-5555.

Penn and Teller
Rio. **Map** 3 B3. 9pm Sat–Wed. **Tel** (702) 777-7776.

Terry Fator
The Mirage. **Map** 3 C3. 7:30pm Mon–Thu.
Tel (702) 792-7777.

Headliner Shows

Britney Spears: Piece of Me
Planet Hollywood. **Map** 3 C4. 7:30pm Tue–Sat. **Tel** (702) 777-2782.

Donny and Marie
Flamingo Las Vegas. **Map** 3 C3. 7:30pm Tue–Sat. **Tel** (702) 733-3333.

Elton John – The Million Dollar Piano/ Celine Dion/Rod Stewart/Reba, Brooks & Dunn
Caesars Palace. **Map** 3 B3. 7:30pm, days vary. **Tel** (877) 723-8836.

Jennifer Lopez: All I Have
Planet Hollywood. **Map** 3 C4. 7:30pm Tue–Sat. **Tel** (702) 777-2782.

Wayne Newton: Up Close and Personal
Bally's. **Map** 3 C3. 7:30pm Wed–Sat. **Tel** (877) 603-4390.

Broadway Shows

Broadway
Smith Center for the Performing Arts. 361 Symphony Park Ave. **Map** 3 C3. Shows and times vary.
Tel (702) 930-8223.

The Bronx Wanderers
Bally's. **Map** 3 C2. 5pm Mon, Wed, Fri & Sat.
Tel (702) 967-4567.

Music and Performing Arts Venues

Las Vegas's music venues have always been famous for their atmosphere, grandeur, and quality. Some of the most impressive concert halls and auditoriums can be found in the mega-resorts located both on and off the Strip. Built on a majestic scale, these venues provide the perfect backdrop for performances by superstars such as Lionel Richie, Dolly Parton, Alanis Morissette, Tony Bennett, and Wayne Newton, to name a few.

Las Vegas also has a thriving theater, classical music, and dance community. The University of Nevada and Las Vegas's performing arts centers regularly host shows by the Nevada Ballet Theater, the Las Vegas Philharmonic, and several acclaimed classical artists.

Popular rock 'n' roll venue, The Joint, Hard Rock Hotel

Popular and Rock Music Concerts

Arguably the best place to experience a rock concert is **The Joint** at the Hard Rock Hotel. The 4,000-seat hall has great acoustics and features table, balcony, and theater seating, as well as plenty of space for standing guests too. Many notable rock stars have played here, including Alanis Morissette and the Rolling Stones. A close second is the Pearl Concert Theater at The Palms, a 2,500-seat venue that attracts big names such as Gwen Stefani. Situated between Monte Carlo and New York-New York, the **T-Mobile Arena** at The Park is the largest entertainment venue in Las Vegas with 20,000 seats. The Rolling Stones, Billy Joel, Coldplay, and Kanye West are among the artists who have performed here.

The **Garden Arena** at MGM Grand has one of the city's largest auditoriums and can seat up to 17,000 people. Only the most renowned headliners are called to perform at the Arena. In the past, this list has included Eric Clapton and Rod Stewart.

Another spacious venue is **The AXIS** at Planet Hollywood Resort & Casino. In addition to hosting mainstream performers and groups such as Styx, Lionel Richie, and Earth, Wind and Fire, the 7,000-seat theater has also showcased Broadway shows such as *Chicago* and *Rent*. Britney Spears and Jennifer Lopez headline shows that take place here quite frequently. The most lavish concert hall in Las Vegas is the **Colosseum** at Caesars Palace. The auditorium's rich architecture is reminiscent of a European opera house, and it periodically hosts concerts. Some of the regular headliners are singers Celine Dion, Elton John, Rod Stewart, and comedian Jerry Seinfeld.

Another terrific venue is the **House of Blues** *(see p143)* at Mandalay Bay. The nightclub books the best blues, jazz, and rock performers, who perform on a small floor surrounded by a tabled seating area and a balcony with theater seats. Among the top-notch stars who have played here are Bob Dylan, Taylor Dane, Etta James, Al Green, the Go-Gos, and Seal.

The **Smith Center for the Performing Arts** opened in 2012 in downtown's Symphony Park. Its Reynolds Theater and Cabaret Jazz performance halls host numerous productions of

Grand interior of the Colosseum concert auditorium, Caesars Palace

An actor in a production at UNLV's Performing Arts Center

Broadway shows, dance, jazz, orchestra, and pop music. It is home to the Las Vegas Philharmonic and Nevada Ballet Theatre.

Most of the hotels in Las Vegas have at least one showroom. Beyond the resorts, there is only one concert venue of note: the **Thomas & Mack Center** on the University of Nevada, Las Vegas (UNLV) campus, which hosts occasional music concerts.

Theater

Las Vegas has a flourishing theater arts community who stage their productions either on the UNLV campus, in public library auditoriums, or at schools throughout the city. UNLV's Performing Arts Center features the **Judy Bayley Theater**, a 500-seat theater that frequently presents events such as the Best of the New York Stage Series that features prominent jazz, cabaret from "the city that never sleeps", and Broadway artists such as Kristin Chenoweth, Dianne Reeves, and Ramsey Lewis. Also on the UNLV campus, **Black Box Theater** is an intimate, 175-seat center used for intimate theatrical events staged by amateur university groups and departments.

There are numerous amateur theater groups in Las Vegas that hold classes and conduct workshops, as well as produce several theatrical plays each year.

The **Las Vegas Little Theater** presents a range of contemporary dramas, while the **Rainbow Company** features family-oriented productions from a company of 40 members between the ages of 10 and 18. Recent classics have included *Cheaper by the Dozen, One to Grow On* and *A Year with Frog and Toad*.

Community centers that often host productions by local theatrical groups include the **Clark County Library Theater** on Flamingo Road, the **Clark County Amphitheater**, the **Summerlin Library Performing Arts Center**, and the **Charleston Heights Arts Center**. During summer, award-winning musicals are performed under the stars at the **Super Summer Theatre**, located in Red Rock Canyon at Spring Mountain Ranch State Park, about 20 miles (32 km) west of the Strip.

Classical Music and Ballet

The primary site for operas, symphonies, and ballet productions in Las Vegas is the **Artemus Ham Concert Hall** on the UNLV campus. It is also the home of The UNLV Chamber Music Series and frequently presents shows by various touring companies. The 2,000-seat theater has a 500-seat balcony, a huge stage, and movable orchestra towers. The university's highly celebrated annual cultural event, Charles Vanda Master Series, takes place here and features some of the biggest names in classical music and dance. Artists such as Leontyne Price and Itshak Perlman have visited Las Vegas as part of the series, as have such groups as the Vienna Chamber Orchestra and Moscow Grigorovich Ballet.

DIRECTORY

Popular & Rock Music Concerts

The AXIS
Planet Hollywood.
Map 3 C4.
Tel (702) 785-5555.

Colosseum
Caesars Palace. **Map** 3 B3.
Tel (702) 731-7110.

Garden Arena
MGM Grand. **Map** 3 C4.
Tel (702) 891-1111.

House of Blues
Mandalay Bay. **Map** 3 C5.
Tel (702) 632-7600.

The Joint
Hard Rock Hotel.
Map 4 D4.
Tel (702) 693-5000.

Smith Center for the Performing Arts
361 Symphony Park Ave.
Map 1 C3.
Tel (702) 749-2000.

T-Mobile Arena
The Park. **Map** 3 B-C4.
Tel (800) 840-9227.

Thomas & Mack Center
UNLV. **Map** 4 D4.
Tel (702) 739-3267.

Theater

Black Box Theater
UNLV. **Map** 4 E4.
Tel (702) 895-2787.

Charleston Heights Arts Center
800 S Brush St.
Tel (702) 229-6383.

Clark County Amphitheater
500 S Grand Central Pkwy.
Map 1 C3.
Tel (702) 455-8175.

Clark County Library Theater
1401 E Flamingo Rd. **Map** 4 E3. **Tel** (702) 507-3400.

Judy Bayley Theater
UNLV. **Map** 4 E4.
Tel (702) 895-2787.

Las Vegas Little Theater
3920 Schiff Dr.
Tel (702) 362-7996.

Rainbow Company
821 Las Vegas Blvd N.
Map 2 E2.
Tel (702) 229-6553.

Super Summer Theatre
6375 NV-159, Blue Diamond. **Map** 2 E2.
Tel (702) 579-7529.

Summerlin Library Performing Arts Center
1771 Inner Circle Dr.
Tel (702) 507-3860.

Classical Music and Ballet

Artemus Ham Concert Hall
UNLV.
Map 4 E4.
Tel (702) 895-2787.

Nightclubs, Lounges, and Bars

No city in the world has more to offer in the form of after-dark excitement than Las Vegas. From hip hotel nightclubs to punk discos and from flashy bars to retro dance clubs – it's all here, basking in neon, blinking until dawn. For decades the city's nightlife revolved around the hotel casinos, but the nightclub scene is no longer the exclusive province of the gaming resorts. As the city has grown, so has the number of nightclubs, sports bars, cowboy saloons, and other after-dark haunts. Among the plethora of new nightlife, Las Vegas has spawned a new genre of pub, the ultra lounge. These upscale bars are often chic, exclusive, and on top of everyone's "A" list.

Party atmosphere on the dance floor at Hakkasan

Hotel Nightclubs

Intrigue *(see p63)* at Wynn Las Vegas is a popular hot spot for the nocturnal set, featuring an open-air dance floor and 90-ft-(28-m-) high waterfall.

Marquee at The Cosmopolitan is centered around the resort's pool, and is a massive megaclub with seven bars, an elevated dance floor, and views of the Strip. There's also a daytime beach club and eight cabanas, each with a private spa and an infinity plunge pool.

XS at Encore, currently the highest grossing nightclub in the world, draws some of the biggest crowds with more than 40 A-list DJ celebrities like Avicii, Zedd, will.i.am, and Diplo. The club's design was inspired by the curves of the human body and features gold leaf sculptures of female torsos.

A magnet for visiting celebrities, **Hakkasan** has picked up where Studio 54 left off, with a constant flow of top DJs such as Tiesto, Fergie, Steve Aoki, and Calvin Harris. The five-level club includes a restaurant, an elevated DJ booth with floor-to-ceiling LED screens, a marble-panelled private members club, and the Pavilion, an oriental themed area with a garden.

Hyde Bellagio has an expansive terrace with an ideal vantage point overlooking the Fountains of Bellagio. Designed to represent an opulent Italian villa, it offers an early evening experience, opening at 5pm.

Drai's has a massive 4,500-person capacity, with the most state-of-the-art high definition LEDs in production, including a towering 80-sided LED disco ball. It sometimes detonates custom rooftop firework shows from its perch atop The Cromwell's 16th floor.

Vanity at Hard Rock Hotel & Casino is one of the most fashionable and sexy nightclubs in town. A popular spot for locals, the club is powered by up-and-coming DJs spinning indie, electronic, rock, and pop sounds. The 14,000-sq-ft (1,301-sq-m) nightclub features a sunken dance floor, two marble bars, 50 VIP booths, an outdoor terrace including five cabanas with direct pool access, and a women's lounge. The rich decor is guaranteed to bedazzle – adorned with pearls and crystals fused with bronze and gold, surrounded by antique mirrors. At the center is a cyclone chandelier with over 20,000 crystals, each lit with color-changing LED lights.

Stand-Alone Nightclubs

Las Vegas is home to a couple of highly popular, non-resort nightclubs with a number of different rooms to dance away the night in. Located at Town Square, **Blue Martini** is a restaurant, bar and nightclub, all rolled neatly into one elegant package. It's the place in town to sip a martini and watch one of the live bands that perform nightly.

Located next to the Fremont Street Experience, is **Downtown Cocktail Room**, a sophisticated and swanky gathering place. The cleverly disguised door is marked only by a tiny Downtown sign and the speakeasy atmosphere is part of the appeal. There are DJs Tuesday through Saturday.

Ultra Lounges

Most of the ultra lounges in the city have a private club atmosphere with plush furnishings and frequent live entertainment. One of the most exclusive is **Ghostbar** at the Palms. Located on the hotel's 55th floor, the bar offers stunning views of the Strip.

Neon lighting and futuristic setting at Ghostbar, Palms Hotel

Sports fans watch the screens at Bally's lounge sports book

Sports Bars

Virtually all the casinos in Las Vegas that have a substantial sports book also have a bar either in or adjacent to the book. Most have wide-screen TV monitors to view the sporting action. Among the best are at The Palazzo, Bellagio, Caesars Palace, Bally's, Gold Coast, and Westgate Las Vegas. Perhaps the quintessential sports bar is **Lagasse's Stadium** at The Palazzo, complete with a sports book, more than 100 HD TVs, luxury boxes, plush stadium-style seating, and billiard tables.

Las Vegas has many non-casino sports bars as well, such as **PT's Pub**, with more than 20 locations.

Waterfalls, giant Buddha statues, and an artificial sandy beach are the major features of Asian-themed club **TAO** at The Venetian. At the top of the hotel, it is open daily during pool season and plays host to an incredible party scene during the day. Enjoy magnificent views from the terrace.

Surrender at Encore Las Vegas is an extension of the resort's Andrea's restaurant, and guests can move from dining to dancing as the evening progresses. A large 90-ft snake is positioned behind the club's back bar, and go-go dancers perform on poles surrounding the VIP tables. An impressive roster of resident DJs includes Marshmello, RL Grime, and Diplo. By day it becomes Encore Beach Club, with cabanas, bungalows, infinity dipping pools, palm trees and balconies overlooking the Strip.

One of the best spots to enjoy live music is the **House of Blues** at Mandalay Bay. Its intimate Southern folk-style setting is complimented by the jazz and blues musicians who play here.

For something a little different, head to **Minus 5 Ice Lounge**. Vodka is the drink of choice and comes served in ice glasses. There are also ice sculptures and ice furniture.

Western Saloons

For a real taste of the Wild West, head for any of the many saloons and bars that Las Vegas has to offer. With its great live bands, **Stoney's Rockin' Country** is the hotspot for country aficionados. Another local favorite is **Saddle N Spurs Saloon**, with weekly two-step and line-dancing lessons, while the hottest Wild West bar is **Gilley's Saloon** with its bikini bull riding and live music.

DIRECTORY

Hotel Nightclubs

Drai's
The Cromwell Las Vegas.
Map 3 C3.
Tel (702) 777-3800.

Hakkasan
MGM Grand. **Map** 3 C4.
Tel (702) 891-7888.

Hyde Bellagio
Bellagio. **Map** 3 C3.
Tel (702) 693-8300.

Intrigue
Wynn Las Vegas. **Map** 3
C2. **Tel** (702) 770-3375.

Marquee
The Cosmopolitan. **Map** 3
C4. **Tel** (702) 333-9000.

Vanity
Hard Rock Hotel & Casino.
Map 4 D4. **Tel** (702) 693-5222.

XS
Encore Las Vegas. **Map** 3
C2. **Tel** (702) 770-0097.

Stand-Alone Nightclubs

Blue Martini
Town Square, 6593 Las
Vegas Blvd S. **Map** 4 D2.
Tel (702) 949-2583.

Downtown Cocktail Room
111 Las Vegas Blvd S.
Map 2 D3.
Tel (702) 880-3696.

Ultra Lounges

Ghostbar
Palms Hotel & Casino.
Map 3 A3. **Tel** (702) 942-7777.

House of Blues
Mandalay Bay.
Map 3 C5.
Tel (702) 632-7777.

Minus 5 Ice Lounge
Mandalay Bay.
Map 3 C5.
Tel (702) 632-7714.

Surrender
Encore Las Vegas.
Map 3 C2.
Tel (702) 770-3633.

TAO
The Venetian.
Map 3 C3.
Tel (702) 388-8588.

Sports Bars

Lagasse's Stadium
The Palazzo.
Map 3 C3.
Tel (702) 607-2655.

PT's Pub
1089 E Tropicana Ave.
Map 3 D4.
Tel (702) 895-9480.

Western Saloons

Gilley's Saloon
Treasure Island.
Map 3 C2.
Tel (702) 894-7111.

Saddle N Spurs Saloon
2333 N Jones Blvd.
Tel (702) 646-6292.

Stoney's Rockin' Country
6611 Las Vegas Blvd S #160.
Tel (702) 435-2855.

Gay and Lesbian Venues

With a vibrant and ever-flourishing gay community, Las Vegas has much to offer its gay visitors in the way of entertainment and recreation. The city's Gay Quarter, also known as Paradise Fruit Loop – though not on the scale of LA's West Hollywood or San Francisco's Castro district – is mainly concentrated along Harmon Avenue, Paradise Road, and the Naples Drive areas. It consists of a cluster of businesses, bars, nightclubs, and restaurants – all conveniently located a stone's throw from each other. Another popular area among the local gay population is Commercial Center, a past-its-prime shopping center at the corner of Sahara Avenue and Maryland Parkway. In addition, Las Vegas's Gay and Lesbian Community Center sponsors frequent social events and is a venue for various gay group meetings.

A performer at the famous gay hangout, Piranha Nightclub

Information Sources

Las Vegas is home to more than 75 organizations representing the interests of the city's gay population. Publications such as **Q Vegas**, a monthly magazine serving the gay and lesbian community, does an excellent job of providing information about local bars, restaurants, workshops, local politics, support groups, professional services, events, and more. Copies of the magazine are available in all gay bars, bookstores, and coffee shops, and online at QVegas.com. Various websites, including Gayvegas.com and Gay.vegas also provide extensive information. These sites offer advice on lodging, nightlife, and restaurants in Las Vegas.

The main support group in Las Vegas is **The Center**, which frequently sponsors social events, and is a gathering place for various gay and lesbian groups. It also provides free and confidential HIV tests. The **Lambda Business and Professional Association** offers an online business directory and also a support and development group for gays.

Gay Quarter

One of the best places to get local news and information on gay-related events and happenings is the city's well-stocked bookshop, **Get Booked**. Located in the heart of the Gay Quarter, this small shop features a collection of gay, lesbian, and feminist print material. These include journals, magazines, flyers, and newsletters. The store hosts readings and book signings of local LGBT authors.

Just a few blocks away is **Piranha Nightclub**, a popular dance club with daily themed events. It often stays open until sunrise and has a tank with live piranhas.

Just around the corner of Naples Drive is the entrance to **Freezone**, one of Las Vegas's most popular gay bars. Mondays and Tuesdays are reserved for Karaoke at this club, while Thursday is Boyz Night. On Fridays and Saturdays, Freezone stages the *Drag Madness* show at 10pm. This exciting dance party usually lasts till the small hours of the morning.

The gay scene has also extended out to East Tropicana. At Tropicana and Pecos is **The Las Vegas Eagle**, a staple in the Las Vegas gay bar scene. Open 24 hours, it is known for its underwear nights, which take place on Tuesdays and Fridays, while Karaoke is on Tuesdays.

Also at Tropicana is the **Goodtimes Bar & Nightclub**. Set in the old Liberace Plaza, and open 24 hours, it is a quiet gay bar by day, but at night it becomes a nightclub with an active dance scene that lasts till dawn. The club also hosts contests and drag shows.

Decorated in a rustic style, **FunHog Ranch** attracts a

Get Booked, a comprehensive bookstore for gay and lesbian literature

Gay Parade

good crowd with its festive atmosphere and central location. While fetish and leather wear is strongly encouraged, it is not compulsory. The staff at Fun[log are renowned for their friendly service.

Commercial Center

The center has four good bars, each with its own unique ambience. **Spotlight Lounge**, which has become very popular with locals since it opened in 1998, offers everything from casino games to free beer nights. Known as probably the friendliest gay bar in town, Spotlight Lounge welcomes everyone regardless of their backgrounds.

There's a different kind of hospitality at the **Badlands Saloon**, a small neighborhood country-western bar, which is also the original home of the Nevada Gay Rodeo Association. The Saloon hosts a bingo event for the benefit of local charities on Tuesdays.

Situated at the beginning of the Arts District, formerly known as Snick's Place, **Bastille on 3rd** is considered the oldest gay bar in the city. Also the only gay bar in downtown Las Vegas, it offers a clean, fun

A unique road sign, Las Vegas

atmosphere, friendly staff, reasonable prices, and custom signature cocktails.

True to its name, **The Phoenix**, has risen from the ashes of its predecessor, The Escape Lounge. Open 24 hours daily, the hi-tech lounge offers a spacious bar and dance floor, DJ nook, outdoor patio, and a massive projection screen for patrons to watch their friends play video games. Weekly events include underwear night on Tuesdays, *American Horror Story* Viewing Party on Wednesdays, Karaoke on Thursdays and Sundays and the *Phired up Phridays* live drag performance on Fridays.

Off The Strip

Located a little way east of the Strip and open 24 hours daily, **The Garage** will appeal to car and automobile enthusiasts, with a mechanical theme and impressive interiors that resemble a car garage. Cozy booths make it the perfect den for those looking for a relaxed and laid-back atmosphere. There is also a shuffleboard, a collection of pool tables, darts, TVs, and video games for entertainment. Drink specials are offered daily, and two for one on any drink from 11am to 7pm.

Slightly to the west of the Strip is **Charlie's Las Vegas**, a country-and-western men's nightclub. The Men of Charlie's is a social group that donates money to different charities. Charlie's hosts fundraisers and has a happy hour twice a day (times vary). Theme nights are a regular and popular feature on the social calendar, ranging from Latin dance to underwear night. Karaoke takes place on Mondays, free line dance lessons are offered on Thursdays, while Fridays are reserved for the *Studs and Suds*, a revue of wet go-go dancers showering on stage.

OUTDOOR ACTIVITIES AND SPORTS

Beyond the lure of the Las Vegas casinos and malls lies some of the country's most magnificent wilderness waiting to be explored by hikers and rock climbers, anglers, bird-watchers, skiers, and snowboarders. From the pine-fringed creeks of Red Rock Canyon and the alpine forestry of Mount Charleston to the blue-green grandeur of Lake Mead, enthusiasts will find a never-ending source of outdoor adventures.

Besides these outlying areas, many of which lie within an hour's drive from Las Vegas, the city's resorts and clubs offer a wide range of facilities for activities such as tennis, basketball, cycling, rollerblading, swimming, and jogging, to name a few. Add to this Las Vegas's internationally renowned, superbly designed golf courses and you have a recreational menu more diverse than any of the city's legendary buffets.

Hotel Recreation and Health Clubs

Most of the resorts in Las Vegas present a variety of sports-related opportunities to their visitors. These include tennis, racquetball, basketball, and volleyball courts, as well as swimming pools and jogging tracks. Those who prefer running on grass can opt for the local parks or the athletic fields at University of Nevada, Las Vegas (UNLV). Some hotels, such as Westgate Las Vegas, offer scenic, meandering paths – ideal for cyclists and roller bladers.

Las Vegas also hosts numerous health clubs. One of the city's premier fitness centers is the **Las Vegas Athletic Club**. It contains all the usual gym equipment, along with virtual-reality exercise machines.

Hiking and Rock Climbing

One of the best destinations for hiking and rock climbing is Red Rock Canyon *(see p82)* – just a 20-minute drive from Las Vegas. Guides and area maps are available at the canyon's visitor center. Most of the hikes are 2–3 mile- (3–5 km-) long hikes over moderate terrain. One of the most popular hiking trails is at Pine Creek Canyon, where you can trek past the sweet-smelling pinion pines to a meadow with the ruins of a historic homestead. Visitors can also take a close look at the area's geological history on the Keystone Thrust trail, a moderate 3-mile (5-km) walk to the older gray dolomite on top of the younger red-and-buff sandstone. The sheer rock faces of the mountains entice many climbers as well. Contact **Jackson Hole Mountain Guides** for information on guided climbs. Another favorite location is Mount Charleston *(see p83)*, which is a 45-minute drive from Las Vegas. The hiking trails here vary from easy, half-hour walks to two-day

Sheer sandstone cliffs at Red Rock Canyon

treks. Most of the trailheads are accessible by car and have water and restroom facilities. One of the trails leads to Deer Creek Road (State Route 158), which is a short distance from the Desert View Scenic Outlook – a point that offers a breathtaking panorama of the valley and dry lakebeds below. The 1–2 hour hike to the top of Cathedral Rock, which provides spectacular views of Kyle Canyon, is also worth a visit. Check with the **Mount Charleston Ranger Station** for directions and maps before starting. Most of the trails are open throughout the year, but some are closed during winter and early spring. Be sure to follow the marked trails, especially at higher elevations. The vertical cliffs can be dangerous and have claimed lives.

Water Sports

The scenic shoreline of Lake Mead *(see p84)* is one of the most sought-after destinations for water sports, sailing, waterskiing, and white-water rafting. The 11-mile (18-km) stretch of Colorado River from Hoover Dam to Willow Beach is open year-round to rafts, canoes, and kayaks, but the best times for canoeing, kayaking, and rafting are spring and fall. A permit from the **US Bureau of Reclamation** is required for river rafting. Further information can be obtained from the visitor center at Lake Mead. Those who do not have their own equipment can rent boats and related supplies at the

Las Vegas Boat Harbor and several other shops lining the marinas on the lake.

A fisherman on the shores of Lake Mead Recreational Area

Fishing

It is open season on fishing all through the year at Lake Mead, where anglers will find an abundance of catfish, trout, bluegill, crappie, and striped bass. Anglers consider the Overton arm of Lake Mead *(see p84)* an ideal location for striped bass. Also worth trying are Calico Basin, the Meadows, Stewart's Point, and Meat Hole.

Fishing is excellent along the Colorado River, south of Hoover Dam, and extending to Laughlin and Bullhead City as well. The cold water below Davis Dam, near Laughlin, is also a good spot, while the area above the dam on Lake Mohave is noted for its bass and rainbow trout.

A fishing license is required by all anglers 12 years of age and older. Non-resident fishermen can purchase a year-long license, but at almost double the cost of a resident fishing license, which requires a minimum six months' residency. Fishermen can also purchase a one-day fishing permit. Baits, tackles, fishing lines, and other goods, as well as licenses can be obtained from marinas and equipment stores such as **Las Vegas Bass Pro Shops** and **Big 5 Sporting Goods**.

Bird-Watching

Although many southern Nevada wilderness areas are suitable for bird-watching, the grounds of **Corn Creek Field Station** at the Desert National Wildlife Range are some of the most frequented.

The natural springs of Corn Creek have formed upper and lower ponds that are connected by a gurgling brook. This small, rugged oasis boasts an astonishing selection of bird life. The fruited mulberry trees attract pine crossbills, tanagers, grosbeaks, and orioles. Other species, such as Wilson's warblers, western bluebirds, flycatchers, and Cooper's hawks, can also be seen. The bird life at this sanctuary is so diverse that the Audubon Society, a wildlife conservation organization, has included it as part of its Adopt a Refuge program.

Winter Sports

The snow-laden slopes of Mount Charleston are a sought-after location for a wide array of winter sports. These include skiing, snowboarding, and snowmobiling. Visitors can also enjoy magnificent cross-country skiing at Lee Canyon, Scout Canyon, Bristlecone Trail, and Mack's Canyon. Most of the resorts at Mount Charleston run snow-making equipment from November through April, depending on the weather conditions. There are also plenty of equipment rental outlets although resort packages usually include skis, lift passes, and lessons as well.

DIRECTORY

Health Clubs

Las Vegas Athletic Club
2655 S Maryland Pkwy.
Map 4 E1.
Tel (702) 822-5822.

Hiking and Rock Climbing

Jackson Hole Mountain Guides
8221 W Charleston, Suite 106.
Tel (702) 254-0885.
w jhmg.com

Mount Charleston Ranger Station
Tel (702) 515-5400.

Water Sports

Las Vegas Boat Harbor
Hemenway Harbor, Lake Mead.
Tel (702) 293-1191.
w lasvegasboatharbor.com

US Bureau of Reclamation
PO Box 61470, Boulder City.
Tel (702) 293-8000.

Fishing

Big 5 Sporting Goods
2797 S Maryland Pkwy.
Map 4 E1.
Tel (702) 734-6664.

Las Vegas Bass Pro Shops
Silverton Hotel, 8200 Dean Martin Drive. **Tel** (702) 730-5200.

Bird-watching

Corn Creek Field Station
Desert National Wildlife Refuge, Hwy 95, 8 miles west of Kyle Canyon Rd.
Tel (702) 879-6110.

Skiers and tourists at a snow-covered resort on Mount Charleston

Golf

Las Vegas's year-round warm weather makes it a golfer's paradise, which attracts both amateurs and professionals. Within easy driving distance of the Strip resorts are more than 35 beautifully designed golf courses, many internationally acclaimed, some positioned in the midst of spectacular scenery. Although almost a third of these are private, the city has many public courses as well. There are essentially two types of courses in Las Vegas – the standard 18-hole courses found in most communities, and the desert golf course or "target" course, in which only tee boxes, fairways, and greens are maintained and the surrounding natural desert landscape is left intact.

The fairway at Las Vegas National Golf Club

General Information

A large number of golf courses in Las Vegas are private, so players will need to be acquainted with a club member in order to book a tee time. It might be better to plan ahead and get a decent tee time at one of the city's public tracks. Most courses accept reservations up to seven days in advance. The winter and spring months are the busiest seasons for golf so try to make bookings as far in advance as possible. Visitors can rent golf clubs from pro shops at the golf course or at selected stores in town such as the **TaylorMade Golf Experience** or the **Las Vegas Golf and Tennis**. The dress code on the course is casual, though most require collared shirts and no cut-off jeans. Soft spikes are a must.

Many courses will charge at least $100 a round, and most clubs expect a cart to be used, which is an additional cost. However, there are a few layouts where a round can be played for less than $50. You may also find some real bargains during the hot summer months of June, July, and August when prices are at their lowest.

Some hotels offer golf packages to their guests. Check with the booking office or concierge upon arrival.

Las Vegas Courses

The city's municipal golf course, **Angel Park**, offers players the chance to enjoy the challenge and beauty of two Arnold Palmer-designed 18-hole courses, known as the Palm and the Mountain. The park's Cloud Nine course offers 12 holes and a par-3 layout with replica holes from the world's most famous par 3s.

If you were wondering what "target" courses are like, visit the **Badlands Golf Club**. The scenic 27-hole course is built around picturesque desert arroyos. This target course was designed by Johnny Miller and is not for the faint of heart as it demands immense accuracy over its 7,000-yard (6,400-m), par-72 layout.

Just steps away from the Mandalay Bay and Four Seasons hotels, the **Bali Hai Golf Club** features thick stands of palm trees, big water hazards, tropical plants, and flowers, all set in a South Seas design.

The **Las Vegas National Golf Club** was established in 1961. This par-72 course has a classic layout with trees, grass fairways, and deep greens. It was also the scene of Tiger Woods' first PGA (Professional Golf Association) victory in 1996. Bargain hunters can get a great round of golf for under $100 at **Las Vegas Paiute Golf Resort**, located on the Snow

The expansive, beautifully maintained grounds at Angel Park Golf Club

Greens at Legacy Golf Club, overlooking Nevada's desert landscape

DIRECTORY

Angel Park
100 S Rampart Blvd.
Tel (702) 254-4653.
W angelpark.com

Badlands Golf Club
9119 Alta Dr. **Tel** (702) 363-0754.
W badlandsgc.com

Bali Hai Golf Club
5160 Las Vegas Blvd S.
Map 3 C5. **Tel** (702) 450-8000.
W balihaigolfclub.com

Black Mountain Golf Course
500 Greenway Rd, Henderson.
Tel (702) 565-7933.
W golfblackmountain.com

Las Vegas Golf and Tennis
4711 Dean Martin Dr.
Tel (702) 892-9999. W lvgolf.com

Las Vegas National Golf Club
1911 E Desert Inn Rd. **Map** 4 F2.
Tel (702) 734-1796.
W lasvegasnational.com

Las Vegas Paiute Golf Resort
10325 Nu-Wav Kaiv Blvd.
Tel (702) 658-1400.
W lvpaiutegolf.com.com

Legacy Golf Club
130 Par Excellence Dr.
Tel (702) 897-2187.
W thelegacygc.com

Painted Desert
5555 Painted Mirage Rd.
Tel (702) 655-2570.
W painteddesertgc.com

Royal Links Golf Club
5955 E Vegas Valley Dr.
Tel (702) 450-8000.
W royallinksgolfclub.com

Shadow Creek Golf Club
3 Shadow Creek Dr, N Las Vegas.
Tel (702) 399-6495.
W shadowcreek.com

TaylorMade Golf Experience
6730 Las Vegas Blvd S.
Tel (702) 896-4100. W taylormadegolfexperience.com

Wynn Las Vegas Golf Course and Country Club
3131 Las Vegas Blvd S. **Map** 3 C2.
Tel (702) 770-4653.
W wynnlasvegas.com

Mountain Indian Reservation 20 miles (32 km) from the Strip.

The exclusive **Royal Links Golf Club** was designed to simulate play on some of the finest courses on the British Open rotation. Tee times here are somewhat pricey, with rates typically around $200.

The enormous 18-hole par-70 **Wynn Las Vegas Golf Course and Country Club** is set right on the Strip. It is exclusively for the use of guests at the luxury resort. Topgolf, located behind the MGM Grand, has a great golf driving range and simulator facility.

Farther Afield Courses

Designed by golf course architect, Jay Morrish, **Painted Desert** is the former site of the Nevada Open and is consistently rated as one of the best-maintained public courses in Nevada. The course is set within a natural desert habitat with challenging greens and roughs, and there are also several lakes that come into play. The desert areas provide a beautiful setting not found in many courses. The clubhouse provides a wide range of facilities, including a restaurant and a golf shop.

Rated among the best 100 courses in the US, the 7,200-yard (6,580-m), par-72 **Legacy Golf Club** course in Henderson features wall-to-wall turf, two lakes, rolling terrain, and plenty of trees. A notable highlight is

the Devil's Triangle, where a canyon creek runs through the 11th, 12th, and 13th holes, spoiling many fine tee shots. Players who master the triple header walk away calling it "Amen Corner."

The **Black Mountain Golf Course** in Henderson is a good course for beginners, but still has plenty of sand bunkers and two lakes to keep the game interesting. Established in 1959, the course is peppered with cacti and Joshua trees. The green fees here are usually under $100.

The **Shadow Creek Golf Club**, located in North Las Vegas, is the only course in Southern Nevada to have earned a place in *Golf* magazine's survey of the world's top 100 courses. The layout at Shadow Creek was designed by world-renowned golf course architect Tom Fazio and hotelier Steve Wynn. The woodland-style course is private, and only guests staying at any of the MGM Mirage properties – including MGM Grand, The Mirage, Bellagio, and ARIA – are allowed to play here.

Tiger Woods

Major Tournaments

The Shriners Hospitals for Children Open *(see p34)* continues a long history of professional golf in Las Vegas. The tournament was the first in the history of the PGA Tour to offer a $1 million purse and the

first non-major to offer a $5 million purse. The three-day, 72-hole event features amateurs along with tour professionals.

GAMBLING IN LAS VEGAS

Despite its growing fame as an all-round adult amusement park, Las Vegas remains famous for its casinos. More than 42 million visitors come to the city every year and, on average, each spends about $80 gambling every day. Do not come expecting to make your fortune; with a combined annual income of $16 billion, the casinos appear to have the advantage.

The secret pleasure of gambling is the lure of the unknown – you never know what the next card will be. Casinos know this and aim to keep you playing for as long as possible. Free drinks are available for gamblers, but it is not a good idea to gamble without a clear head. Before you start, decide on an amount that you can afford to lose and be sure to stick to it. For a first-timer, the casino can seem daunting, but, with a basic understanding of the rules *(see pp152–7)*, most of the games are relatively simple. Some hotels have gaming guides on their in-house TV channels and Las Vegas's visitor center supplies printed guides. Several large casinos give free lessons at the tables.

Row upon row of slot machines on the gaming floor of New York-New York casino *(see p45)*

General Information

You need to be at least 21 years old to gamble in Las Vegas, so be sure to carry some ID at all times if you look young. Children are not welcome on the casino floor at any time. If you hit a substantial slot jackpot, the casino will ask for identification, usually a driver's license, and will note down your Social Security number. This is in keeping with certain IRS regulations regarding jackpots of $1,200 or more. Nonresident winners are subject to a with-holding tax of 30 per cent to be deducted from the jackpot winnings before payment. All Las Vegas casinos deal in the same basic commodity – a chance to beat the odds. As the casino enjoys a statistical advantage in every game, the longer you expose yourself to it, the greater your chance of losing. The house advantage is the result of a combination of things – the odds or percentages inherent in the game, rules tailored to favor the casino, payoffs at less than actual odds, or predetermined payoffs like those in slot machines. The casino's edge may be small, as in baccarat, blackjack, and sports betting, or enormous, as in keno and the wheel of fortune, but it still generates billions of dollars a year in gambling profits. In rare instances it can be highly profitable for the gambler too.

Tipping is common in a casino, but is not a requirement. It can be to your advantage to tip when you first sit down at the table, as it is a good idea to get the dealer on your side. It is casino etiquette to tip the dealer if you are winning at the tables. Slot winners usually tip the change person about 5 to 10 per cent of their winnings.

Poker chips

Guests placing bets on the roulette table at a casino in Las Vegas

Anatomy of a Casino

Every casino has a main cashier, also known as the main cage by the staff. This is where players can establish credit, cash checks, and redeem their chips and vouchers for cash. The cage, however, will not sell you chips, which you must purchase from the dealers when you "buy in" – the amount of cash you use to enter a game – at the various tables. In addition to the main cage, most casinos have

Casino player's card

other satellite cashiers. Slot machines usually take only paper money or vouchers bought from the cashier. Nearly every casino has a slot club, which awards its members various types of freebies for a required amount of play. Ordinarily, slot club members accumulate points while playing, and then redeem their points for free meals, room discounts, merchandise, and any other benefits that might be on offer. There is no charge for joining a slot club and you can get more information about it at the slot promotions or redemption booth located in the casino.

You can also expect to find automated teller machines (ATMs) placed at several points in most casinos. But you will rarely, if ever, find any clocks in the casino. The hotel executives want their customers to play as long as possible, so clocks are never part of the decor. The same is true for windows. You will not get the chance to see a sunset through a glass window as the casinos want time to stand still during the entire gambling experience.

Gambling Etiquette

Much of the etiquette in the casino stems from common courtesy. However, there are some guidelines that should be kept in mind. If you are browsing among table games – blackjack, Caribbean Stud, and poker – note that the chairs are for players, not observers. If you want to watch a game, it is best to stand in the back or to the side of the players. This is not so true in other areas of the casino, such as the slot floor, keno lounge, or sports book. Here, sitting is generally okay, although it is not uncommon for slot players to request that you either play or leave if there aren't any machines free.

Most disputes arise at the slot machines. Players often leave to get a drink, wash their hands,

Tips

- Always play within your means. That is, only gamble with money you can afford to lose.
- Gambling is meant to be an enjoyable form of entertainment. Hence head for the tables where players are talking and laughing. Chances are, a row of glum faces means that you are in for an equally dull time.
- Dealers can prevent inexperienced gamblers from making silly mistakes and will usually explain the finer points and intricacies of the game if asked.
- Slots is one of the easiest games and a lot of fun too. But take the time to understand what you are betting and what it takes to win. This philosophy should extend to all the other games as well.

Casinos Offering Gaming Lessons

Boulder Station
Daily. Poker: 2pm.

Circus Circus
Daily. Blackjack: 10:30am;
Roulette: 11:30am;
Craps: 12:30pm.

Excalibur
Daily. Poker: noon;
Roulette: 11am and 7pm;
Blackjack: 11:30am and 7:30pm;
Craps: noon and 8pm.

Gold Coast
Fri–Sun. Craps: 11:30am.

Golden Nugget
Daily. Poker: 10am;
Craps: Mon–Wed 10am, Thu–Sun
10am and noon;
Pai Gow: 10am;
Roulette: 11:30am;
Blackjack: 11am.

Luxor
Daily. Roulette, Craps,
and Blackjack: all at noon.

Mandalay Bay
Daily. Poker: 2pm.

Monte Carlo
Daily. Craps: 11am.

The Palazzo & The Venetian
Sun–Fri. Craps: 11am & 7pm
(plus Sat 11am);
Blackjack: 11:30am, 11:30am &
7:30pm (plus Sat 11:30am);
Roulette: 11:45am & 7:45pm
(plus Sat 11:45am).

South Point
Tue, Thu. Craps: 10:15am
(plus Sat 11:15am).

Stratosphere
Sat and Sun. Poker: 8am.

or buy cigarettes, and find someone else at "their" machine when they come back. Always ask a change person or floor supervisor to baby-sit your machine while you are away. They are usually happy to do it.

Since everything in the casino is recorded by the "eye in the sky" security system, do not hesitate to take any disputes to a higher authority – the casino manager. The tape will tell the tale and resolve the issue.

Craps

Often the most fun game on the floor, a sense of camaraderie develops in craps because players are betting either with or against the "shooter" (whoever has the dice) on what the next number rolled will be. The aim of the shooter's first roll, or "coming out," is to make 7 or 11 in any combination (say 3/4, 5/6) to win. A roll of 2, 3, or 12 is craps; everyone loses and the shooter rolls the dice again. If a total of 4, 5, 6, 8, 9, or 10 is rolled, this becomes the "point" number, and the shooter must roll this number again before rolling a 7 to win. Craps etiquette says that you place your money on the table rather than handing it to the dealer; wooden holders around the table will keep your chips. Always roll with one hand; the dice must hit the end of the table. All betting and laying down of chips must be completed before the next roll.

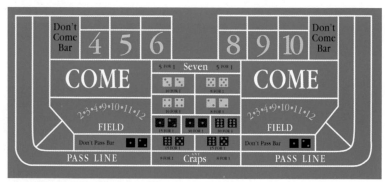

Craps table seen from above, showing the various boxes and areas for the many bets

Bets

Craps can seem confusing as there appears to be a lot going on at any one time; this is largely due to the wide variety of bets it is possible to lay. If you are a beginner, the following bets are the best ones to lay.

Laying bets during a craps game

The Pass Line Bet

In this, you are basically betting that the shooter will roll a 7/11 on the first roll in order for you to win. The odds at this point are even, so if you do win you get the same amount you laid down. If a point number is rolled, the shooter has to throw the same number before he rolls another 7. Since there are more ways to roll a 7 than any point number, it pays to take the odds once the shooter has a point, which means placing an additional bet behind your pass line bet. This will pay you the true house odds if the shooter rolls his point. The odds change according to the number, so check with the dealer first.

The Don't Pass Bet

This is the opposite of a pass line bet. The aim here is for the shooter to lose by throwing a 2 or 3 on the first roll, or by rolling a losing 7, which happens before he makes his point number.

The Come Bet

This is an optional bet you can make during the game, when your money comes to the next number that rolls. For example, if the point is 6 you make a come bet, and the shooter rolls an 8. Your come bet "comes" to the 8, and now you have two numbers in play. You can also take odds on a come bet.

The Place Bet

Another way of getting additional numbers is by making a place bet. In this case, you simply pick the number you want and make a place bet on that number. The advantage of place bets is that you pick the number yourself and you can remove your bet at any time. The disadvantage is that the casino charges you from 50 cents to $1 for each $5 bet you place.

Slot Machines

Slots of every kind dominate Las Vegas casinos. The simple one-armed bandit, where pulling a handle spins the reels and a win results from a row of cherries or some other icon, has been largely superseded by computerized push-button machines offering a confusing variety of plays. There are basically two kinds of slots; flat-top machines and progressive machines. A flat-top machine has a range of fixed

One-armed bandit slot

payouts depending on different arrangements of winning symbols. There will usually be a choice of stakes, and if you hit a winning display you will win less if you play a low stake than if you play the limits.

On progressive slots, you give up smaller jackpots in exchange for winning a progressive jackpot. To be eligible for the progressive jackpot, the

Slot machines lined along the casino floor at Excalibur hotel

maximum number of coins allowed must always be played. The payout on these machines increases as you play, and the rising jackpot figure is displayed above each machine. The biggest payout is currently from the Megabucks slots, which operate all across Nevada. A software engineer from Los Angeles playing at Excalibur at the Desert Inn won almost $40 million on a machine there in March 2003.

Virtually all slot machines in casinos now take only vouchers or paper money. A player inserts $1, $5, $10, $20 or $100 bills, or vouchers for money he/she has won on other machines into the receptor of a machine. When play stops, the machine issues a paper voucher for the amount of money that has been won, or not spent, which the player can cash in.

Slot machine at Caesars Palace

players to control dozens of cards at one time. Bingo is a relatively inexpensive game. Sessions often cost $4 to $5 and players get free drinks and can play at practically any time of day. Typically, casinos offer a series of sessions, of one or two hours duration, that begin at 9am and run on until 11pm. Arizona Charlie's offers bingo sessions all day at odd-numbered hours at both of its locations. New cards must be purchased for each session. Winnings can be huge. Casinos such as Sam's Town, Fiesta, and Station Casinos have instituted progressive jackpots, often reaching six figures. These jackpots are usually placed on a cover-all game. That is, all the numbers must be covered within a certain number of balls. Most of the cover-alls start with around 46 to 48 numbers, and the casino adds one number per week until someone hits it.

Slot Machine Tips

- Always play the machine limit because if you win, you will receive the maximum amount.
- Wins on both types of machine allow you to rack up credits, which you can use for subsequent bets. Monitoring your display of credits will help keep track of how much you are spending. If your original stake was 10 quarters and you win 30, using credits allows you to decide to walk away when the credit display is down to 20, leaving you 10 quarters up.
- Join a slot club. Most casinos have clubs that offer a range of incentives to get you to play with them; which range from cash back to various discounts. Members are also issued an electronic-strip plastic loyalty card.

Bingo

A very popular game with Las Vegans is bingo. In fact, generally the city's bingo halls are located in off-the-Strip casinos, such as Gold Coast. Plaza is the only casino located downtown that has a bingo hall.

Bingo is a very simple game. Players purchase their cards and mark off numbers as they are called out. Numbers are usually marked with a dauber, but some casinos also offer electronic bingo tabulators that allow

A live bingo session at a hotel in Las Vegas

Blackjack

This card game is one of the most popular games on the floor; casino blackjack tables offer minimum bet games from $2 to $500. The game is played against the dealer and whoever gets closest to a total card value of 21 without going over is the winner. Cards are worth their numerical value, with all the picture cards worth 10 and an ace worth 1 or 11. Hands that have aces are called "soft" hands and the ones without aces are known as "hard" hands.

Dealing cards to players at the blackjack table, Monte Carlo

Generally, the dealer will deal from a "shoe" – a box containing up to six decks of cards. Each player receives two cards face up. The dealer also gets two cards – one face up and one face down. Players must not touch the cards and should use hand signals to indicate if they wish to "hit," scratch the table with their forefinger to

Ideal cards for blackjack

receive another card or "stand," wave a flat hand over their cards. Players can also "double down," double their bet or "split," a hand that has two cards of the same value can be separated into two hands, each with individual bets. Once each player has decided to stand or hit the 21 limit, the dealer turns over his second card and plays his hand, hitting 16 or less

and standing with 17 or more. This is an essential part of blackjack's "basic strategy." The assumption here is that the dealer's second card will be a 10 and that the next card in the shoe will also be a 10. This is because there are more tens in the deck than any other card – there are 96 tens in six decks.

Big Six or Wheel of Fortune

One of the oldest games of chance, the Wheel of Fortune, also known as Big Six, is easier to play than the more intensive table games.

The ornate wooden wheel is 6 ft (1.8 m) in diameter with a pointer attached to it, and is divided into nine sections. Each of these sections is further divided into six pockets. This gives the wheel a total of 54 pockets, each holding a symbol you can bet on.

Out of these, 52 contain symbols of US currency bills of $1, $2, $5, $10, and $20 denominations and the two remaining symbols are of a joker and the casino's logo. The wheel's symbols are reproduced on a table layout. The players choose any of these symbols and place their bet on it. A dealer spins the wheel. When it stops, the number that the pointer is aimed at wins. The payoff is a multiple of the currency amount the player bet on. For instance, a $1 bet on a $2 symbol wins $2, a $5 bet on a $10 symbol wins $50, and so on. Bets placed on the casino logo and joker, usually pay at 40 to 1 – so a winning bet of, say, $2 on any of these symbols wins a payoff of $80.

Basic Blackjack Strategy

Blackjack's basic winning strategy, based on computer-generated studies, is given below. It tells the player when to hit, stand, double down, or split pairs, depending on the dealer's up card. Using basic strategy is permitted in casinos, and many dealers even advise gamblers on how to play.

1. Hit or Stand: With a hard hand – no aces – against the dealer's 7 or higher, the player should hit until he/she reaches at least 17. With a hard hand against the dealer's 4, 5, or 6, stand on a 12 or higher; if against the dealer's 2 or 3, hit a 12. With a soft hand, hit all totals of 17 or lower. Against the dealer's 9 or 10, hit a soft 18.

2. Doubling Down: Double down on any 11, no matter what the dealer shows. Double down on 10 when the dealer shows anything except a 10 – the dealer's "10" includes picture cards. Double down on 9 when the dealer shows 2, 3, 4, 5, or 6. Double down on a soft 17 (ace + 6) if the dealer shows 2, 3, 4, 5, or 6. Double down on a soft 18 (ace + 7) if the dealer shows a 3, 4, 5, or 6. Double down on a soft 13, 14, 15, or 16 against the dealer's 4, 5, or 6.

A winning hand on a blackjack table

3. Splitting Pairs: Always split aces and 8-8. Never split 5-5 or 10-10. Split 4-4 against the dealer's 5 or 6. Split 9-9 against the dealer's 2, 3, 4, 5, 6, 8, or 9. Split 7-7 against the dealer's 2, 3, 4, 5, 6, or 7. Split 6-6 against dealer's 2, 3, 4, 5, or 6. Split 2-2 and 3-3 against dealer's 2, 3, 4, 5, 6, or 7.

Poker

Over the last few years, the popularity of poker has skyrocketed in Las Vegas, largely due to events such as the World Poker Tour, Las Vegas's World Series of Poker, and numerous other celebrity tournaments.

Unlike blackjack and Caribbean Stud poker, "live" poker is not played against the casino but against other players. The casino simply provides the dealer and charges a rental for the seat at the table, which is actually a percentage taken out of every pot – this is called the "rake." The skill

at winning at poker lies in the ability to not only judge the quality of the poker hand, but also the quality of the opponent's hand and penchant for bluffing. Although not every poker player is a novice-eating shark, many of the regulars are experts, so beginners should test the waters in a low-stakes game or take a few lessons before taking on the pros. Even after lessons, it might be a good idea to watch a game for a while to understand the method of play.

There are basically two poker games played in Las Vegas – seven card stud and Texas Hold 'em. In recent years, Texas Hold 'em has become more popular, perhaps because it is usually the championship game in most tournaments.

Essential ingredients of a poker game

Seven-Card Stud

Most beginners start with this game. The dealer gives each player two cards face down and then one card face up. The player with the lowest card showing makes the first bet. Other players can either match the bet, increase it, or withdraw. Another card is dealt face up, and the player with the highest hand showing starts this round of betting. This is repeated until six cards have been dealt face up. Finally the seventh card is dealt to those who have remained in the game, and the final round of betting begins. During this "showdown," players may "raise" a bet up to three times. When the last bet is "called," the dealer asks for a showing of hands and the highest hand wins.

An excellent poker hand

Texas Hold 'em

This game is very similar to seven-card stud except only two of the seven cards are dealt to each player; the other five are dealt face up and used collectively by all the players.

The dealer gives each player two cards face down. The player next to the dealer starts the betting and the other players have to match the bet or withdraw.

The dealer discards, or "burns," the top card from the deck, then deals three cards face up in the center of the table – this deal is called the "flop." A round of betting occurs again. The dealer burns another card and adds a fourth face-up card, known as the "turn" card, to the center. Once again, a round of betting takes place. Finally, a fifth face-up card, called the "river" card, is dealt to the center. A final round of betting occurs, along with a showdown and revealing of hands. Once again, the highest hand wins.

Strategy

Texas Hold 'em's strategy is based on your first two cards. Most pros agree that if you do not have any of the combinations below, drop out.

1. A pair of aces or a pair of kings: Hold and bet from the first round.

2. A pair of queens or jacks: Hold and cover all bets until the fourth up card is dealt. If the value of your hand has not increased, drop out.

3. Two high-value cards – ace, king, or queen: Hold and cover all bets until fourth up card is dealt. If your hand has not improved, drop out.

4. Two high-value cards of the same suit: Hold until the fourth up card. If your hand has not improved, drop out.

5. A small pair – 10s or less: Hold until the fourth up card. If the value of your hand has not increased, drop out.

Poker Hands

Several versions of poker are played in Las Vegas casinos. You should know the hierarchy of poker hands to play any of these. From the lowest to the highest, the hands are as follows: pair – two cards of the same value; two pair – two separate pairs; three-of-a-kind – three cards of the same value; straight – five cards of any suit in sequence; flush – any five cards of the same suit; Full House – three cards of the same value and a pair; four-of-a-kind – four cards of the same value; straight flush – any five-card sequence of the same suit; and finally royal flush – ace, king, queen, jack, and ten of the same suit.

Caribbean Stud Poker

A type of five-card stud poker played on a table with a layout like a blackjack table, where the aim is to beat the dealer. There is a progressive jackpot where winnings increase according to a player's hand. Players win all or part of a progressive jackpot with a royal flush, straight flush, four-of-a-kind, full house, or flush.

Pai Gow Poker

Combining the Chinese game of Pai Gow with American poker, this game has a joker card that is used as an ace or to complete a straight or flush. Players have to make the best two-card and five-card hand to beat the banker's two hands.

Poker chips

Let It Ride® Poker

In this game, players do not compete against the dealer or each other. They try to get a good hand by combining three cards dealt to them with the dealer's two "community" cards that are revealed during play. Players can remove up to two-thirds of their bet during play if chances for a win seem grim.

Video Poker

No other casino game has gained the popularity that video poker has enjoyed over the past few years. It is the game of choice for locals, those who live and work in Las Vegas, and generates up to 75 per cent of the revenue in some casinos. There are several reasons for video poker's popularity. The first is that people can play at their own pace, without pressure from dealers, croupiers, or other players. Secondly, there is an element of skill in video poker. Decisions must be made which, unlike slot machines, will determine whether and how much you can win. And, most importantly, there is the chance of hitting the jackpot.

The basic video poker game is five-card draw poker, in which the machine "deals" five cards to the player. The player can then decide to "hold," keep those cards or "draw," replace some or all the cards. The winnings are based on the value of the poker hand.

Initially, the game started as jacks or better poker, in which the minimum payback was based

A dealt hand on a video poker machine, Las Vegas

on a pair of jacks or better – a pair of queens, kings, or aces. Today, there are many variations of video poker, including deuces wild poker, joker wild poker, and bonus poker, to name a few.

In 1998, inventor Ernie Moody pioneered a multi-hand concept called Triple Play Draw Poker. This new game allows the player to play three hands at once by dealing three rows of five cards. The first two rows are dealt face down, and the bottom row is dealt face up. The player then chooses the cards they want to hold from the bottom hand, and those cards automatically appear in the corresponding spaces in the top two hands. After hitting the "draw" button, the player gets three different draws from three different decks. So players who hold three-of-a-kind from the bottom deck, have three different chances to get four-of-a-kind.

Adding to the game's popularity is the fact that when dealt a big hand like a royal flush, players receive three times as much as they did on the older, single-hand video poker games. Many players say that after playing Triple Play, they can never go back to playing regular video poker. Triple Play poker has since given birth to Five Play, Ten Play, Fifty Play, and Hundred Play Poker.

Although it might be inconceivable to play such a large number of hands at once, the game's manufacturer has made it easier by offering the game in small denominations – 1 cent and 2 cents per hand.

Pai Gow Poker dealer laying out the table at Palace Station casino

Three-Card Poker

This card game debuted in 2002 and by 2004 had more placements than Let it Ride® and Caribbean Stud combined. Virtually every casino in North America and the United Kingdom offers Three Card Poker.

In this game, players compete against the dealer and against a bonus paytable. The bonus bet, called Pair Plus, is the key to the game's popularity. It is so strong that several other games have borrowed it – 3-5-7 Poker, Pai Gow Mania, and Boston 5.

Players win the Pair Plus bet if their three-card poker hand contains a pair or better. Payouts increase for hands like flushes, straights, and three-of-a-kinds. The top hand, a straight flush, pays 40-1. And unlike bonus bets in five-card games, Pair Plus winners are easy to get.

The game against the dealer is simple. Players place an ante – a poker stake that goes into the pot – and receive their cards. They may fold or make an additional bet equal to their ante. The dealer then reveals his hand. If he qualifies – has a queen-high or better – the dealer pays the winners who have higher cards than him and takes the bet of the losers. If the dealer doesn't qualify, players win their ante as well as the secondary bet money.

Roulette

Roulette is quite a simple game but with a great variety of bets. A ball is spun on a wheel containing numbers 1 to 36 divided equally between red and black, plus a single and a double zero, colored green. Each player's chips are a different color so they can be easily identified on the table. The aim is to guess the number that will come up on the spin of the wheel. Bets are placed on the table that has a grid marked out with the numbers and a choice of betting options. The highest payout odds are

Croupier setting up roulette in a private gaming room

35 to 1 for a straight bet on one number such as 10 black. You can also make a "split bet" on two numbers that pays 17 to 1 if either number comes up.

The most popular bets are the outside bets that are placed in the boxes outside the numbered grid. These only pay even money, but allow you to cover more numbers such as Odd or Even, Red or Black, First 18 Numbers or Second 18 Numbers. You can also make a Column Bet covering 12 numbers, which pays 2 to 1.

Roulette wheel

Baccarat

A variation of *chemin de fer*, baccarat is played at a leisurely pace with eight decks of cards, the deal rotating from player to player. The object of the game is to guess which hand will be closest to 9: the player's or the banker's. You can bet on either hand.

Keno

One of the easiest games to play, keno is a close relative of bingo. Out of the 80 numbers on a keno ticket, players may choose up to 20. A range of bets is possible and winning depends on your chosen numbers coming up. The prize depends on the amount of numbers matched.

A game of keno in progress at Circus Circus

Race and Sports Book

Giant video screens adorn these areas of the casino, where you can bet on almost any sport, such as car racing and boxing tournaments. The race book is for betting on thoroughbred horse racing and features live coverage from racetracks across the US. The sports book covers the main sporting events taking place all over the country, as well as the major championships staged in Las Vegas itself. Sports fans can watch the progress of their team on the nearby TVs.

Two cards in each hand of baccarat

WEDDINGS IN LAS VEGAS

Apart from its fame as one of the most popular entertainment destinations in the country, Las Vegas is also widely acclaimed as the wedding capital of the world. Each year, more than 110,000 couples, including several celebrities, such as Britney Spears and Sinéad O'Connor, tie the knot here, which is about one-fifth of all the marriages that take place in the nation. The city has dozens of stand-alone chapels *(see pp30–31)*, many of which are converted Victorian homes decorated with bells and cherubs. Most of the resorts also have at least one chapel. Weddings in Las Vegas can range from simple civil affairs and exotic themed events to full-blown, lavish extravaganzas. While some chapels hire an Elvis impersonator to croon a few tunes to the newlyweds, others offer romantic hot-air balloon rides over the city or the Grand Canyon. Those in a hurry can even get married at a 24-hour drive-through chapel. In addition to the quick, easy, and relatively inexpensive ceremonies, couples getting married here find it a great place to spend their honeymoon as well.

A marriage certificate from the State of Nevada

Legalities

The requirements for a marriage license in Las Vegas are less stringent than those in other parts of the US. No blood tests are needed, nor is it necessary to wait a set period after the license has been issued. The only prerequisite to marriage is that you must be at least 18 years of age. Those aged between 16 and 18 must have parental consent. To obtain a license, both partners must appear at the **Clark County Marriage License Bureau**. Civil ceremonies are performed one block from the courthouse in the office of the **Commissioner of Civil Marriages**. The cost of a license at both these places is $77 and must be obtained at the Marriage Bureau. A civil ceremony costs $75 (credit card only). Be prepared to produce your social security number and proof of identity such as a driver's license, certified copy of birth certificate, passport, or military ID. If using a birth certificate, an additional proof of identity is required; all other documents are acceptable on their own. Divorced applicants must know the month, day, year, city, and state where the final decree was granted, but no papers are necessary. Couples planning to tie the knot on Valentine's Day or New Year's Eve, two of the year's most popular days for weddings, should get their licenses well in advance in order to avoid long queues at the County Clerk's office.

Indoor Spectaculars

Perhaps the most elaborate weddings in Las Vegas take place at **Bellagio** *(see pp50–51)*. The resort's two romantic and elegant chapels have a stained-glass window behind the altar, while ornate lamps, chandeliers of amethyst, and Venetian glass complement the pastel shades of the furnishings and the flower-decked passages. Weddings here are expensive and couples can spend up to

Fresh flowers adorning the richly decorated interiors of the wedding chapels at Bellagio

A newly married couple at the elegant chapel at Bellagio

$25,000 for a lavish ceremony that includes every service right down to the exquisite flower petals that carpet the aisle. Personalized services are also available for room reservations as well as for the wedding and reception planning.

Couples can also take advantage of any of the hotel's wide variety of wedding packages. One of the most exclusive is the Cosa Bella Wedding Package. This offers spa treatments for the bride and groom, hair and make-up services at the salon, an impressive penthouse suite for three nights, dinner at the five-star Picasso restaurant or at Prime, and two tickets to Cirque du Soleil's production, "O" (see p136).

Couples can exchange vows at **Planet Hollywood Resort & Casino** (see p48), formerly known as the Aladdin, where Elvis Presley wed Priscilla in 1967. The hotel has a chapel that is adorned with arches and columns, soft desert colors, hand-painted murals, and an art glass display by Dale Chihuly. It can accommodate up to 65 guests.

At the **MGM Grand** (see p46), couples can tie the knot in the Forever Grand's Legacy Chapel. The chandeliered halls here offer a stunning backdrop.

Wynn Las Vegas (see pp62–3) has some of the nicest wedding rooms in the city, decorated in warm tones with elegant fabrics and hand-blown glass chandeliers. The Lavender Salon seats 120 guests, the Lilac Salon has room for 65, and Primrose Court is an outdoor venue for 40 guests. Personal consultants help to plan every aspect of the wedding.

Another favorite Las Vegas wedding venue is the Chapel in the Clouds at **Stratosphere** hotel (see p65). Located in the resort's tower, 800 ft (244 m), above the ground, this claims to be the country's highest wedding chapel, and presents a breathtaking view of the city's bright lights as the backdrop to proceedings.

Forever Grand's Legacy Chapel, MGM Grand

Outdoor Extravaganzas

Although the Southern Nevada desert is far from any seashore, tropical-themed weddings are hugely popular in Las Vegas. These usually take place at resorts that feature lush, landscaped areas, which have been artistically designed to resemble an exotic island. The **Flamingo** (see p53), for instance, hosts weddings in its charming garden gazebo chapel, and offers cascading waterfalls, palm trees, and fresh flowers. Couples can choose from several wedding packages, which often provide wedding coordinators, a leather bound album, a pianist or violinist, champagne and toasting glasses, and a two-night stay in the hotel's lavish Royal Suite.

The Garden of the Gods pool complex at **Caesars Palace** (see p52) makes for an impressive pastoral backdrop with its striking terraces, fountains, and waterfalls. And at the **Treasure Island – TI** resort (see p58), couples can marry on the poolside or on the deck of the TI Song Ship in Siren's Cove. The ceremony is performed by the ship's "captain" while guests watch from the adjacent patio. A pirate may even swing down from the crow's nest to deliver the rings to the couple.

One of the most beautiful settings for an outdoor wedding is at **JW Marriott Hotel** in Summerlin. The wedding arbor is set among dense trees in a lush garden with a cascading waterfall as a backdrop. Outdoor packages include white garden chair seating and a reception.

Equally tranquil and far from the neon lights is **The Grove** in Centennial Hills. Happy couples can exchange al fresco vows in an outdoor gazebo, almond orchard or an arbor by a pond, amid beautiful landscaped gardens with vistas of mountain ranges in the distance. Reception packages include gourmet menus prepared by The Grove's on-site chefs, and a wedding DJ to get the party in full swing.

Wedding procession outside Little White Chapel

Unusual Weddings

Most chapels in Las Vegas seek to offer something different and unique in order to separate themselves from the rest of the crowd. For instance, the **Little White Chapel** has a reputation of hosting rather unconventional weddings. For the bride and groom who are either acting on impulse or are in a huge hurry, the chapel offers a Drive-Up Wedding Window, where they can exchange vows without leaving the front seat of their car. The window never closes and an appointment is not necessary. The chapel also offers the "Weddings on Wheels" program, where a minister travels to a location chosen by the couple in order to perform the ceremony.

Many chapels in Las Vegas feature a range of themed weddings. The **Viva Las Vegas Wedding Chapel** probably performs more themed marriages than any other – between 15–20 ceremonies each day. One of its most popular weddings is the Blue Hawaii package, which comes complete with a tropical set, dancing hula girls, theatrical fog, and of course, a singing Elvis. For couples who want something more exotic, there is an Egyptian wedding, where King Tut performs the service, and a Camelot wedding

in which Merlin the Magician conjures up the nuptials.

New York-New York (see p45) offers couples the chance to reserve one of the most exhilarating wedding experiences on the Strip. The "Weddings on the Coaster" package allows couples the chance to say "I do" on the roller coaster, featuring its 180-degree "heartline" twist-and-dive maneuver and reaching speeds of 67 mph (107 km/h). Package rates begin at $600 with weddings available Sunday through Thursday (10:45am or 11:15pm) and Friday and Saturday (10:15am or 12:15am) – weather permitting. Couples can take the plunge with up to 14 guests. It is also possible to tie the knot atop the High Roller, the world's largest observation wheel, at **The LINQ Hotel & Casino** (see p53).

A large number of resorts also offer weddings that tie into their theme, if they have one. The **Excalibur** (see p44) extends its King Arthur's castle theme into the chapel, where couples can dress in medieval outfits.

Elvis impersonator, Little White chapel

The canals at **The Venetian** (see pp60–61) are worked into some wedding ceremonies, which can be performed on a gondola, or on one of the bridges.

Unusual weddings are not confined to the earth-bound. **A Special Memory** offers airborne marriages that include helicopter and hot-air balloon rides. The chosen craft hovers over Las Vegas, Grand Canyon, or Valley of Fire State Park. **Helicopter Weddings Las Vegas** will elevate nuptial vows with its helicopter wedding packages. One package whisks couples via helicopter to the awe-inspiring Grand Canyon, where they are set down on the floor of the canyon, adjacent to the Colorado River. The couple exchanges vows on the riverbank, after which they are flown back to their hotel. Another package flies the betrothed high above the glittering Strip at night, where they are wed by an airborne minister. Serving as a spectacular backdrop are dramatic views of Paris Las Vegas's Eiffel Tower, Luxor's pyramid, and the fountains at the Bellagio.

Wedding and Honeymoon Packages

One of the reasons so many couples choose Las Vegas for their wedding is that they have a

An Egyptian-themed ceremony in progress at the Viva Las Vegas Chapel

A newlywed couple stepping out of a helicopter

built-in honeymoon destination at their fingertips. Virtually all the hotels in the city offer wedding and honeymoon packages. These include a bottle of champagne, optional breakfast in bed, a reception in the banquet hall, tickets to production shows, spa treatments, dinner at one of the hotel's restaurants, and of course, accommodation in a honeymoon or master suite.

The cost of these packages can vary from season to season. For instance, a week-long honeymoon during the annual giant CES (see p35) convention, which attracts thousands of delegates, may cost two to four times more than it might during the preceeding or following week. As far as accommodations are concerned, the general rule is that the farther away you are from the Strip, the less expensive the rooms are likely to be. However, since there are exceptions to this rule, it would be a good idea to check the hotels websites or your travel agent for any special deals.

Wedding Planning

The hotel wedding chapels usually have a planner or staff member who will make all the arrangements, including the photographer, florist, pianist, limousine service, harpist,

albums, boutonnieres and bouquets, refreshments, and so forth. Couples can also hire professional services to handle all the details. These companies will typically find a chapel or venue, arrange for the ceremony, book the honeymoon, and provide the flowers, wedding cake, photographer, limousine, music, champagne, balloons, and a garter for the bride – in fact, almost anything the marrying couple may want. One of the most well-known wedding planners in the city are **Las Vegas Weddings**, who have been arranging weddings and honeymoons since 1973.

Sign at Viva Las Vegas Wedding Chapel

Gay and Lesbian Weddings

Las Vegas has a thriving gay and lesbian community. Though the state approved a constitutional amendment banning same sex marriages in 2002, the ban was struck down by the 9th US Circuit Court of Appeals and, as of June 2015, same sex marriages are now legal throughout the US. All but one wedding chapel now perform weddings for LGBT couples. **EnGAYged** is a company that provides free booking services for LGBT weddings and lists of LGBT-friendly businesses.

DIRECTORY

Legalities

Clark County Marriage License Bureau
201 Clark Ave. **Map** 2 D4.
Open 8am–midnight daily.
Tel (702) 671-0600.
🆆 co.clark.nv.us

Commissioner of Civil Marriages
330 S Third St. **Map** 2 D5.
Open 9:30am–8:45pm Fri, 12:30–8:45pm Sat, 2–6pm Mon–Thu, 9am–5pm Sun.
Tel (702) 671-0577.

Weddings Venues

A Special Memory
800 S 4th St.
Tel (702) 384 2211.
🆆 aspecialmemory.com

The Grove
8080 Al Carrison St. **Tel** (702) 645-5010. 🆆 the-grove.com

Helicopter Weddings Las Vegas
🆆 helicopterweddings lasvegas.com

JW Marriott Hotel
221 N Rampart Blvd. **Tel** (702) 869-7777. 🆆 marriott.com

Little White Chapel
1301 Las Vegas Blvd S. **Map** 2 D5.
Tel (702) 382-5943.
🆆 alittlewhitechapel.com

Viva Las Vegas Wedding Chapel
1205 Las Vegas Blvd S.
Map 2 D5. **Tel** (702) 384-0771/(800) 574-4450.
🆆 vivalasvegasweddings.com

Wedding Planning

EnGAYged Weddings
Tel (702) 737-6800.
🆆 engaygedweddings.com

Las Vegas Weddings
2550 E Desert Inn Rd #562.
Tel (800) 322-8697.
Tel (702) 737-6800.
🆆 lasvegasweddings.com
🆆 las-vegas-weddings.co.uk

CHILDREN IN LAS VEGAS

Las Vegas hosts a variety of attractions for children. Most hotels and resorts feature activities that cater to the younger generation. From the thrill rides at Stratosphere and Circus Circus's Adventuredome to the *Tournament of Kings* show at Excalibur and the massive Shark Reef aquarium at Mandalay Bay, there is plenty to satisfy a child's never-ending quest for adventure and fun. Some resorts also offer day care facilities for young children while their parents are busy. The city has several non-hotel attractions, including a lion habitat, a huge arcade at GameWorks, a chocolate factory, and the famous Discovery Children's Museum, which showcases interactive exhibits tailored to spark a child's imagination. Las Vegas has numerous outdoor activities for kids of all ages too, such as miniature golf, skateboarding, swimming, and biking. Las Vegas is not only a city for adults.

Traveling with Children

There are a few general guidelines that are helpful when traveling with children. Book your accommodations well in advance, and ensure the hotel or motel has the extra crib or cot you require. The more expensive resorts provide babysitting services and children's clubs offering supervised activities. Remember to carry everything you might need – diapers, food, toys, and extra clothes for kids and parents alike. A first aid kit is always a good idea. The glare of the desert sun can be harmful to young eyes so carry sunglasses and hats.

Sources of Information

For updates and special promotions on upcoming activities around the city, the *Las Vegas Kids' Directory* magazine is a good source of information. This free monthly publication carries a month-to-month calendar of no-cost or low-cost child-oriented events. The magazine can be picked up at any local library and at most supermarkets.

Children's Discounts

The long-established custom of allowing children to stay for free in their parents' hotel room can no longer be taken for granted. While some hotels still allow young children to share the room at no extra cost, many others require an added charge, usually no more than $10 or $12 per person. Be sure to check with the resort and booking agent in advance. Most restaurants also provide reasonably priced children's menus, although do not expect to find any at the more exclusive dining rooms. Many museums, shows, and special events offer discounted rates or free admission to children of a certain age and below. Check with the establishment you plan to visit since this varies from place to place. Children also receive reduced fares on the city's public transportation systems.

Day Care and Baby-Sitting Services

Several hotels in the city will provide or arrange for licensed baby-sitting services. Sitters are typically available 24 hours a day and will come to the hotel room, often equipped with toys, games, books, and videos to entertain your children. It is a good idea to make reservations for the sitters in advance.

Some hotels also maintain day care centers for the children of guests as well as those of their casino personnel and other staff. These centers generally require a written consent form from the parents, and cater mostly to children who are pre-school aged and past the diaper stage.

Moreover, **Station Casinos** and **Coast Casinos** – two of Las Vegas's most prominent gaming corporations – also operate child care centers in select hotels. These are available to toddlers and children up to 12 years of age, and required that the parent remain on the property while the child is in the center, up to a maximum of five hours. At Coast Casinos, the minimum age for children is 3 years, and it is necessary for the child to be potty trained. Boulder Station, features the **Kids Quest** center that tends to children aged 6 weeks to 12 years. The center is open to all tourists, not just hotel guests, and offers many

Tournament of Kings show at Excalibur

Day care workers looking after children

The drinking age in Nevada is 21, so anyone who looks under this age may be asked for some form of identification when purchasing alcohol. It is advisable to carry identification around with you at all times. In addition, Las Vegas has a 10pm curfew, so minors – those younger than 18 – must be off the street by that time or be accompanied by either a parent or a legal guardian.

Hotel Attractions

One of the most exciting destinations in Las Vegas is **Shark Reef** (see p43) at Mandalay Bay. This enormous aquarium houses a wide selection of marine life including sharks, Komodo dragons, reptiles, and various species of tropical fish. Kids especially enjoy the petting section where they can touch eels, jellyfish, stingrays, and small sharks.

forms of entertainment such as movies, arts and crafts, a jungle gym, Nintendo games, table tennis, board games, a pre-school room, and more.

Parents can also contact independent baby-sitting services such as **Artsy Nannies**, whose sitters will come to your room, and **Around the Clock Child Care** – all are professional sitters trained in administering CPR or mouth-to-mouth resuscitation.

City Taboos

It is important to remember that Las Vegas is, first and foremost, an adult playground. Games of chance beckon everywhere – from the slots at the corner convenience store to the baccarat rooms at the mega resorts. Although the

gambling halls attempt to keep restaurants, shops, and other general attractions separate from the adult games, the trip sometimes invariably requires a walk through parts of the casino. Visitors younger than 21 cannot tarry, so the stroll must be brisk. Parents are not permitted to wager or place bets at any of the tables while youngsters are in tow.

Most of Las Vegas's production shows are geared toward adult audiences. In general, the earlier of the day's two shows will be less racy than the late edition, when many of the showgirls become "uncovered."

Many clubs offer adults-only entertainment. Children below the age of 18 are not allowed anywhere near strip clubs or gentlemen's clubs.

The **Adventuredome** (see pp66–7) at Circus Circus is another popular children's attraction in Las Vegas. This indoor amusement park has an extensive array of rides and games designed to keep kids entertained for hours. They can ride the Canyon Blaster, a looping, corkscrewing roller coaster or practice rock climbing on a formidable indoor mountain face. Also available are laser tag, miniature golf, and carnival midway games.

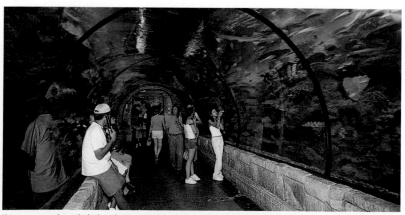

Visitors gaze at predatory sharks through a transparent glass barrier, Shark Reef, Mandalay Bay

A thrilling spin on Chaos, Adventuredome, Circus Circus

Kids also enjoy the exhilarating ride on Chaos, which spins its passengers at varying speeds. Moreover, the mezzanine above the Circus Circus casino presents circus performances such as trapeze artists and tightrope walkers, and a midway filled with games.

Another hot spot on the Strip is **Excalibur** (see p44), which, below its casino, houses Fun Dungeon, a "fun zone" of carnival games enticing youngsters in games of skill. One of the highlights here is the *Tournament of Kings* show – a wholesome family entertainment where guests can enjoy a meal while watching jousting knights, and exciting sword play.

The **Popovich Comedy Pet Theater** at the V Theater at Planet Hollywood (see p48) is a family show featuring an amazing cast of 30 cats, dogs, parrots, geese and mice and internationally renowned juggling and comedy by Gregory Popovich. The show is offered Tuesday to Saturday at 4pm.

Siegfried & Roy's Secret Garden and Dolphin Habitat (see p58) at The Mirage is one of the city's must-see attractions. This delightful facility, created by famed conservationists, is home to several lions and threatened white tigers. Designed to resemble the natural habitat of these magnificent big cats, the lush, landscaped environment of the garden provides exceptional

viewing opportunities. The stunning and spacious Dolphin Habitat is where a family of Atlantic bottlenose dolphins can be observed at play.

Older kids can head over to the SoBe Ice Arena at **Fiesta Rancho Casino Hotel**. In keeping with National Hockey League regulations, the rink measures a massive 31,000 sq ft (2,880 sq m) and is home to several youth and adult leagues. SoBe offers figure skating and ice hockey facilities, as well as skate rental and private rooms that can be hired for birthday parties. Skate School is held every Tuesday and Saturday and is open to all ages.

If you count white-knuckle adventure as fun, the Strip offers many roller coaster and thrill-rides. A gut-wrenching ride at Stratosphere Tower (see p65) is

The hair-raising Big Shot ride at the Stratosphere Tower

the **Big Shot**, which is located on the observation deck and shoots passengers 160 ft (49 m) up into the air. Riders for this must be at least 48 inches (4ft) tall. Probably the best roller coaster in town is **The Big Apple** at New York-New York (see p45). To experience the thrill of riding a high-speed zipline, visit **SlotZilla Zip Line** at the Fremont Street Experience (see p75).

GameWorks

In the Town Square Mall a few miles south of the Strip, GameWorks is the ultimate arcade complex. This massive facility is the brainchild of movie mogul Steven Spielberg, Sega Enterprises, and Universal Studios. This 7,000-sq-ft (650-sq-m) flagship located underneath the AMC theater offers hundreds of arcade games, an eight-lane bowling alley, eSports arena, and a devoted space for multi-player online computer gaming.

Museums

Art, science and a lot more come alive at the **Discovery Children's Museum** (see pp78–9), located in downtown Las Vegas.

The nine themed exhibition halls include The Summit, a 13-level climbing structure with hands-on experiments exploring machines, air pressure, flight, magnets, electricity and light; Water World, which is all about the movement and power of water; Toddler Town, for ages 5 and under; Patents Pending, where children use trial and error to design and engineer inventions; Eco City, looking at how people can live and work together in an environmentally friendly community; and Young at Art, hands-on investigations of color, line, shape, texture, and form.

The **Las Vegas Natural History Museum** (see p79) exhibits sharks, dinosaurs, and other creatures. Its Young Scientists' Center showcases interactive displays, and kids can also pet a 13-ft (4-m) long python and dig for fossils in the museum's workshop.

Facade of the Discovery Children's Museum

Waterparks

In 2013, **Wet'n'Wild Las Vegas** opened a new location about 25 minutes from the Strip. This waterpark offers more than 25 slides and attractions. On the other side of town is **Cowabunga Bay**, which opened in 2014 in Henderson, and includes a wave pool, 8 water slides and a 1,200-ft (366-m) long lazy river. Both parks are open April through September.

Las Vegas Mini Gran Prix

This venue has plenty to do, with a games arcade, 90-ft (23-m) Super Fun Slide, and a selection of rides, but the main attractions are its four tracks. These cater to all ages, offering vehicles ranging from Kiddie Karts, for children who are 38 to 54 inches (3 ft to 4.5 ft) tall, to Gran Prix Cars, for adults with a driver's license.

Lion Habitat Ranch

Although the Lion Habitat at the MGM Grand has closed, the lions are still Las Vegas residents. Their home is 10 miles south of the Strip in Henderson. It has 45 cats, most of which were born at the ranch, plus ostriches, emus, cockatoos, and macaws, and a young giraffe. Handlers are very informative, and visitors are welcome Friday to Monday from 11am to 3pm in winter and from 10am to 2pm during summer.

Sports and Outdoor Attractions

Many hotels, including **Gold Coast**, **Fiesta Rancho Casino Hotel**, and **Sam's Town** have bowling alleys, and provide special equipment and prices for kids.

Youngsters who like to roller skate or rollerblade can visit **Crystal Palace**, which operates two skating rinks in the Las Vegas area, or head for one of the many municipal parks in town. These parks feature a host of innovative attractions, such as bicycle courses, skateboard paths, water playgrounds, and more.

The city's most popular park is **Sunset Park**, which has joggers' paths, basketball, volleyball and tennis courts, a place to fly kites and sail boats, a dog park, and a massive lake with ducks and fish.

The **Wetlands Park** is partly a designated Nature Preserve. This wildlife habitat has beautiful trails, viewing ponds, and a visitors' center.

Parents can also take their children on trips to wilderness areas close to the city such as Mt. Charleston and Lake Mead.

DIRECTORY

Around the Clock Child Care
Tel (702) 365-1040.

Artsy Nannies
Tel (702) 448-4352.

Coast Casinos
w coastcasinos.com

Cowabunga Bay
900 Galleria Dr, Henderson.
Tel (702) 850-9000.
w cowabungabay.com

Crystal Palace
4680 Boulder Hwy.
Tel (702) 458-7107.
3901 N Rancho Dr.
Tel (702) 645-4892.
w skatevegas.com

Fiesta Rancho Casino Hotel
2400 N Rancho Dr.
Tel (702) 631-7000.

Kids Quest
4111 Boulder Hwy, Boulder Station Hotel. Tel (702) 432-7569.

Las Vegas Mini Gran Prix
1401 North Rainbow Blvd.
Tel (702) 259-7000.
w lvmgp.com

Lion Habitat Ranch
382 Bruner Ave, Henderson.
Tel (702) 595-6666.
w thecathouse.us

Sam's Town
5111 Boulder Hwy.
Tel (702) 456-7777.
w samstownlv.com

Station Casinos
w sclv.com

Sunset Park
2601 E Sunset Rd, E Ave.

Wetlands Park
7050 Wetlands Park Lane at E Tropicana Ave.

Wet'n'Wild Las Vegas
7055 S Fort Apache Rd.
Tel (702) 979-1600.
w wetnwildlasvegas.com

Volleyball game at Sunset Park

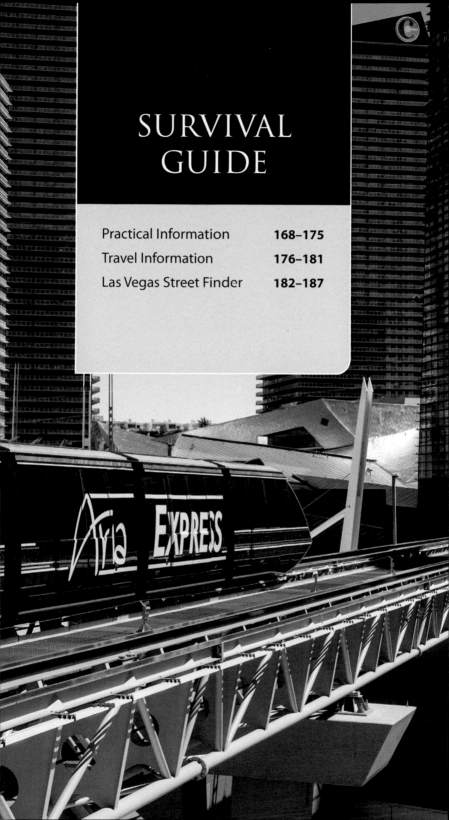

SURVIVAL GUIDE

PRACTICAL INFORMATION

As one of the world's most popular playgrounds, Las Vegas attracts millions of visitors each year. Lavish resorts and casinos, spectacular shows, and the frantic pursuit of around-the-clock entertainment, are just some of the amusements that tourists never seem to tire of. The city's surrounding wilderness, harsh and cruel in some places but always fascinating and beautiful, offers a wide variety of outdoor activities such as swimming, hiking, horseback riding, waterskiing, fishing, camping, snowboarding, and white-water rafting. With so much to choose from, it is a good idea to do some advance planning, and there is plenty of information available to tourists.

Exterior of the Las Vegas Convention Center, Las Vegas

When to Go

Las Vegas is a popular year-round destination. The most comfortable times to visit are during spring and fall, when the days are sunny without being too hot. Summer is extremely hot with an average July temperature of 40° C (105° F). Winter is unpredictable; some days are warm, while others are cold with nighttime temperatures below freezing. It has been known to snow on rare occasions.

Avoid planning your trip during conventions as rates are high and traffic is heavy.

Visas and Passports

Citizens from Australia, New Zealand, the UK, and many other European countries can visit the US without a visa if staying 90 days or less. Visitors must apply for entry clearance via the **Electronic System for Transport Authorization**. Applications should be made at least 72 hours before travel (there is a charge). Canadians are required to show a passport or other approved identification. Entry requirements are prone to change. Visitors should always check with the nearest US embassy.

Travel Safety Advice

Visitors can get up-to-date travel safety information from the **Foreign and Commonwealth Office** in the UK and the **Department of Foreign Affairs and Trade** in Australia.

Tourist Information

The **Las Vegas Convention and Visitors Authority** (see p134) provides excellent information and has a detailed website. Other useful websites include **vegas.com** and **lasvegas.com**. The **Nevada Commission on Tourism** provides information on scenic, recreational, and historic sites.

Opening Hours and Admission Prices

Casinos in Las Vegas remain open around the clock, as do some restaurants, bars, and gift shops. Museums and galleries tend to keep more regular hours. Most museums, parks, and other attractions charge an admission fee. Many sights offer discounts to families and children. ID-carrying students and senior citizens can also profit from the discounts at some attractions.

Etiquette and Smoking

Visitors under 21 cannot loiter in casinos. General photography is permitted, but filming of any gaming activities is not allowed. Smoking is prohibited in public areas and restaurants, but is permitted in bars that do not allow guests under 21. You must be 18 to purchase cigarettes.

Taxes and Tipping

The sales tax rate in Las Vegas is 8.15 per cent (see p126), and there is a 12 per cent tax on hotel rooms. When tipping at restaurants, leave 15–20 per cent of the total bill. As a guideline, give hotel personnel $1–2 for each bag of luggage they handle. If using concierge services, a $5 tip is appropriate, and $2 a day for housekeeping. A small bet for the dealer is the usual method of tipping at gaming tables, and a small tip is appropriate for keno runners and slot attendants. Give taxi drivers $1–2 for a short trip, or follow the 15–20 per cent rule, whichever is greater. All MGM properties charge for parking unless you are staying at one of their properties.

Travelers with Special Needs

Travelers with accessibility issues are well catered for in Las Vegas. All the hotels and restaurants provide facilities for the disabled (see p135). Visitors can expect ramp access, accessible slot machines, and disabled-friendly washrooms in all hotels and casinos. All city buses, the monorail, shuttles, and some taxis are wheelchair-accessible.

◀ The ARIA Express is a monorail system servicing the ARIA, Crystal City, Vdara and Bellagio resorts in Las Vegas

The **Society for Accessible Travel & Hospitality** offers advice to disabled travelers.

Traveling with Children

Once strictly a haven for adults, Las Vegas now provides entertainment for the entire family *(see pp162–5)*. A handful of shows are geared toward children, such as the *Mack King Comedy Magic Show* at Harrah's *(see p58)*.

Children from four and under to under 18 years are eligible for discounts. Some hotels provide babysitting services and children's clubs. Many restaurants offer low-priced children's menus.

Senior Travelers

Las Vegas is an ideal destination for older travelers. A wide range of discounts are available to people over the age of 50. Seniors over 60 years of age receive 50 per cent off fares on RTC public buses. The **National Park Service** offers a Senior Pass that reduces the cost of park tours and services. **Road Scholar** arranges educational trips, with economical lodgings and meals for anyone over 55, while the **American Association of Retired Persons** offers travel discounts to members.

Gay and Lesbian Travelers

Las Vegas has liberal attitudes regarding homosexuality. There are bars and nightclubs that cater to gay clientele such as FunHog Ranch and Piranha Nightclub. The Wynn/Encore hotels are considered two of the more gay-friendly hotels. See pages 144–5 for more information or visit the **QVegas** website.

Traveling on a Budget

Book in advance for the best accommodation options, or stay outside the city in somewhere like Henderson. Look out for two-for-one coupon books such as the Entertainment Book. Websites like **Cheapo Vegas** offer many deals and tips, and half-price tickets for shows are often sold at kiosks. Several free shows can be found in the main tourist areas, such as the water and light shows at Bellagio or the erupting volcano at The Mirage.

Casinos in downtown Vegas and locals casinos accept the lowest minimum wagers and many also offer single deck blackjack. By joining a casino's players' club you can get free slot play, discounts, and often free merchandise.

When dining, the best deals are available after 11pm and during happy hours, which are usually in the late afternoon or early evening. Caesars has a buffet pass that allows you to eat at any or all of the different buffets at their seven properties during a 24-hour period starting at $59.99.

For student travelers, some travel organizations, such as **STA Travel USA**, offer special package deals.

Responsible Tourism

Hotels on the Strip are improving their eco credentials. The **CityCenter** development earned prestigious awards for its environmental design and construction. The complex has a combined heat and power system that traps excess heat to warm hot water for hotel use. CityCenter also uses efficient irrigation systems, low-flap taps, provides priority parking for hybrid vehicles, and has limos powered by natural gas.

Las Vegas leads the nation in terms of solar production per capita, with many businesses and homes converting sunshine into electricity. There are several weekly farmers' markets with produce grown locally.

DIRECTORY

Visas and Passports

Electronic System for Travel Authorization
w cbp.gov/travel/international-visitors/esta

Travel Safety Advice

Australia
Department of Foreign Affairs and Trade
w dfat.gov.au/smartraveller.gov.au/

UK
Foreign and Commonwealth Office
w gov.uk/foreign-travel-advice

Tourist Information

Las Vegas Convention and Visitors Authority
3150 Paradise Rd, Las Vegas.
Tel (702) 892-0711.
w lasvegas.com

Nevada Commission on Tourism
w travelnevada.com

Travelers with Special Needs

Society for Accessible Travel & Hospitality
347 Fifth Ave, Suite 610, New York, NY 10016.
Tel (212) 447-7284.
w sath.org

Senior Travelers

American Association of Retired Persons (AARP)
3200 E Carson St, Lakewood, CA 90712.
Tel (888) 687-2277.
w aarp.com

National Park Service
w nps.gov

Road Scholar
11 Ave de Laffayette, Boston, MA 02111.
Tel (800) 454-5768.
w roadscholar.org

Gay and Lesbian Travelers

w qvegas.com

Traveling on a Budget

Cheapo Vegas
w cheapovegas.com

STA Travel USA
Tel (800) 654-9510.
w statravel.com

Responsible Tourism

CityCenter
w www2.citycenter.com

Personal Security and Health

Las Vegas is a relatively safe place to visit as long as some general safety precautions are observed. In contrast to large urban centers, the crime rate in town is relatively low, but it is wise to be aware of areas that might not be safe at night, in particular the area around Stratosphere Hotel, east and west of Las Vegas Boulevard, and several blocks on either side of Fremont Street. When driving in the desert regions outside of Las Vegas, take a reliable map, as well as a good compass, and follow the advice of local rangers and visitor information services. These sources provide invaluable guidelines for survival in the wilderness and safety procedures to be followed by those engaging in outdoor activities. Also, heed any flash flood warnings.

Metropolitan policeman on duty on the streets of Las Vegas

What to be Aware of

Like any major city, Las Vegas has a criminal element. Casino visitors are often targets for robbery because it is likely they are carrying large amounts of money. Although the local police department and hotel security place a high priority on keeping tourists safe, it is wise to observe a few basic rules. Never wear expensive jewelry, hold huge sums of cash, or keep your wallet in your backpocket, as these

Fire engine

Police car

Paramedics vehicle

are the main temptations for pickpockets. Avoid certain parts of the city while you are sightseeing. Downtown is generally safe, but it is not advisable to wander from the well-lit hotel and shopping areas, particularly north of Fremont Street and east of Maryland Parkway. Another district to avoid is the area west of the Strip, known as the "naked city." It is not somewhere to explore, especially at night. Otherwise, follow the rules of common sense, keeping your valuables close at all times. While driving, be sure to lock expensive belongings in the trunk, and to park only in well-lit areas.

In an Emergency

In an emergency situation, dial 911 from any telephone. The operator will dispatch police, fire, or emergency medical services. The Nevada Highway Patrol, Las Vegas Metropolitan Police Department, Henderson Police, North Las Vegas Police, and Park Service Rangers all have the authority to arrest lawbreakers.

If you are in a casino-hotel resort, contact the hotel operator or hotel security. Security personnel are well trained in emergency medical treatment.

Lost and Stolen Property

Although lost and stolen property may not be recovered, it is necessary to report all incidents to the police in order to make an insurance claim. Telephone the **Police Non-Emergency Line** to report the loss or theft, and they will issue you with a police report so that you can make a claim with your insurance company. The major resorts can be very helpful in holding lost property. To report and claim a lost item, call the hotel's main switchboard number.

If a credit card is missing, call the credit company's toll-free number immediately. Report lost or stolen traveler's checks to the issuer. If you have kept record of the checks' numbers, new checks can usually be issued quickly.

If you lose your passport, contact the nearest consulate. They will be able to issue a temporary replacement. However, if you are traveling on to another destination, you will need a full passport. It is also useful to hold photocopies of your driver's license and notarized passport photographs if you are considering an extended visit or need additional identification.

Hospitals and Pharmacies

The **University Medical Center of Southern Nevada** (UMC) is the city's primary provider of emergency medical care. UMC is the only hospital in Nevada with Level 1 Trauma and Burn Care centers. The hospital also has a Flight for Life medivac helicopter and operates facilities across the city for non-emergency medical care. All hospitals with emergency rooms can be found in the Community Pages at the front of the telephone directory and in the Yellow Pages. In private hospitals you may be required to provide evidence of your ability to pay before a doctor will agree to treat you. **Access Emergency Dental Care** can help with urgent dental issues.

Nonprescription painkillers and other medicines can be bought at drugstores, but prescription drugs can be dispensed only from a pharmacy. Pharmacies can be found at CVS and Walgreens stores; both have locations on the Strip. Ask at your hotel for 24-hour pharmacies. Carry extra supplies of any prescribed medication you take.

CVS/pharmacy

Pharmacy logo

Outdoor Hazards

Due to its location in the Mojave Desert, visitors to Las Vegas can expect extreme temperatures and weather conditions. Sudden summer storms can cause flash floods, especially along the major washes. The **Regional Flood Control District** can answer questions about a specific wash. Monsoon rains occur usually in the late summer months and used to cause major flooding, but since the 1990s several flood retention basins have been built. These greatly limit flooding in the urban areas.

Visitors may obtain the latest weather information from the ranger stations in the national parks, and by listening to the reports on local radio and television channels. If you are planning a hike in wilderness territory, always inform someone where you are going and when you expect to return.

The dry heat of the region's summers can often be underestimated by visitors, and hikers especially are advised to carry with them at least a gallon (4 liters) of drinking water per person for each day of walking. If you plan on hiking or indulging in other outdoor activities during the summer, wear an effective sunscreen and a sunhat.

Watch out for venomous snakes and scorpions. They are nocturnal but can be spotted during daytime in fall and spring and mostly hide under rocks and in crevices during the heat of the day. If bitten, seek medical help immediately.

Travel and Health Insurance

The United States has excellent medical services, but they are expensive. Visitors are strongly advised to take out comprehensive medical and dental coverage. All US hospitals are required by law to treat anyone with a medical emergency regardless of their ability to pay or whether or not they have health insurance, but that does not prohibit them from demanding payment.

DIRECTORY

Emergency Services

All Emergencies
Tel 911 to alert police, fire, or medical services.

Police Non-Emergency Line
Tel (702) 828-3111.

Lost Property

Lost or Stolen Credit Cards (Toll free)

American Express
Tel (800) 528-4800.

Diners Club
Tel (800) 234-6377.

MasterCard (Access)
Tel (800) 627-8372.

VISA
Tel (800) 336-8472.

Hospitals and Pharmacies

Access Emergency Dental Care
2585 S Jones Ave,
Las Vegas, NV 89146.
Tel (702) 319-4734.

University Medical Center of Southern Nevada
1800 E Charleston Ave.
Tel (702) 383-2000.

Outdoor Hazards

Regional Flood Control District
Tel (702) 685-0000.
Ⓦ ccrfcd.org

Consulates

The consulates closest to Las Vegas are found in California.

Australian Consulate
Century Plaza Tower, 19th Floor,
2049 Century Park E, Los Angeles,
CA 90067. **Tel** (310) 229-4800.

British Consulate
11766 Wilshire Blvd, Suite 1200,
Los Angeles, CA 90025.
Tel (310) 481-0031.

Canadian Consulate
550 S Hope St, 9th Floor,
Los Angeles, CA 90071-2627.
Tel (213) 346-2700.

New Zealand Consulate
2425 Olympic Blvd, Suite 600E,
Santa Monica, CA 90404.
Tel (310) 566-6555.

Young couple walking in the desert sun near Las Vegas

Banking and Currency

Aside from the risk of gambling away all of your money in the casinos, you should encounter no problems with financial transactions in Las Vegas. Foreign travelers can exchange currency at hotel cashiers and major banks. Automated teller machines (ATMs) are at virtually every casino in Las Vegas and can be found throughout the city, enabling visitors to make cash withdrawals 24 hours a day. Credit cards are a more common form of payment. In fact, most hotels and car agencies will not book a room or car without a credit card. Carrying some small change for tips and minor purchases is recommended.

Wells Fargo Bank, a prominent bank in Las Vegas

Banks and Bureaux de Change

Bank opening times can vary in Las Vegas, but generally they are open between 9 or 10am and 5 or 6pm. Most major US banks are represented in Las Vegas, including Chase, Wells Fargo, Bank of America, Bank of the West, and Citibank.

Most hotel cashiers and major banks exchange foreign currency and cash traveler's checks, though always ask if any special fees apply before you make your transaction. McCarran International Airport has foreign currency exchanges where traveler's checks can also be changed. Checks bought in US dollars are accepted as cash in many restaurants, hotels, and stores, and visitors will not be subject to a transaction fee. A passport or valid US driver's license is required as identification when using traveler's checks. Before departing for the US, consult a currency exchange website, such as www.xe.com, to check up-to-the-minute rates.

ATMS

All credit, charge, and debit cards can be used to draw money from an ATM, but a password or PIN will be required. ATMs are usually found at casinos, banks, bus stations, airports, and convenience stores. Withdrawing cash on a debit card costs less

Automated teller machine (ATM), open 24 hours a day

than doing it on a credit or charge card. The most common international systems are Cirrus and Plus. This is usually indicated on the card. If you are unsure, check which ATM system your card can access, and how much you will be charged for each transaction with your bank and credit card company. Withdrawals from ATMs may provide a better foreign currency exchange rate than cash transactions.

Credit and Debit Cards

Credit and charge cards are practically essential when traveling in the US. The cards are accepted as a guarantee when renting a car (see p181), and are used to book tickets for most forms of entertainment. The most widely used cards are **VISA**, **American Express**, **MasterCard**, and **Diner's Club**. Contact your card provider prior to travel to inform them of your plans and ensure there will be no problems using your card.

American Express charge cards

Currency

American currency has 100 cents to the dollar. Bills are all the same size and color, so check the number before paying. Smaller denominations are preferred at businesses in small towns and remote gas stations. These smaller enterprises will often refuse to change a bill worth more than $20.

Large $500–10,000 bills are no longer printed but are still legal tender, usually found in the hands of collectors. The $1 coin is also still legal but is rarely seen in circulation. Always carry cash for giving tips, and to pay public transportation and taxi fares.

Coins

American coins come in 50-, 25-, 10-, 5- and 1-cent pieces. Gold-tone $1 coins, though rarely in use, are in circulation, as are the State quarters, which feature a historical scene on one side. Each value of coin has a popular name: 25-cent pieces are called quarters, 10-cent pieces are called dimes, 5-cent pieces called nickels, and 1-cent pieces called pennies.

25-cent coin (a quarter)

10-cent coin (a dime)

5-cent coin (a nickel)

1-cent coin (a penny)

Bank Notes (Bills)

Units of currency in the United States are dollars and cents. There are 100 cents to a dollar. Notes come in $1, $5, $10, $20, $50, and $100s. The $5, $10, $20, $50, and $100 bills in circulation include security features with subtle color hues and improved color-shifting ink in the lower right hand corner of the face of each note.

DIRECTORY

American Express
Moneygram US only
Tel (800) 543-4080.

Check replacement
Tel (800) 221-7282.

Stolen credit and charge cards
Tel (800) 528-4800.

Diner's Club
Check replacement and stolen credit cards
Tel (800) 234-6377.

Thomas Cook (and MasterCard)
Check replacement and stolen credit cards
Tel (800) 223-9920.

VISA
Check replacement
Tel (800) 227-6811.
Stolen credit cards
Tel (800) 336-8472.

1-dollar bill ($1)

5-dollar bill ($5)

10-dollar bill ($10)

20-dollar bill ($20)

50-dollar bill ($50)

100-dollar bill ($100)

Media and Communications

Las Vegas is well-connected to the rest of the world and its communication systems are, usually, both efficient and affordably priced. Telephone, mail, and Internet services are all readily available in Las Vegas, providing fast and efficient services to destinations both local and international. In addition, Las Vegas has a daily newspaper and a plethora of visitor magazines that offer information on ongoing and upcoming events, as well as special discount coupons.

International and Local Calls

With the proliferation of cell phones, public pay phones are fairly hard to find in Las Vegas. Where payphones are available, instructions for use are included on the front.

All numbers within a local area have ten digits, including the 702 area code for Las Vegas.

To dial long-distance, add a one and the three-digit area code in front of the seven-digit number. The cost of a local call within the same area code is between 35 to 50 cents for three minutes. Long-distance calls are to any number outside the area code you are in and cost less at off-peak times, generally in the evenings and at weekends. Be aware that if you use your hotel telephone you may find you are charged at a much higher rate.

International numbers are preceded by 011, then the country code, followed by the city code (dropping the initial 0), and the number.

International calls can be made from a pay phone, but you may need a stack of change to dial direct and will be interrupted by the operator for more money when your time runs out. It is easier to buy a phonecard from one of the major telephone companies such as **AT&T**. These can be obtained from hotels, convenience stores, and vending machines.

Cell Phones

Most of the major cell phone service providers are represented in Las Vegas, so virtually any cellular phone will function here. The most prevalent cell services are **T-Mobile**, **AT&T**, **Verizon**, and **Sprint**, all of which have cell phone towers throughout the Las Vegas area. The towers are designed to look like tall pine or palm trees, and with numerous locations it is fairly easy to obtain reception. However, many casinos either block reception or prohibit

AT&T logo

cell phone use in their gaming areas.

If you forget to bring your phone, pre-paid cell phones can be purchased for as little as $10, and 30 minutes of airtime for an additional $10. **Tracfone** is a good example, and can be purchased in most convenience and chain department stores. It is also possible to rent a cell phone by the day or week from stores such as **Bearcom**. To dial long-distance, add a one and the three-digit area code in front of the seven-digit number.

Useful Dialling Codes

- To make a direct-dial call in Las Vegas or outside the local area code, but within the US and Canada, dial **1** then the area code.
- The area code of all telephone numbers in Clark County is **702** or **725**; this includes Las Vegas, Mount Charleston, Laughlin, Searchlight, and Mesquite. The area code in the rest of Nevada is **775**.
- For international direct-dial calls, dial **011** and the appropriate country code. Then dial the area code, omitting the first 0, and the local number.
- For international operator assistance, dial **01**.
- For local operator assistance, dial **0**.
- **800**, **877**, and **888** indicate a toll-free number.

Internet and Wi-Fi

Most hotels and coffee shops offer free Wi-Fi to people with their own laptop or device, and it is also available at McCarran Airport. All **Starbucks** branches, of which there are more than 100 in Las Vegas, offer free Wi-Fi. In addition, the five largest branches of the public library have computers that are free for library card holders. Faxes can be sent from most hotels, as well as from post offices.

Virtually every cell phone functions in most areas of Las Vegas

Access to the Internet is available in many locations across the city

Postal Services

Within the US, all mail is first class and generally takes between one and five days to arrive at its destination. The correct zip (postal) code usually ensures a swifter delivery.

International mail sent by air takes between five and ten days to arrive, but parcels that are sent at the surface parcel rate may take as long as four to six weeks. There are two special parcel services run by the federal mail – Priority Mail promises faster delivery than normal first class mail, while the more expensive Express Mail guarantees next-day delivery within the US and up to 72 hours delivery for international packages. Several private international delivery services offer swift, next-day delivery for overseas mail, the best known being **DHL** and **Federal Express**. Like all major cities, there is a Las Vegas Main Post Office, as well as many smaller local offices. If you have the correct value of postage stamps, both letters and parcels can be mailed in any one of the many mailboxes around town. These are generally dark blue and have the collection times posted on them. Any hotel will also be happy to place your mail in their outgoing bin.

It is possible to buy postage stamps from vending machines, convenience stores, and even some hotels.

Newspapers and Magazines

The best-selling national newspaper, *USA Today*, is popular in Vegas because many hotels offer it free to their guests. For local news, the *Las Vegas Review-Journal* is invaluable. It includes a weekly supplement on Fridays, *Neon*, with entertainment and museum event listings. Magazines such as **Las Vegas Weekly** and **Vegas Seven** contain restaurant profiles, show reviews, and shopping guides, as well as many discount coupons. These publications are free and can be found in many tourist locations including hotel lobbies and restaurants.

A customer outside a Starbucks coffeehouse, Las Vegas

Television and Radio

Las Vegas has several radio stations, covering a wide range of genres including sports, talk, news, and music. The television market in Las Vegas is similar to most major cities – all the main networks are represented here. Most hotels and motels provide at least the network channels, as well as PBS, CNN, and HBO.

DIRECTORY

International and Local Calls

AT&T
Tel (212) 387-5400.

Cell Phones

AT&T
Tel (800) 331-0500.
w att.com

Bearcom
Tel (702) 740-2800.
w bearcom.com

Sprint
Tel (866) 866-7509.
w sprint.com

T-Mobile
Tel (800) 866-2453.
w t-mobile.com

Tracfone
Tel (800) 867-7183.
w tracfone.com

Verizon
Tel (800) 256-4646.
w verizonwireless.com

Internet Cafes

Starbucks
w starbucks.com/
coffeehouse/wireless-internet

Postal Services

DHL
Tel (800) 225-5345.
w dhl.com

Federal Express
Tel (800) 463-3339.
w fedex.com

Las Vegas Main Post Office
1001 E Sunset Rd.
Tel (800) 275-8777.

Newspapers and Magazines

Las Vegas Weekly
w lasvegasweekly.com

Vegas Seven Magazine
w weeklyseven.com

TRAVEL INFORMATION

Despite its location in a remote part of the Mojave Desert, Las Vegas is easily reached by two major highways, Greyhound buses, and several commercial and charter airlines. It is one of the few Southwestern cities that services non-stop international flights, while its position in southern Nevada puts the city at the hub of brief commuter flights from

Los Angeles, San Francisco, Phoenix, and Denver amongst others. Once there, traveling around town can be a challenge because the streets are a maze of traffic, gridlock, and road construction. Helping facilitate travel around town are a large fleet of taxis, a highly efficient municipal bus system, two trams, and a monorail.

Plane arriving at McCarran International Airport

Arriving by Air

Located just 1 mile (1.6 km) from the Strip, **McCarran International Airport** is one of the busiest airports in the US – millions of passengers fly into Las Vegas each year. In addition to servicing about 35 domestic airlines, McCarran accepts direct flights from international carriers, including **American Airlines**, **British Airways**, **AeroMexico**, **Air Canada**, **Virgin Atlantic**, **Hawaiian Airlines**, and **Korean Airlines**. McCarran is also the largest operation base for **Allegiant Air** and **Southwest Airlines**. Allegiant offers direct flights and charters to small cities that have limited passenger airline services.

Airports

The one main airport for charter and group travel in Las Vegas is McCarran International Airport. The traffic at McCarran includes more than 1,100 flights a day, with direct flights to nearly 80 cities in the US, Europe, and Asia. Las Vegas is also one of the few non-West Coast

cities to offer direct flights to the Hawaiian Islands. Apart from domestic and foreign airlines, the airport is also served by a helicopter service, two commuter lines, and, depending on the season, up to 20 charter flights.

Passengers arriving at this well-designed airport should have no problem locating the baggage claim area, even though it is sometimes a long walk from the gate. The Ground Transportation section is situated just outside baggage claim. This is a focal point for taxis, hotel shuttles, city buses, and courtesy shuttles provided by car rental companies *(see p181)*.

For travelers with time to spare, McCarran features many attractions such as a shopping arcade and an aviation museum. Gambling can start at the airport, which has 1,300 slot machines throughout its terminals.

Some of the hotels allow travelers to check their luggage and print boarding passes.

Most charter flights arrive and depart from the **Atlantic Aviation** terminal, located right behind McCarran.

On Arrival

Travelers using the waiver scheme must register online with the Electronic System for Travel Authorization (ESTA) at https://esta.cbp.dhs.gov/esta well in advance of departure. If you are not a US citizen or resident, you must present your passport and visa, along with completed customs declaration forms, to immigration officials before claiming your baggage. Adult nonresidents can bring in a limited amount of duty free goods. These include 0.2 gallons (1 liter) of alcohol, 200 cigarettes, 100 cigars. Cuban cigars are allowed if purchased for personal use while on a visit to Cuba, and up to $100 worth of gifts. Cash amounts over $10,000 should be declared, but there is no legal limit on the amount of money brought into the US. Travel requirements change, so check what documentation you need before traveling.

Getting to the City

The city is located only 1 mile (1.6 km) away from the airport. The Las Vegas Monorail has not yet expanded to the airport, so the options for getting to and from the city are taxi services such as Uber or Lyft which transport travelers to and from the airport, shuttles, or the city buses. Shuttles are the most reasonable option, with fares of around $7 to the Strip resorts and $9 to downtown hotels. Shuttles run 24 hours a day and reservations are not needed for travel to the Strip and downtown. Some off-Strip resorts offer free shuttle

Two major highways allow road access to Las Vegas

transportation to and from the airport for guests. Hotels on the Strip are prohibited by the county from offering free airport transportation.

Tickets and Fares

If you are traveling from outside the US, research the market well in advance of your trip, as the least expensive tickets are usually booked early. This is particularly so during busy seasons, which are between June and September, as well as around New Year.

Although several travel websites offer bargains on last-minute bookings, direct flights to Las Vegas are more likely to be booked in advance through an airline or travel website. The McCarran Airport website offers a list of all the airlines with flights to Las Vegas, along with their phone numbers and web addresses. Travel agents can also advise. Fly-drive deals, where the cost of the ticket includes car rental are also a low-priced option, as is booking an APEX (Advanced Purchase Excursion) fare, which must be bought at least seven days in advance.

Arriving by Car

Las Vegas is connected to the rest of the country by two major highways – Interstate 15 and US Highway 95. Heading southwest, I-15 is the major connector to Southern California and the city of Los Angeles, which is about 270 miles (434 km) from Las Vegas. All the major hotels, McCarran International Airport, and the Las Vegas Convention Center have exits along I-15, which also connects the Strip with the downtown area.

Another way to reach Las Vegas from Southern California is to take I-40 across the desert to Needles, California, then proceed north on US 95 to the Colorado River resort town of Laughlin that is situated about 100 miles (161 km) south of Las Vegas. For more information on road travel, see pp180–81.

Arriving by Bus

Though it may not be the fastest mode of travel, a **Greyhound** bus provides a relatively inexpensive and often leisurely way to visit Las Vegas. Buses arrive daily from Los Angeles, Phoenix, Salt Lake City, Denver, Reno, and San Diego.

A typical Greyhound bus

Getting Around Las Vegas

Most of the visitor districts in Las Vegas are concentrated in three areas – the Strip, downtown, and the Convention Center – so a rental car is unnecessary unless you plan to visit the outlying areas. The city's transportation, which includes a municipal bus system, monorail, and elevated trams, is an efficient and inexpensive (sometimes free) way to commute among the resorts and other tourist attractions. Several free shuttles transport guests between sister properties, such as Bally's/Harrah's/Rio. Taxis are plentiful and can be found at most casinos and hotels.

Stratosphere and Mandalay Bay and also travels to Fremont Street in downtown Las Vegas. Tickets can be purchased on buses or at Deuce ticket vending machines at each bus stop on the Strip. These buses can take up to an hour to travel from the Strip to downtown Las Vegas. Downtown Express buses travel from the Strip to downtown with fewer stops. Tickets must be purchased at the bus stops, not on the bus.

Buses offer an inexpensive means of traveling along the Strip

Green Travel

The city's fleet of **Regional Transportation Commission** (RTC) buses includes double-decker buses, compressed-natural-gas-fueled vehicles, and hybrid electric vehicles. There are bike racks on the front of all RTC vehicles, and the transit system carries more than 40,000 bikes each month, so while cycling on the city's streets is difficult *(see p179)*, traveling with your bike is not. **Yellow Checker Star** operates more than 900 propane-powered taxis in Las Vegas, making it the largest alternative-fueled taxi fleet in the country. Several major car rental companies offer hybrid car rentals, with fuel-efficient models.

Buses

The RTC operates more than 50 scheduled bus routes throughout Las Vegas. Most of these begin operations at 4:30am and continue running until 1am. Some routes – including services to the airport, along the Convention Center corridor on Paradise Road, and the busy Strip to downtown route – operate 24 hours a day. All buses have bicycle racks and hydraulic lifts for wheelchair-users.

Bus fares are inexpensive – $2 each way on all residential routes and $6 on the Strip – and can be bought on board. Seniors above the age of 60, those with a disability, and youngsters between the ages of five and 17 can ride for half-fare, while children under five years old ride free. A reduced rate ID card is required for these special fares. Frequent riders can buy a 24-hour, 3-, 15-, or 30-day pass, which must be bought at a transit center such as **Bonneville Transit Center** or an **Albertsons** store before boarding.

Big Bus Tours offers hop-on hop-off tours in a London-style double-decker bus departing approximately every 30 minutes between 10am and 6pm, with 20 stops on the Strip.

The Deuce double-decker bus stops at every hotel and casino along the Strip between

Elevated Trams and Monorail

Free elevated trams operate between certain hotels – one links the Excalibur, Luxor, and Mandalay Bay hotels; another connects The Mirage and Treasure Island resorts; and a third links the Monte Carlo to CityCenter, and the Bellagio.

The **Las Vegas Monorail** runs mainly on the east side of the Strip along a 4-mile (6-km) route which extends from the SLS Las Vegas stop down to the MGM Grand. There are seven stations on the system: the MGM Grand; Bally's/Paris Las Vegas; Flamingo/Caesars Palace; Harrah's/The LINQ; Las Vegas Convention Center; Westgate Las Vegas; and SLS Las Vegas. It takes 15 minutes to travel the length of the Strip in a safe and comfortable environment. Single ride tickets cost $5, an all-day pass is $12, and three-day passes for unlimited rides are $28. You can buy tickets at the vending machines found at each stop. The monorail operates from 7am to midnight Monday, 7am to 2am Tuesday to Thursday, and from 7am to 3am Friday to Sunday.

Monorail linking various hotels along the Strip

Walking

Walking may well be the best way to travel along the 3-mile (5-km) long Strip and the downtown area. The sidewalks here are wide and the terrain is flat so you will not have to tackle any hilly areas during your outing. Walking also offers you the option of exploring the major sights and shopping areas without worrying about the traffic or spending time searching for a parking place. Expect a lot of walking between resorts.

Traffic streams along the Strip day and night

Driving

Vehicles are driven on the right-hand side of the road in the US, except on one-way streets (see p180). If driving in town, be prepared for heavy traffic and fast driving. Avoid the rush hours from about 7 to 9am and 4 to 7pm. Congestion on the Strip begins late morning and continues until after midnight. Many hotels and casinos on the Strip and in downtown provide free parking in high-rise garages, and almost all hotels offer free valet parking services except for MGM Resorts properties. The city also has many huge parking lots and garages. When parking on the street, be sure to read all the signs about restrictions to avoid incurring fines or having your vehicle towed away.

Taxis

Las Vegas has more than 3,200 taxis but they are usually clustered around the hotels, Convention Center, and airport. The basic rate is an initial charge of $3.50, $2.76 a mile, and 54 cents a minute when waiting at a red light. An additional $2 fee is charged for a departure from the airport. The maximum per cab is five people. A taxi ride from the airport to the Strip costs about $16–25, and $20–25 from the airport to downtown. It is illegal for taxis to stop on the street if flagged, so it is best to go to a taxi stand at a resort. When traveling from the airport, be sure to insist that the driver does not take the 215 airport tunnel to get to the Strip, as this longer route will add miles and $8–12 to your fare.

Limousines

Perhaps the ultimate Las Vegas travel experience is the limousine. It is possible to rent a range of these vehicles, including stretch and superstretch versions that are fitted out with a cocktail bar, stereo, TV, telephone, moon roof, and even a Jacuzzi. The average cost for a limo and driver starts at $50–55 an hour, a stretch limo costs about $55–60, while a superstretch costs about $80 an hour. Among the many operators in Las Vegas are **Bell Trans**, **Las Vegas Limousines**, **Presidential Limousines**, and **24–7 Entertainment Limousines**.

Cycling

Las Vegas is not a very bike-friendly city because of heavy traffic congestion. Though cycling along the main arteries is not advised, riding through the residential neighborhoods and in outlying areas, such as Red Rock Canyon and Lake Mead, can be pleasant and scenic. Many streets in the residential areas of Las Vegas have designated bike lanes, but there are none in the tourist areas, and biking along the congested Strip is not recommended. Be sure to wear a safety helmet when cycling and carry water, especially during the summer heat. **Las Vegas Cyclery** conducts guided tours in desert and mountain areas beyond the Strip and downtown.

DIRECTORY

Green Travel

Regional Transportation Commission
300 N Casino Center. **Tel** (702) 228-7433. **W** rtcsnv.com

Yellow Checker Star Transportation
Tel (702) 873-2000.

Buses

Albertsons
1300 E Flamingo Rd. **Tel** (702) 733-2947. **Map** 4 E3.

Big Bus Tours
Tel (702) 685-6578.
W eng.bigbustours.com/lasvegas/home.html

Bonneville Transit Center
101 E Bonneville Ave. **Map** 2 D4. **W** rtcsnv.com

Monorail

Las Vegas Monorail
3960 Howard Hughes Pkwy. **Map** 4 D3. **Tel** (702) 699-8200. **W** lvmonorail.com

Taxis

Desert Cab
Tel (702) 386-9102.

Whittlesea Blue Cab
Tel (702) 384-6111.

Limousine Services

24–7 Entertainment Limousines
4200 W Russell Rd. **Map** 3 A5. **Tel** (702) 616-6000.
W 24-7limousines.com

Bell Trans
1900 Industrial Rd. **Map** 1 C5. **Tel** (702) 739-7990.
W bell-trans.com

Las Vegas Limousines
5010 S Valley View Blvd. **Map** 3 B4. **Tel** (702) 888-4848.
W lasvegaslimo.com

Presidential Limousines
2030 Industrial Rd. **Map** 1 C5. **Tel** (702) 731-5577.
W presidentiallimolv.com

Cycling

Las Vegas Cyclery
10575 Discovery Dr. **Tel** (702) 596-2953.
W lasvegascyclery.com

Traveling Outside Las Vegas

Many visitors are surprised to learn of the numerous sights and attractions located just a short distance from the bright lights of Las Vegas. The panoramic wilderness of southern Utah, California, and Arizona surrounds the city and forms a landscape filled with awe-inspiring canyons and parks, such as The Grand Canyon and Zion National Park. As public transportation to these places is limited, renting a vehicle is often necessary. The area is served by a network of well-maintained roads, from multi-lane highways to scenic routes.

Snow-topped peaks along a scenic route

What You Need

Nevada law requires proof of insurance and a valid driver's license from another state or an international driver's license. Drivers must have their license with them and carry the car rental contract if renting the vehicle.

Interstates and Highways

The main interstates and highways in Southern Nevada are the I-15, which links California, Nevada, and Utah, and the US 95, which runs north and south from Northern Nevada to Arizona. The 215 beltway extends around three fourths of the outer ring of the Vegas Valley with connections to the 95 and I-15 freeways, and a section linking the I-15 to the airport. Driving northeast from Las Vegas along the I-15 leads to the Valley of Fire State Park, the border town of Mesquite, Nevada, and St. George, Utah, about 95 miles (153 km) from Las Vegas. Close to St. George are the magnificent national parks of southern Utah, Dixie National Forest, and the quaint town of Cedar City, home to the annual Utah Shakespearean Festival, held in late summer.

Traveling south on US 95 takes visitors to Lake Mead, Hoover Dam, and Boulder City, about 30 miles (48 km) from Las Vegas. Driving north on US 95 leads to Tonopah, Reno, and Lake Tahoe, about 450 miles (724 km) from Las Vegas. Many hamlets and towns along this route offer tourists a taste of the Wild West. For the Grand Canyon, travel east on US 93 until the city of Kingman and then take US highways 40 and 64 to the canyon's national park. The South Rim of the canyon, which is easier to access via road than the North Rim, is a five-hour drive from Las Vegas.

Rules of the Road

Law requires that the driver and passengers wear seat belts. Highway speed limits vary from state to state, but in no instance are speeds in excess of 75 mph (120 km/h) permitted. Cars that pull trailers or campers are restricted to 55 mph (90 km/h). Always be aware of the posted speed limits because they vary from state to state, and can be altered because of ongoing construction or weather conditions. The highway patrol in Nevada and other states are in charge of enforcing the highway laws and speeding violations are usually accompanied by a strict fine. Also note that drivers can be cited for driving too slowly on the interstates and hitchhiking is illegal in Nevada. The most serious offence, however, is driving under the influence of alcohol or other substances. The legal limit is 0.08 BAC (Blood Alcohol Concentration) and heavy penalties are exacted from those who violate these laws. Moreover, it is illegal to pass a stationary school bus when students are boarding and departing or when the bus is flashing its red lights.

Unless a sign says otherwise, you can turn right after stopping at a red light if there is no oncoming traffic, and the first vehicle to reach a four-way stop sign junction has the right of way. You can get maps and more information on driving rules from your car rental agency or the **American Automobile Association** (AAA).

For exploring any of the remote wilderness areas surrounding Las Vegas, it is important to check if a four-wheel-drive vehicle is required. Many of the backcountry areas can be accessed only by "fire roads," which are unpaved or dirt roads. Maintenance agencies, such as the US Forest Service at Mount Charleston and the Bureau of Land Management at Red Rock Canyon, can provide maps and tips.

Plan your route and carry up-to-date maps. If you are traveling between remote locations, let the park warden or caretaker know about your itinerary. Check the road conditions before you start by calling the **Nevada Highway Patrol**, and be aware of seasonal dangers such as flash floods, which can occur with little warning in the Southern Nevada desert. Do not drive off-road unless in a specially designated area.

Fill your tank before entering remote areas

Gas and Service Stations

Generally, gas prices are higher in remote locations than in the heart of the city. Most gas stations are self-service, in which case you must pay before filling up. Be sure to fill your tank before driving across remote areas.

Breakdown Services

Membership services, such as the American Automobile Association (AAA), will quickly come to your assistance in the event of a breakdown or running out of gas. Also, calling 911 will connect you with the Highway Patrol or Park Service Rangers, who will assist stranded motorists.

Hertz

Hertz car-rental logo

Car Hire

Visitors from abroad must have an international driver's license. Although it is legal to rent a car to those over the age of 21, most rental companies charge extra to those under 25. It is also essential to have a credit card to pay the rental deposit as few companies are willing to accept a cash deposit. There are many car rental companies in Las Vegas. Most of the major businesses such as **Alamo**, **Avis**, **Enterprise**, and **Hertz**, have outlets at the airport and at most major hotels as well. Rental rates vary but the average price for an economy car runs in the range of $41–9 a day. Added to the rental rate are an airport surcharge, sales tax, a $3 per day consumer facility charge, and license tag fee. If renting a car outside of the airport, the surcharge and $3 facility charge can be saved, but some companies will charge a fee for picking up a car elsewhere. For an extra $20–23 you can purchase the collision damage waiver, which saves you from being charged for any visible defects on the car. Travelers can opt for a BMW, Mercedes, Ferrari, or even a Rolls Royce, but these cars command a rent of $89–3,500 a day. Most rental cars have automatic transmission. Child seats or cars for disabled drivers must be arranged in advance.

Guided Tours

Several companies, such as **Pink Jeep Tours** and **Grand Canyon Discount Flights & Ground Tours**, provide guided tours to Hoover Dam, Lake Mead, Red Rock Canyon, Valley of Fire and Grand Canyon. Among the most popular excursions are air tours from Las Vegas to the Grand Canyon, in helicopter or by small plane. Alternatively four-wheel drive tours, bus tours, rafting, horseback, and even jet ski tours are also available. Most packages include pick up and drop off at your hotel and a meal.

DIRECTORY

Useful Numbers

American Automobile Association
4100 E Arkansas Ave, Denver, CO 80222.
Tel (303) 753-8800.
w aaa.com

Nevada Highway Patrol
Tel (702) 486-4100.

Car Hire

Alamo
Tel (702) 263-8411/ (800) 327-9633.
w alamo.com

Avis
Tel (702) 531-1500/ (800) 331-1212.
w avis.com

Enterprise
Tel (702) 795-8842/ (800) 736-8222.
w enterprise.com

Hertz
Tel (702) 262-7700/ (800) 654-3131.
w hertz.com

Guided Tours

Grand Canyon Discount Flights & Ground Tours
Tel (800) 871-1030/ (702) 629-7776.
w gcflight.com

Pink Jeep Tours
Tel (888) 900-4480.
w pinkjeeptours lasvegas.com

Visitors with Pink Jeep Tours enjoying a spectacular canyon view

LAS VEGAS STREET FINDER

The map references given in this guide for all sights, hotels, casinos, restaurants, shops, and entertainment venues refer to the Street Finder maps on the following pages only. The map below shows the area of Las Vegas covered by the four Street Finder maps, including the sight-seeing areas, which are color-coded.

The key, set out below, indicates the scale of the maps and shows what other features are marked on them, including post offices, bus stations, monorails, trams, tourist information centers, police stations, and hospitals. An index of the street names can be found on the opposite page.

Glittering lights and a busy cross-section of streets along the Las Vegas Strip

Scale of Maps 1–2

| 0 meters | 800 |
| 0 yards | 800 |

Scale of Maps 3–4

| 0 meters | 800 |
| 0 yards | 800 |

Key to Street Finder

- Major sight
- Other sight
- Other building
- International airport
- Las Vegas Monorail
- Free tram
- Bus station
- Tourist information
- Hospital
- Police station
- Railway
- Highway
- Pedestrian street
- Monorail/Tram route

Street Finder Index

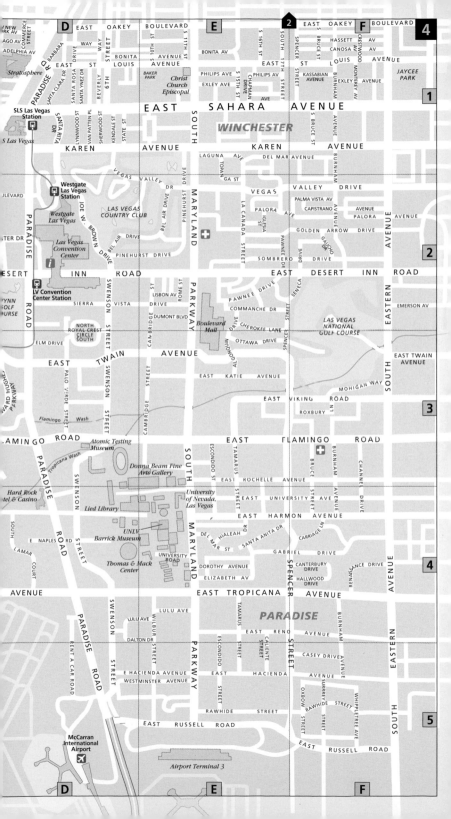

General Index

Page numbers in **bold** type refer to main entries
18b Arts District 12, **78**